D1878685

THE ANTIQUITIES OF SIND
WITH HISTORICAL OUTLINE

ARCHAEOLOGICAL SURVEY OF INDIA. VOLUME XLVI, IMPERIAL SERIES.

THE ANTIQUITIES OF SIND

WITH HISTORICAL OUTLINE

BY

HENRY COUSENS, M.R.A.S.,

LATE SUPERINTENDENT, ARCHAEOLOGICAL SURVEY OF INDIA, WESTERN CIRCLE

GYAN

Published by

Gyan Publishing House
5, Ansari Road
Daryaganj, New Delhi-110002
Phone: 011-47034999, 9811692060
E-mail: books@gyanbooks.com

Distribution Network
gyanbooks.com
India, USA, Canada, UK, Australia, France

© Publisher

All rights reserved. No part of this work may be reproduced, stored, adapted, or transmitted in any form or by any means, electronic, mechanical, photocopying, micro-filming, recording or otherwise, or translated in any language, without the prior written permission of the copyright owner and the publisher.

ISBN : 978-81-212-2216-7 (PB)
First Published, 1929

2nd Impression 2021

Printed at: Gyan Press, Delhi.

The book is sold subject to the condition that it shall not, by way of trade or otherwise, be lent, resold, hired out, or otherwise circulated without the prior publisher's written consent.

The Antiquities of Sind with Historical Outline
Author: Henry Cousens

ARCHÆOLOGICAL SURVEY OF INDIA. VOLUME XLVI. IMPERIAL SERIES.

THE ANTIQUITIES OF SIND

WITH HISTORICAL OUTLINE

BY

HENRY COUSENS, M.R.A.S.,

LATE SUPERINTENDENT, ARCHÆOLOGICAL SURVEY OF INDIA, WESTERN CIRCLE

BHARTIYA PUBLISHING HOUSE

B-9/45, PILKHANA, SONARPUR, VARANASI

LANTERN ON THE DOME OF SHAH BAHARO'S TOMB AT LARKHANA.

PREFACE

At present it is not possible to write an exhaustive monograph on the antiquities in Sind, for there are still many buried remains awaiting the pick and the shovel, and as to excavation and exploration we cannot yet write "Finis," for this class of work has but only begun in that province. Many promising sites, lighted upon more by accident than intent, have not been touched; and, no doubt, others are still lying perdu in the sandy wastes to the east, the north-east, and in the Kairpur State. The Western Circle for Archæology is so large, that it is difficult for the Superintendent to give more than a small moiety of his time to any one district; nor have we had much help, in this respect, from local officials, the forbidding nature of the country, and its indifferent means of travel, not being calculated to induce any but an enthusiast to risk a possible unprofitable journey. For these reasons Sind has been to a great extent neglected, but it is to be hoped that this state of affairs may be rectified ere long and sufficient new material gathered for a supplementary volume of even more interest and importance than the present one.

The explorations described in the following pages were made some years ago when funds for excavation purposes were very limited; and their publication was postponed during the war, the presses being taken up fully with more urgent work. Since I retired in 1910 my successors have added to our knowledge by excavations at Suḍheran-jo-ḍaḍo, Ṭhūl Mīr Rukān, Mīrpūr-Khās and Mohen-jo-dhaḍo. I shall hope to see, in the near future, still more of this work taken in hand, for I am convinced that interesting results will reward the trouble. A further volume, more interesting than this, might well follow, which would enlarge our knowledge of Sind long before the Arab invasion but the exploration of the many sites, eminently deserving of further investigation, will require much time and money, and I would most earnestly appeal to Government to help all they can in its accomplishment before the villagers, who are fast digging out the bricks and foundations, leave not even a memory behind. A special excavation officer and staff for Sind is necessary if any real progress is to be made.

TUNBRIDGE WELLS
January, 1925.

H. C.

CONTENTS.

B

CONTENTS.

LIST OF PLATES.

LIST OF TEXT ILLUSTRATIONS.

SIND, ITS RIVERS AND ANTIQUITIES.

SIND is a land of sepulchres and dust, of "holy" shams and "holy" humbugs. When the good old times under Hindu rule gave way to Muḥammadan domination, the principal concern of its rulers seems to have been for the selfish pleasures of the living and the glorification of their dead. It has been a country very fruitful in the production of *pīrs* or holy men; and, though some of these have, no doubt, been earnest disciples of the Prophet, many more have made it a cover for base and selfish motives. "It notoriously swarms with sanctified beggars and impostors, and contains, according to the current saying, no less than 100,000 tombs of saints and martyrs, besides ecclesiastical establishments, which, under the Talpurs, absorbed one-third of the entire revenue of the state."[1]

Save upon the coast, it is not a very desirable country to sojourn in; the intense heat for the greater part of the year, its disagreeable dust storms and dreary aspect, the difficulty of procuring supplies, and the troublesome means of locomotion—especially its humpity-dumpity camel riding—make it anything but a comfortable land to travel over when away from the rail. Consequently, its architectural treasures which, in many cases, lie far off the beaten track, are not often visited, except, in a very cursory manner, by officials when they happen to be in their near neighbourhood. It is little pleasure, except to the enthusiast, to wander about, under a broiling sun, over ancient brick and dust heaps, choked with a dust-laden atmosphere, in search of possible remnants of the glory of other days.

Sind has been compared to Egypt, inasmuch as it is a dry and almost rainless country, the length of which is traversed by a single great river, the Indus, whose waters, especially at the seasonal inundations, are made to irrigate the land and produce cereal and other crops in abundance. Its present great system of irrigation canals, which are taken off the main stream, in the extreme north of the province, are spreading a network of arteries over the whole surface of the country, converting vast desert wastes of fine alluvial deposit into rich productive soil. But this great river, which is the main channel into which the rivers flow that drain the Panjāb, did not always occupy the bed in which it flows to-day. No other river had, perhaps, through the ages, shifted its course more as it cut its erratic way through the level plains of Sind. There is hardly a tract between the confines of the Rājputānā desert on the east, and the

---

[1] Elliot's *Appendix to the Arabs in Sind*, 63.

rocky barriers on the west—a width of at least a hundred miles, through which, at one time or another, it has not passed; and not always as a single great stream as now, but, at times, as two or more primary streams with their minor channels, which were ever changing their unstable beds.

In the past, the waters of the many rivers of the Punjāb, flowing towards the south-west, have met at different points between Multān and the north-eastern borders of Sind, when, after running together for a short distance as one stream, they have again separated, before entering Sind, into two or more principal streams. It is, however, only with the main changes that have occurred since the Arab conquest that we are now concerned. Each separate stream has had its own name, which has often changed from time to time and sometimes at the different villages by which it flows.[1] It is this constant shifting of the waters of Sind, and the many names they have been known by, often confused by writers, that have caused most of the trouble in the identification of old city sites which are scattered about, high and dry, over the plains. Native historians, when they have noticed these places, often appear to have had in mind the hydrographic conditions that existed at the time of writing. The Indus, itself, as we now see it, does not seem to have existed until the time when the western branch of the Hakṛāh deserted its channel on the east of the old capital of Alōr for another to the north and west of that place. The whole surface of the country is at present furrowed and cross-furrowed with the beds of ancient channels, and these are being fast levelled up by the shifting sands and dust storms which are so prevalent in these regions. These channels can be easily traced upon the village maps, where the fields, in their fertile beds, being so much smaller and more valuable, show serpentine bands of smaller triangulation than over the country on either side. They may also be noticed in travelling over the country by the more valuable crops, such as indigo, which are grown in them.[2]

Then, again, as these main streams approached the coast, they split up into a great delta of streams cutting their tortuous ways along the lines of least resistance to their respective outlets, where estuaries, which were navigable one year, ceased to be so the next.[3] The corrosion of its banks is still going on apace. Postans, in 1843, writes: "The noise of the falling banks of the Indus, when heard upon the stream upon a calm night, resembles the constant discharge of distant artillery."[4] Immense quantities of mud, held in solution, are brought down by the river, so that the Indus, as we see it to-day, is a thick turbid

---

[1] Elliot's *History of India*, I, 256.

[2] See Raverty's *Mihrān of Sind*, (Journ. Asiatic Soc. Bengal, LXI, Part 1, 1892) 309. Haig says: "Along these channels the land is strewn with the broken brick and pottery, so familiar to the traveller in Sindh, which mark the sites of once flourishing towns and villages" (*Indus Delta country*, 70). As I have shown elsewhere, the areas on the river banks, strewn with pulverised pottery only, which are so frequently met with, rather indicate the encampments of troops on the march.

[3] Captain Wood, who travelled through Sind in 1837-8, and entered the delta by the Hajamari mouth, found the hull of a Dutch brig-of-war embedded in the neighbourhood of Vikkar "affording proof, if any were wanting, of the over-changing course of the Indus" (*A Journey to the Source of the Oxus*, p. 2)

[4] *Personal Observations on Sind*, p. 18.

fast flowing stream. This mud is deposited wherever the current meets with a check, whether from the banks at their bends or the tides of the sea, and so the delta has been always pushing forward its coastline, and is, probably, to-day, at least forty miles further seaward than it was in the time of Muḥammad Qāsim. Raverty says: "A vast deal of the delta is of comparatively recent formation; for the small district dependent on Bādīn was the most southerly part of Sind in Akbar Bādshāh's reign, and now it is over seventy miles from the southernmost part of the delta." And again: "It is supposed, and with very good reason, that the greater part of the delta between Ṭhaṭhah and Karāchi south, has been formed since the Āb-i-Sind or Indus deserted the channel which passed by Naṣr-pūr, and took a more westerly course. There is little doubt, indeed, but that great part of the S͟hāh Bandar district of Sind, as at present constituted, and the southern part of the Jarak district likewise, are of comparatively recent formation." K͟hān-i-K͟hānān Mīrzā 'Abdur-Raḥīm, after the annexation of Ṭhaṭhah, is said to have proceeded from that place, by two easy stages of about fifteen miles each, to Mug͟hal-Bīn to see the great ocean. Hence the name, which means "Mug͟hal's View." [1] Raverty says, a line from near Karāchi to about 20 miles above Lakh-Paṭ will show the limit of the delta in the time of Akbar, while that of the time of the Arab conquest would be represented by a line from a few miles south of Pīr Paṭho and Badīn towards Wāngah, or even much further north-east towards Nawā Koṭ. (See the general map of Sind and the small inset map upon it).

It is, therefore, altogether useless to try to identify ancient sites by the present conditions of the river and delta. The river, as it flows now, cannot go much further westward, as it has already pushed its way right up to the base of the hills on that side for a great part of its course, and it is further restricted where it passes through the rocky barriers, between Rōhrī and Sakhar and down about Jarak. But the enormous force of the current of so great a volume of water may, unless carefully and continually watched, cause it to suddenly break through a weak point into a completely new channel. Major Raverty, who has, perhaps, studied the subject more than any one else, though a bit dogmatic, and inclined to be impatient with those with whom he does not agree,[2] came to the conclusion that, at about the time of the Arab conquest, the great river of Sind was the Hakṛāh,[3] which entered Sind in two streams one of which flowed westward toward Alōr where, meeting with the low ridges running north and south, it turned southward and continued its course to a point about half way down the length of Sind, where the other, the main or eastern branch, which flowed past Wanjrūṭ or Vijnōṭ, met it. Here, they had no sooner joined forces, than they again separated, one branch starting off across Sind past Brahmanābād towards Haidarābād, and thence running south through the

[1] *The Mihrān of Sind*, 317, 468n, and 469n.

[2] In his article on the *Mihrān of Sind and its tributaries*, in Journal the of the Asiatic Society of Bengal, Vol. LXI, a work of great patience and research.

[3] Also called by him the Mihrān of Sind or the Great Mihrān, the Sind Ṣāgar, the Wahindah or Bahinda, the Wahind Sāgar and the Sankrah, from its source to the sea (*The Mihrān of Sind*, p. 466).

delta to the sea. The other, the main channel, kept a southerly course from the point of separation, and ran by the west of 'Umarkoṭ to the Ran of Kachh. This river, from Alōr down to 'Umarkoṭ, is now represented by the Eastern Nārā,[1] which, during the inundations, still received some amount of water after the Hakrāh failed. With the great change in the course of the river at Alōr, the main channel of the Hakrāh, which flowed past Wanjrūt, ceased to flow, owing to the loss of most of its tributaries and failure of others, while the new stream, the Indus, increased in volume and became a great river by the accession of five of those tributaries. This is as Major Raverty supposes things to have been, but it is impossible to fix on any hard and fast courses for these rivers at any time; it is only by carefully collating the statements of different writers, and studying the general contour of the country, that these approximate courses may be guessed at. As an extreme specimen of the inaccuracy of some of these writers may be mentioned the statement made by Al-Jāhiz in his work *Kitābu-l-Amsār wa Ajaibu-l-Buldān,* that the river Mihrān in Sind comes from the Nile, alleging, as proof, that crocodiles live in it.[2]

Raverty places, as shown in his map, a stream, which he calls the Kumbh, running from a little west of Alōr down to Hālā, and another stream bed between this again and the old course of the Hakrāh, but he does not show whence they come, or whither they go on their way through the delta. He says: "It is necessary to mention that there are a number of old channels—indeed traces of them are everywhere met with—between the channel of the Sindhu, Āb-i-Sind, or Indus, as it runs at present, and the channels of the Mihrān of Sind or Hakrā, one of which passes close to Shādad-pūr on the west, and runs towards Bahman-ābād [he puts Manṣūra at Depār Ghāngro] and Mansūriyah. It may be said, in fact, that, at different times, the Mihrān of Sind or Hakṛā has flowed over a great part of Sind, as far west as Shādad-pūr, and this is fully indicated from the many vestiges of ancient towns still remaining on the banks of the old channels..........Among these old channels, probably, is that in which the river so repeatedly mentioned by the 'Arabs, the Kumbh, flowed, which passed between Sīw-istān, the modern Sihwān, and the western branch of the Mihrān of Sind, and into which the Āb-i-Sind or Sindhu may have found its way during its repeated changes."[3] Haig says: "If they are right [that is, Istakhri and Ibn Hauqal] then the Indus at the time of the Arab conquest cannot have been more than 8 to 10 miles east of Sēwan."[4] But since Raverty has depended, more or less, upon his identifications of the positions of Nīrūn and Debal in fixing these courses, which is certainly wrong in the first and very doubtful in the second, his deductions may not be correct;

---

[1] The valleys in the course of this stream are occupied by numerous *dhandhs* or lakes, amounting to nearly four hundred, some being three miles in length. The Western Nārā is on the other side of the Indus running south from Lārkhānā, of which Manchar lake is an expansion (*Sind Gazetter*, 589, [and 686, and Burton's *Sind Revisited*, Chapter XXIX, 269).

[2] Elliot's *History of India*, I, 21.

[3] *Mihrān of Sind*, 466 and 467.

[4] *Indus Delta Country*, 57n. These two writers appear to have visited Sind some time in the first half of the tenth century. *Id.* 65.

and, as I have already shewn in the historical section, native writers, especially those who had not been in Sind, are not always reliable, and their untrustworthiness is increased by the bad habit copyists had of leaving out diacritical marks, which was often fatal to the correct reading of names. "As regards the ancient course of the Lower Indus infinite has been the speculation, the theorization, the dissertation, the argument, and the contradiction upon this much vexed subject."[1]

The Kumbh of Raverty is not mentioned in the *Chach Nāmah*,[2] as translated by Fredunbeg, but a river which seems to have run in its bed, as marked by Raverty on his map, is called throughout the Mihrān. In one case it is called the "Sehun, *i.e.*, the Mehran," and in another the "Sehun, which is called the Mehran." Fredunbeg says "Sehun" is the Arabic name given to the Indus, in fact any great river may be called "Sehun" or "Jehun."[3] That the present river Indus was known as the Mihrān, we are told by Abū-l-Faẓl who says: "At Ṭhaṭhah the Sind is called Mihrān, and all six rivers, in one stream, pass under [the walls of] Bakhar, one portion north and the other south of the fort."[4] The *Á'in-i-Akbarī* says: "All the rivers that disembogue themselves into Sind take its name; but in Tatah the Sind is called Mehran."[5]

One almost fears to disagree with such eminent authorities as Raverty and Haig, yet my own impression, gathered from the historic narratives, even from their own disagreements, is that, at the time of the Arab invasion, there was an important unfordable river flowing through Sind, from north to south, between the Alōr hills and the present line of the Indus, which is called the Mihrān in the *Chach Nōmah*, shown in the two native maps with a loop from it encircling Mansura[6], and which is there labelled the Mihrān. This may have left the Panjāb rivers higher up than the point of departure of the Hakṛāh, and this is indicated by the blue dotted line in Raverty's map. Into this, very possibly, the diverted waters of the Hakṛāh flowed when it deserted Alōr; and its further progress south was, probably, through the Lohano Daryo as shewn in Haig's map.

All authorities, however, are agreed that the western branch of the Hakṛāh, which flowed past Alōr, in the time of the Arab conquest, changed its course somewhat later, and then flowed north-west of Alōr, at some considerable distance from it, subsequently changing its course southward.[7] This change seems to have carried it so far from Alōr that the town became uninhabitable for want

[1] *Sind Revisited* by R. F. Burton, I, 202.

[2] Unless it be his "Kanbah," on the banks of which Sīsam was situated, which was somewhere in the direction of Sehwān from Nirūn.

[3] Ibn Hauqal says, the source of the Mihrān is the river Jeḥūn, جيحون and that it comes out at Multān, passes by the borders of Basmid and by Mansūra, and falls into the sea on the east of Debal (Ouseley's translation, p. 147).

[4] *Mihrān of Sind*, 297.

[5] Gladwin's translation, p. 111.

[6] Ibn Hauqal, who wrote about A.D. 976, says: "He who travels from Mansura to Budha must go along the banks of the Mihran as far as the city of Sadūstan" [Sehwan]. (Elliot's *History of India*, 39).

[7] Cunningham says, this change took place in the reign of king Dāhir, but this statement is quite wrong. It is associated with a king Dalu Rāi, who reigned at Alōr after the invasion, when the Hindus, for a time, recovered much of what had been wrested from them by the Arabs. The story of Dalu Rāi is given under the account of Bakhar.

of water. Later, this river took yet another course, and, inclining to within about four miles of Alōr on the north, cut its way through the rocks between Rōhrī (which did not exist then) and Bakhar, on the south side of the latter, which then probably occupied the present site of New Sakhar, finally cutting a loop channel round what became the fort of Bakhar, converting it into an island.

FIG. 1.—Sassanian coins found near Lārkhānā.

It is not known what the meanings of these names, Sakhar and Bakhar, are; they are probably a catchy repetition such as are often met with in India, as Ankāi and Tankāi, Rāvala and Jāvala, twin forts in the Dakhan.[1] The Indus is called in modern times, by the common people, the Mitho Darya or "Sweet-Water Sea."

Coming down to recent times, an important change in the course of the Indus took place about 1758, when, suddenly breaking through its banks at a point just south of Hālā, it shifted to a new course some 12 to 15 miles to the west, which is at present about three miles west of Haidarābād. The Fulelī channel, since dried up, was then newly formed after this change. A yet later change was reported by Mr. N. Crow, who, writing in the year 1800, says: "By a strange turn that the river has taken within these five and twenty years, just above Tatta, that city is flung out of the angle of the interior Delta, in which it formerly stood, on the main land towards the hills of Baluchistan."[2]

In its general character, climate, population, and natural products, the province of Sind has more affinity with its neighbouring countries on the west than with the rest of Hindustān. The river, running down the middle, divides the country into two parts of very different aspects, that on the west being, for the most part, hilly, culminating in the lofty range separating Sind from Baluchistan, and that on the east being extensive plains, deep in old river silt, the deposit of ages, which gradually merges, further westwards, with the sand hills and desert of Rājputānā. There is still a third division, namely that of the delta, where the Indus, breaking up into a labyrinth of channels, cuts its devious

[1] McMurdo says "The Tohfat-al-Girāni states, that this town (Bhakīr or Bakar) did not exist in the time of the Hindu *Raj*, and that it got its name Bakar ('The Dawn') from Saiyid Muhammad Make, of religious memory, some years after its foundation." (Journ. R. A. S., I, 235).

[2] Elliot's *History of India* I, 393.

ways to the sea through low, flat, and, for the most part, desolate salt wastes and muddy rice land. The country is comparatively bare of forests, such as there is, mostly of *bābul*, lining the banks of the main river, on either side, for considerable distances. The country to the east of the Indus, or rather the belt of alluvial soil which used to be, to a great extent, a waterless desert covered with the camel thorn, has been gradually reclaimed, since the British occupation, for agricultural purposes by a wide-spread system of irrigation canals.

The antiquarian remains in Sind may be divided into three classes. The first consists of prehistoric remains and rude stone monuments of uncertain age. "Flakes" and "cores," constituting the flint implements of the neolithic stone age, are not uncommon, and the valleys among the hills, in the west, contain dolmens, cairns, circles and other specimens of such primitive erections. The second class are the remains of the pre-Muḥammadan, Hindu and Buddhist period, represented now by the ruins of *stūpas*, old cities and forts, which are scattered over the country, more especially along the old, and now dried up, courses of the main streams. The third class consists of the Muḥammadan remains, mostly the elaborate tombs of rulers and saints, those of the latter being always considered of far more importance than those of the former. Indeed, though a true son of Islām may not admit it, the fact remains that a favourite saint's shrine receives more honour, especially among the lower class, than the house of Allah, the mosque itself. Certain it is that these tombs are the rendezvouses of more "holy" men and *badmashes* than most mosques, having fatter revenues and offerings attached to them, and greater numbers of simple pilgrims to be fleeced.

Of the early history of Sind, before the Arab conquest, we know but little, and the only light we have upon early Hindū and Buddhist remains we get, for the most part, from subsequent Muḥammadan writers, and very dim and confused it is. The curtain of oblivion, which is drawn across these long ages, has been occasionally lifted for the moment to give us fleeting glimpses of the panorama of events in the far past. We see Alexander's army fighting its weary way down the whole dusty length of the land at a time when it was divided up between several independent native rulers, and Nearchus collecting his fleet together to lead it down through the tortuous channels of the uncharted waters of the great river to the sea. But the very fleeting glimpse that is vouchsafed to us is, alas! insufficient for us to identify, with any approach to accuracy, the places that they passed through, and so we are left to guess and conjecture to fill in the detail of the passing scenes. But long, long ages before this, we get a peep at the ruler of Sind sending assistance to the Kūrūs in their fight with the Pāndavas during the great Mahābhārata war. Again, through a gap in its impenetrable folds, we see the country, about the sixth century of our era, under the rule of the White Huns, whose barbarian rulers oppressed the people and threw down their gods. Once more, and we see that indefatigable, but tantalising Chinese traveller, Hiuen Tsiang, wandering about the country, amongst the Buddhist establishments of the land, in his patient quest for knowledge. We have reason to hope, however, that beneath the surface, we may yet bring to light some further traces of the life and history of the country during the long silent periods which are as yet shut out from our view.

Owing to the nature of the soil of Sind, the constant drying and silting up of old river courses as the waters change their beds, and the ever-prevalent sandstorms, there must be much yet buried. As it is, the ruined sites of many old cities and encampments are still traceable in the wild wastes of its solitudes among the partly obliterated channels which furrow the country in all directions to the east of the present river. Mr. Bellasis has written : " Besides Brahmanābād, there are the remains of several other cities on or near the supposed ancient course of the river Indus, showing that when that stream flowed by Umarkot into the gulf of Kachh, this older valley of the Indus was a fertile and populous country.

" There is the ancient city of Alor, near Rohri. Of His Highness Mir Ali Murad's territory, which next intervenes, little is known ; but directly you re-enter British territory, the remains of antiquities again appear. Lieutenant Jameson in a recent letter writes : ' I paid a visit to an ancient city in the Naushahro Pargana, but there was nothing to discover. Ruins there are none, the only thing that betrays former civilisation is the vast quantity of old bricks with which the ground is strewed in every direction. There are one or two other places in the Moro Pargana (immediately south of Naushahro), and from their uniform appearance and situation they must have formed a line of cities or towns on or near the banks of the Indus in a former dynasty, when the course of the river lay near them.'

" South again, of these localities is Brahmanabad, and further south, between Khipra and Umarkot, I have heard of other ruins, and the remains of cities ; and again, near the borders of the Rann of Kachh, are the ruins of old Badin. Besides these there may be others, as this part of the country is little known."[1]

Lieutenant Pottinger, writing about 1834, says that, at about 20 miles south or south by east of Khairpūr, they crossed a deserted channel of a very large river, " and after riding along the western bank for some time, the Sindhian Chiefs, who had come to meet and welcome the mission, pointed out to us the ruins of a large city which they called Mihrābpur." In a footnote he says Lieutenant De L'Hoste, on his route from Haidarābād to Khairpūr, and about midway between these two places, passed through part of a country much deserted and covered with jungle, amongst which were the ruins of many towns and villages.[2]

But these remains are fast disappearing. As they consist chiefly of brickbats, the contractors and engineers of the various railways and the many canals in this part of the country, which have been constructed since the above was written, have found in them desirable material for ballast and concrete. Yet, notwithstanding their depredations, some of the sites, such as Brahmanābād and Vijnōṭ, still have much left of their rolling heaps of ruins. In the former place they are in such vast quantities that it would take " seven maids with seven mops " a very long time to get it clear.

---

[1] Account of Brahmanābād, Journ. Bom. Br. R. A. S., V (1857), No. XX.
[2] *On the Present State of the River Indus*, etc., Journ, R. A. S., Vol. I, p. 207.

The identification of these old sites is a problem always fascinating to the student of antiquity; and, in proportion to the lack of reliable evidence to work upon, the more interesting do they become. As there is then less likelihood of being contradicted, one is tempted to build pretty theories and fall back upon a lively imagination, only to be upset, perhaps, on further examination, by some very small but very pertinent and stubborn fact—a carved brick or an inscribed stone—that may very unexpectedly disclose itself. Several old mounds which, from their general innocent-looking surface, gave little hint of their contents, have turned out on excavation to cover the stumps or foundations of old Buddhist *stūpas*, erected, many hundreds of years ago, with much pomp and circumstance, as imperishable monuments, by earnest men who fondly hoped that these, their good deeds, would live after them and go to swell the accumulated merit standing to their credit in the bank of destiny. There are, no doubt, many of these mounds still waiting to catch the eye of the expert and submit to the pick and spade. Of these Burton wrote many years ago: "They are the Round Towers of the land but not belfries; all of them are pegs for tradition, and possibly, at some future time, will be material for archæological discussion."[1]

Of mediæval remains there is practically nothing in Sind, or, at least, little has as yet come to light, save in the far away south-eastern corner, in and about the towns of Virāwah and Nagar-Pārkar. These are noticed in the sections on those places further on. Some sculptured stones from these old temples were brought away many years ago, and were placed in the Karāchi Museum. Fig. 3 shows one of these—a door-jamb from Nagar-Pārkar. But that such

FIG. 2.—The Indus.

[1] *Sind Revisited*, 88.

architectural buildings did once exist in other parts of Sind we know from the references to the great temple at Dewal, the temple material used in the tomb of Jām Nindo at Ṭhaṭhah, the ruins of the Thambuwāro *masjid*, a converted Hindū temple, near Lāhōrī Bandar, and other temples destroyed by the Arabs during their inroads. It is not likely Sind would be without such, and some of them of importance too, since Multān, not so far away to the north, possessed the very celebrated and historical temple of the Sun-god, and Kāthiawād, Gujarāt, and Rājputānā, on the east, were absolutely crowded with them, whose remains excite our admiration at the present day. But Sind had to bear the brunt of the iconoclastic attacks of the Arabs, fresh from the cradle of Islām, and suffered accordingly; and since that time the province had been under the intolerant rule of the Muḥammadans, when the Hindu, so far as his idolatrous practices went, had to lie low.

One of the most interesting discoveries was that made, a few years back, in a field near Mīrpūr-Khās, which was being ploughed, of a very fine standing image in brass, or bronze, of the god Brahmā (Plate II). This, no doubt, belonged to some temple; and, judging from its workmanship and size, a temple of some architectural importance. It would be interesting to know what material was used in pre-Arab days in these buildings—whether it was stone, imported from a distance, or brick, decorated with moulded and carved ornament, such as we find in the remains of the *stūpas* and in the early brick temples found in the eastern districts of the Central Provinces.

This image of Brahmā stands three feet two inches high. It was originally fixed permanently in position by the tenons under the feet, and the two in the back of the figure. It has four clean-shaven faces—those at the back and sides being smaller than the front face—and the hair is elaborately worked. It has but two arms; the left hand may have held a *mālā* or rosary, the fore-finger and thumb being in the position of counting the beads; and the right, which is turned up with the palm towards the body, may have held a book, the *Vedas*. It is very difficult, with a solitary image like this, to arrive at any definite estimate of its age: I should think it belonged to some period anterior to the Arab conquest. The object, hanging over the left shoulder, may, perhaps, be intended for an antelope skin, otherwise he seems to wear but one garment from the waist to the ankles. The sacred thread hangs over his left shoulder. The half-closed eyes look very much like those of some of the Buddha images from the Mīrpūr-Khās *stūpa*. That the worship of Brahmā in mediæval times was followed, despite assertions to the contrary, I have shown elsewhere.[1]

Coming down to the Muḥammadan period we have more light. The Hindū was a bad chronicler of events, but the Muḥammadan was a born scribbler Although we get so much more from the pen of the latter, it is so tainted with religious bias that it is often difficult to separate the wheat from the chaff.

The Arabs destroyed but they did not build. The first invaders from the west, full of zeal for the spread of their newly established religion, laid a heavy hand upon the religious buildings of the Hindūs and Buddhists. After destroying

[1] In an article contributed to the Annual Report of the Archæological Survey of India for 1906-7, 171.

their idol houses, they found in their ruins abundant material with which to erect a few mosques for their immediate requirements, and this is about all they did do in the building line, except the patching up of a few old forts. These, too, were very impermanent structures of which there are now but few traces. The building of such pretentious mausolea, as the later rulers of Sind erected, did not occur to them. They were foreigners and temporary rulers in the land, without their families, men appointed from the far western Khilāfat, who did not altogether look upon the country as their permanent home. But when we come down to the times of the later chiefs we find them building costly shrines for their saints and ostentatious sepulchres for themselves. Sind, being a brick country, these are generally found in that material, stone foundations being used beneath them to enable them to resist the insidious and destructive infiltration of the salts from the soil which quickly disintegrate brickwork. The manufacture of the beautifully moulded and carved brick of the Buddhist period seems to have entirely died out by this time, so these buildings depended for their decoration largely upon the coloured glazed tiles which had been introduced into Sind from Persia, and had become a much patronized industry in its new home. Unlike the Aḥmad Shāhī rulers of Ahmadābād, who adorned their capitals with countless mosques, many of which are among the finest specimens of Indo-Saracenic work in India, to which their tombs took quite a second place, the Sind chiefs thought more of themselves and their own personal grandeur, even in death, than the glory of God. Thus it came about that, with the exception of the great Jāmi'Masjid at Ṭhaṭhah, which they did not build, they have left few mosques that can be counted a credit to them.

Though elaborately emblazoned with enamelled tiles which, with better effect, confined themselves, in the earlier buildings, to two shades of blue and white, but with more gaudy show and a greater multiplicity of raw colours in the later ones, these mausolea cannot be said to be architectural successes. They are rather heavy and clumsy in outline, and, to some extent, are only saved by their elegant finials, and, in a few cases, by the very effective finish to the dome, the ornamental lantern, a very rare feature in India (See Frontispiece). These mausolea are, as a rule, great cubical blocks of masonry surmounted with heavy-looking hemispherical domes. Save for the decorated façade, the other three walls are often bald plastered areas relieved only by rows of shallow panels. There is but one door to most of them, and that too small in proportion to the heavy mass of walling above and around it; and there is seldom a porch, or any advanced shelter, to give a sense of dignity to the entrance. It is but a hole in the wall with its necessary shutters. Yet, notwithstanding these defects, the mere mass makes them to some extent imposing; and, in their more or less neglected state, mellowed by age, they look better, perhaps, than they did when fresh and raw from the builder's hands. Of a more pleasing type are the few stone pillared buildings, decorated with surface carving, after the manner of Fatḥpūr-Sīkrī, the best example of which is the mausoleum of 'Īsa Khān at Ṭhaṭhah. Marble is but sparingly used in Sind, and then only upon grave slabs and railings within the buildings.

It is strange how, in spite of their own canons, the Muḥammadan princes of India have always had such a predilection for these grand buildings wherein to lay their weary bones. The erection of tombs and monuments over graves of Muslims is forbidden by the strict laws of Islām. The grave should not be more than a span high, of unburnt bricks, no mortar or building being permitted. Jābir, an associate of Muḥammad, is represented as saying that the Prophet prohibited the building with mortar on graves, and also the placing of inscriptions upon them.[1] The excuse may be that the mausoleum is but the shelter for the grave, and that the elaborately sculptured tombstone within it is not the true grave, which is usually in the crypt below, and which, as it is not supposed to be seen, conforms more closely to these injunctions. We are told that Nawāb Āmīr Khulil Khān, who is buried on the Makli hill at Ṭhaṭhah, was so peculiar and conscientious a man that he left directions that his body should not be buried within the mausoleum he had built for himself, in his thoughtless days, but near it.

Some of these old buildings have, no doubt, been damaged by earthquake. Captain Wood speaks of the damage done by the great earthquake of 1819 extending as far north as the town of Dhera Dīn Punah,[2] and we know that much havoc was caused by it to the fine old mosques and other buildings of Gujarāt. Lieutenant Alexander Burnes also says it was felt at Sīndrī on the Ran, when it caused great changes and inundations.[3] So impressed would the natives of Sind appear to have been by its great convulsions that they have found in it a very plausible cause for the destruction of well-nigh all the ancient cities of the land. But damage to the glazed decorative tile work, especially the finer specimens at Ṭhaṭhah and Khūdābād near Dādū, has been caused, almost entirely, by the mischievous fingers of the vandal. In other cases, as in the mausoleum of Ghulām Shāh at Haidarābād, it has been caused by inferior work, the tile veneer having separated and fallen from the walls.

FIG. 3.—Door jamb from Nagar-Parkar.

The numismatic antiquities of Sind are very meagre. A few Indo-Sassanian, one or two Indo-Parthian, Kushana, and Kashatrapa, some badly preserved specimens of Arabic coins, imported and local, and a very few small pieces in thin copper, impressed with Sanskrit letters, are about all we have, as yet, for study. The later Muhammadan rulers used Kābul or Delhi coins, being at different times, to some extent, tributary to those powers.

[1] Hughes' *Dictionary of Islam*.

[2] *A Journey to the Source of the Oxus*, 52.

[3] *Travels into Bokhara*, 311.

OUTLINE OF THE HISTORY OF SIND.

FROM THE TIME OF THE ARAB INVASION, A. D. 711.

MATERIALS for the history of Sind, previous to the time of the Arab conquest in A.D. 711, are very meagre indeed, and what exist are contained almost solely in the accounts of a few Arab writers. The most lucid account, though very short, of the country immediately preceding the establishment of Arab rule in the province, is to be found in the *Chach Nāmah* which is a Persian translation of a work written by 'Alī, son of Muḥammad Kūfī, in A.D. 1216. Two later works on the history of Sind—the *Tārīkh-i-Ma'ṣumī* or *Tārīkh-i-Sind* and the *Tuḥfatu-l-Kirām*—were to a great extent based upon the *Chach Nāmah* in their accounts of the earlier periods.[1] The history of Sind, as told by its own historians, with its contradictions and various spellings of names, is very confusing; but this is as nothing to the hopeless tangle caused by the contradictory translations and commentaries of modern writers, each of whom is perfectly convinced in his own mind that he alone is right.

We are able to gather from these accounts that both Buddhism and Brahmanism were flourishing in the country, side by side, when the Arab invasion took place in the beginning of the eighth century; and, as mention is made of monasteries which were, even then, in sore need of repair, Buddhism must have been well established for some centuries before that time as the remains of early *stūpas*, found scattered about the land, clearly indicate.

In this brief outline I do not intend entering upon the many vexed questions connected with the invasion of Alexander the Great, since we have, as far as we know, no remains of his time; and, as the features of the country have so entirely changed with every varying course of its great river, it is now almost hopeless to attempt to identify any of the places mentioned by the historians of his expedition. Nor do Hiuen Tsiang's brief and perplexing references help us much more. A long dark period of a thousand years in which we catch glimmers of the White Huns and other invaders, is as yet untraversed by any but the faintest rays of light. With the Arab incursion comes the dawn of history, and most of the monuments of Sind are connected with a later period.

---

[1] In this account I have chiefly followed the translation by Mīrzā Kalichbeg Fredunbeg, late of the Sind Civil Service. The *Chach Nāmah*, also known as the *Tārīkh-i-Hind wa Sind*, was originally written in Arabic very shortly after the events it records, and was found in the possession of Ismā'īl, son of 'Alī, the Qāzi of Alor, whose ancestors are said to have written it. 'Alī Kūfī, who discovered the manuscript, found it to be "a book adorned with jewels of wisdom and embellished with pearls of morality," which, in translating, he further "adorned with chains of style and ornaments of virtue and religiousness."

In the beginning of the eighth century Sind is said to have embraced all the country between the mountains of Kurdan and Qīkānān, Khandhār, and Sīstān on the north; the sea coast and Debal on the south; Kaśmīr and Kanūj on the east; and by the province of Makran on the west. Its capital was Alor or Aror, where the king resided. "It was a town adorned with various kinds of royal buildings, villas, gardens, fountains, streams, meadows and trees, and was situated on the bank of the river called the Mihrān."

About this time a king, named Sahiras, son of Sāhasi Rāi, reigned over the country. Under him were four provincial governors who resided, respectively, at Brahmanābād, Sīwistān (Sehwan), Iskandah and Mūltān. The fifth, the home province, was under his own immediate control. He is credited with the construction of six mud forts, namely, Uchh, Mathelah, Sewrāi, Māu, Alor and Sīwistān.

An army of the king of Nimruz,[1] a province of Fars in Persia, is said to have invaded Sind and subdued and killed Rāi Sahiras II,[2] who, on the departure of the Persians, was succeeded by his son Rāi Sāhasi II, whose wife was Suhandī. This king had a Prime Minister named Rām, an astute and capable man, to whom he intrusted the government of the country while he spent his days at his ease "in the bedchamber of happiness." Rām, with the king's sanction, employed a certain Brahman, named Chach,[3] son of Selāij, of the town of Alor, to assist him in the discharge of his state duties. On the death of Rām, Chach was promoted to the office of Chamberlain and principal minister in his stead. The queen, Suhandī, on seeing Chach, on an occasion when he had come to see the king on business, fell violently in love with him; but, unlike Potiphar's wife, she was successful in her cajoleries and overcame his protestations, and soon there was a liaison between them. Chach prospered and became the first man in the kingdom, feared and respected by all. On the death of the king, who had no issue, Chach and the queen disposed of his nearest relatives, and Chach himself, usurped the throne.

The late king's brother, Rānā Maharat, king of Chitor, as next-of-kin, claimed the kingdom, and, with an army, set out for Alor, when a general engagement took place in which Chach and Maharat fought a duel, the latter being killed. This, according to the *Tuhfatu-l-Kirām*, took place in the first year of the Hijra or A.D. 622. The marriage of queen Suhandī to Chach immediately followed, and they had issue two sons, Dāhar and Daharsiah, and a daughter called Bāī. Chach appointed his brother, Chandra, to the post of Prime Minister, and left the entire administration of Alor in his hands. He then set out on a tour of his kingdom, in order to make himself personally acquainted with the whole of its districts. He attacked the ruler of the fortified town of Babiah, on the southern bank of the river Bias, and compelled him to fall back upon his other fort of Iskandah. After bringing about the death of this king, he possessed himself of his territory and left a governor in charge

[1] It has been thought that this was Khusrū Nūshīrwān, king of Persia, but Elliot thinks it was no greater potentate than the ruler of Sijistān, or possibly Khusrū Parvēz (A.D. 591-628), king of Persia. Elliot's *Appx.* 172.

[2] The *Tuhfatu-l-Kirām* gives the following list of the kings of this Hindu dynasty: Rāi Diwāil, Rāj Sahiras I, Rāi Sāhasi I; Rāi Sahiras II. and Rāi Sāhasi II. They are supposed to have reigned over a period of 137 years.

[3] Variously written Juj. Muj, Hoj, Tohoteh, Jaj, Hijaj and Chuk.

After this Chach moved on to the attack of Sikkah[1] and Multān. The ruler of Multān appealed for aid to the king of Kaśmīr, but, getting none from him, abandoned the fort and withdrew with his men to the mountains of Kaśmīr, towards which place Chach continued his victorious march, and there marked out the boundary between the two kingdoms. Returning to Alor, and spending a year there, he started for his southern provinces, directing his steps towards the fortified towns of Mudapūr (or Budhapūr) and Sīwistān (Sehwan), crossing the Mihrān[2] at a village called Wahtaet (or Dihayat) on the boundary between Brahmanābād, which included the district of the Sammahs, and Alor.[3] After taking Sīwistān he proceeded against Agham Luhānāh, the ruler of Brahmanābād,[4] where, after defeating him in the field, he spent a year in the siege of his fort. Agham had a friend, a monk, named Sāmānī[5] Budhgui (or Budh Rakhū), that is one protected by Buddha, who was supposed to bear a charmed life. "He owned an idol-house or temple, which was called Budh Nawwihar. It contained several idols. He was the chief monk of the place, and was well known for his devotion and piety, and all the people of that part of the country obeyed him. Agham professed his faith, and had taken him as his spiritual guide." The Sāmānī, though professedly occupied in his temple with his sacred books, found time to interest himself in state affairs, and, on the death of Agham, which took place about this time, he was anxious about the trend of affairs when Agham's son succeeded to the chiefship. He consulted his books to ascertain the decree of fate, when he learnt that the country was to come under the rule of Chach. Eventually the fort fell.

On account of the interference of the Sāmānī in causing the siege to be so protracted, through his practice of magic and sorcery, Chach swore to skin him as soon as he could lay hands on him. The opportunity was not long in coming, for Chach pretended to visit the monk in a friendly way at his temple which was a little way off from the city ; but, instead of encompassing his assassination as he had arranged, Chach was so amazed and dumb-founded at the Sāmānī's coolness and reception of him that he came away without carrying out his object. During Chach's visit the Sāmānī occupied himself in stamping clay votive tablets. Chach "found him sitting on a chair busily engaged in prayers, and with some hard clay in his hands with which he was making idols. He fixed a sort of seal on the idol, and the image of Budh appeared on it. The idol being now complete he placed it on one side." All this time he took no notice of the presence of Chach, though he had divined the object of his visit. While at Brahmanābād Chach married Agham's widow, the mother of Sarhand, and gave the daughter of his nephew Dahiyah (or Daharsiah) to Agham's son.

---

1 Opposite Multān, on the other side of the river.

2 The *Chach Nāmah* always calls the river, which flowed between Alor and Sehwan, the Mihrān. See the section on the rivers of Sind.

3 It is very likely that Chach, when on his march from Alor to Sīwistān, commenced the building of the fort of Rāwar or Rāor, of which more presently, somewhere on the east bank of the river between Alor and the reach opposite Lārkāna.

4 The province of Brahmanābād, at this time, appears to have extended down to Debal and the sea.

5 The term Sāmānī was a title given to Buddhist ascetics, but it seems also to have been applied to Buddhists holding positions of authority, such as the Sāmānī or head-man of Nīrūn, when Muḥammad Qāsim took that town.

Chach, being now rather taken with the Sāmānī, offered to do anything for him that he might wish. To Chach's request the Sāmānī replied: "As you are determined to do some charitable act and add to your good deeds know that the temple of Budh Nawwihār here is an ancient religious institution. For some time past, owing to the vicissitudes of time, some parts of the structure have suffered injury. It should, therefore, be built anew, and you should spend your own funds in laying a fresh foundation. In this matter alone can I implore your help."

Chach remained at Brahmanābād settling the affairs of the province. Upon the Jats and Lūhānahs he imposed certain restrictions. These were that they should not carry swords, except on occasion of urgent necessity; that their under garment should be o woollen cloth; that they should not wear velvet or silken cloth; that they might use scarves of cotton thread, of black or red; that they must ride horses without saddles; that they must walk about bare-headed and bare-foot; that, when going out of their houses, they must take dogs with them; that they must supply firewood to the ruler of Brahmanābād; that they must serve him in the capacity of guides and spies; that, if they distinguished themselves in carrying out these injunctions, they would be considered trustworthy and honest; that they must live in harmony and co-operate with king Agham's son, Sarhand, who was being left in charge of the city; and that, if an enemy invaded the country, they should consider it their duty to stand by him and fight for him.

Chach then turned his attention to the demarcation of his boundaries in the direction of Kirmān, and marched to Armā'īl, which town was then in the hands of a Buddhist Sāmānī descended from the agents of Rāi Sahiras, king of Hind. Thence he went on to the district of Makrān and returned by way of Armā'īl and Kandā'īl[1] to Alor, where, after a reign of forty years, he died at his capital, or, as Mīr Ma'ṣūm puts it, he folded up the carpet of his life.

It was in the 36th year of his reign that one Mughairah commanded an expedition from Arabia against Sind, but he was killed before the walls of Debal. This event is put in the eleventh year of the Hijrah (A.D. 632).

Chach was succeeded by his brother Chandar (or Chandra), who had already been appointed heir-apparent and his deputy at Alor, who was also a monk and who promulgated the Buddhist religion. Mattah, the ruler of Sīwistān, took advantage of the religious and peaceful nature of Chandar to induce the king of Kanūj to join him in attacking, dethroning and seizing upon his kingdom. They prevailed upon the king of Kaśmīr to join them, who, at that time, was a grandson of Chach by his daughter. The allied troops approached Alor by way of the fort of Dew Dhanaz (or Dew Dhanush) and Band Kāhūyeh where they stayed a month and busied themselves in offering prayers to Budh. Chandar prepared to meet his foes by sending Daharsiah (Dharasimha), a son of Chach, to defend Brahmanābād, while he, with Dāhir, the younger son of Chach, shut themselves in the fort of Alor and set its defences in order. The combined armies, however, were

[1] Also written Armabel or Armabelah and Kandhābel or Kandhār.

unsuccessful in their enterprise and were obliged to return discomfite to their own countries

After a reign of seven years, during which he ruled the state wisely, Chandar died, and was succeeded by Dāhir, while Durāj, son of Chandar, established himself at Brahmanābād.[1] But Durāj's rule at Brahmanābād did not exceed one year, when Daharsiah took possession of that place. He married Agham's daughter and remained at Brahmanābād for some five years. Sōhan, king of Bātiah, in the country of Ramal,[2] sent messengers to Daharsiah asking for the hand of his sister in marriage, upon which, Daharsiah sent his sister to his brother at Alor in order that he might give her to Sōhan. But Dāhir first consulted a famous astrologer who declared that the stars said that she should never leave the fort of Alor, and that no one should marry her but the king, who would then acquire the kingdom of Hindustān. Dāhir at first met the idea of marrying his sister with great repugnance, but, as it would mean the loss of the kingdom of Hindustān if he thwarted the prediction of the stars, he eventually, with the connivance of his nobles, married her to his sword,[3] but did not consummate the marriage. This unnatural act brought about a quarrel with Daharsiah who straightway marched against Dāhir at Alor. On arriving at that place he demanded the surrender of the fort, declaring that Dāhir held it as his agent, and there could not be two crowned heads in one country. Daharsiah, however, while endeavouring to arrest his brother, was taken ill with smallpox and died. Dāhir thereupon took possession of his treasury, married his widow, Agham Lūhānah's daughter, and, proceeding to Brahmanābād, settled there. Daharsiah ruled for thirty years.

Dāhir installed Chach II, the son of Daharsiah, as his father's successor, and marched by way of Sīwistān to Rāwar, where, one account tells us, he stayed long enough to see the fort completed, which had been commenced by his father Chach.[4] He spent in it the four months of summer, as it was a very pleasant city with a salubrious climate and with sweet water. He fixed his winter quarters at Brahmanābād, where he spent the four months of winter, the remaining four months of spring he spent at Alor.

After Dāhir had been reigning some eight years in peace, his territory was invaded by the king of Ramal. Now there was a man, an Alāfī Arab, of the tribe of Banī Asāmah, who, in his own country, had killed 'Abdu-r-Rehman, son of Ash-Ās, for running away from battle, and who had come, out of fear of the Khalīfah's punishment, and joined Dāhir, with five hundred Arab followers, to serve under him. Dāhir, with the aid and at the counsel of this man, fell upon the enemy at night, completely defeated them, and took 80,000 prisoners

[1] Mīr Ma'ṣūm makes Dāhir succeed Chach direct, and says nothing about Chandar, nor does he mention Durāj.

[2] In the *Tuhfatu-l-Kirām* this is Raumalrāi, king of Kanūj, and not king of Ramal.

[3] Marriage to the sword constituted a perfectly legal marriage among Rājput princes. It was resorted to in cases when, the auspicious day for the wedding having arrived, the bridegroom, being absent in the field or from other unavoidable cause, was not able to be present at the ceremony.

[4] The completion of this fort is also ascribed to Daharsiah. If that be true, he probably finished it when on his march against his brother, in order to have a place to fall back upon in case of his plans miscarrying. The climate of the place may have been influenced by the proximity of the Kingri lake and other expanses or *dhandhs* formed by the river in the neighbourhood.

and 50 elephants. It is said that Dāhir was for slaying all the prisoners, but their lives were spared on the advice of his *wazīr*, who dwelt upon the nobility of a victorious king pardoning those who fall into his hands. He seems to have been so pleased with his *wazīr* for this advice that he decreed that, as the latter had no children to perpetuate his name, it should appear on the reverse of Dāhir's coins just as his own did upon the obverse.

After the expedition under Mughairah, already referred to, Usmān, son of Affān, who succeeded 'Umar in the Khilāfat, despatched an army to Kandā'īl and Makrān under the command of 'Abdullāh, son of Āmīr, with instructions to gather all possible information concerning Sind. 'Abdullāh sent Hākim, son of Hāilah Abdī, for the purpose, who returned with such discouraging accounts of the province and its people that he gave up all thoughts of invading it. Another expedition was sent out during the Khilāfat of 'Alī, the son of Abī Tālib, which was entrusted to Hāris, the son of Marrah. It got as far as Makrān and Kīkānān, where the latter town was reduced, when the martyrdom of the Khalīfah caused it to return.

When Muāwiyeh, son of Abīsafiyān, succeeded to the Khilāfat, he sent 'Abdullāh, son of Sawād, with 4,000 men to Sind, appointing him Governor thereof and chief administrator in those parts. He said that in Sind there was a mountain (or hilly country) called Qīkānān,[1] where fine big horses were to be found, and whence spoils had been brought on previous occasions. The people there were very cunning, and, in the shelter of their rugged defiles, had become refractory and rebellious. Muāwiyah also sent 'Umar, son of 'Abdullāh, to effect the conquest of Armā'īl, and ordered 'Abdullāh, son of Āmīr, to proceed to Basrah, and join Kais, the son of Hāshim Salmī in the operations in Ammān and Ardbīl. Each of these officers was to take 1,000 selected men with him. 'Abdullāh, son of Sawād, first marched against Qīkānān which he attacked, the tribesmen opposing him in the mountain passes. They eventually succeeded in defeating him and putting his army to flight, he himself being killed.

When 'Abdul Malik, son of Marwān, sat in the seat of the Khalīfahs, he placed the government of Hind and Sind in the hands of Hajjāj, the son of Yūsuf Sakfi, and governor of 'Irāq.[2] When Walid, the son of 'Abdūl Malik, became Khalīfah, in A.D. 704, it is said that the king of Sarandeb (Ceylon) sent valuable presents from the "Island of Pearls" by sea, in a small fleet of boats, to Hajjāj, together with some Abyssinian male and female slaves. Some Musalmān women, on a pilgrimage to Makka, accompanied them.[3] But, owing to storms these boats were cast up upon the coast of Sind ("the coast of

---

[1] This name is spelt in different ways. Bilāduri changes the two ق s *kwāfs* of other writers to two ک s *kāfs*, while the *Chach Nāmah* spelling is rendered by Elliot, Kaikānan, and by Fredunbeg, Kīkānān.

[2] This Hajjāj seems, from all accounts, to have been a fiend incarnate, though a capable man in other respects. Muḥammad Qāsim, whom he sent to conquer Sind was the very opposite, and he was always reproaching the latter for not carrying out a more wholesale slaughter of the conquered people.

[3] Bilāduri tells us the present to Hajāj, from the "Island of Rubies" were certain Muḥammadan girls, who had been born there, and were the orphan daughters of merchants who had died. (Elliot's *History*, I, 118). Mīr Ma'sūm says nothing about Ceylon. He says the Khalīfah sent his agents to Sind to buy Hindustāni female slaves, and other things, and that, on the return journey, these were way-laid and robbed at Debal Bandar "now called Tatta" (Malet's *Mir Ma'sūm*, 6).

Debal ") where a band of pirates seized them. When this came to the ears of Hajjāj, he sent a message to Dāhir demanding the release of these Musalmān women and the return of the presents.[1] Dāhar replied that the pirates were very powerful and were not amenable to his commands. The Khalīfah then sent a punitive expedition against Sind, which, sailing by the sea of Ammān, arrived at the fortified town of Nīrūn (Haidarābād). Bazīl, who commanded this expedition started out with 300 men, which was reinforced by a large army sent on to him by Muḥammad Hārūn: with these combined forces he marched towards Debal.[2] The people of that town sent a man to Dāhir at Alor informing him of the arrival of the Arabs, which caused him to despatch, with all haste, his son Jaisiah[3] in command of 4,000 horsemen and camelry to the relief of the town. Bazīl had already fought with and defeated the local troops, but Jaisiah engaged him and defeated and killed him.

Upon hearing of the death of Bazīl, the people of Nīrūn feared that the Arab troops would, in their retreat northwards, set upon them and sack the town out of revenge for their commander's death; so the Sāmānī governor of the town lost no time in tendering his submission, and offered to pay tribute regularly to the Khilāfat. In this he was successful, and obtained pardon on condition of his releasing all the prisoners.

It was at this juncture that Muḥammad *bin* Qāsim,[4] the Arab conqueror of Sind, first came to notice; and his appointment to the chief command of the expedition, fitted out for the subjugation of the province, though only seventeen years of age, shows the casual way in which such important and responsible posts were filled. It is stated that when Hajjāj determined to send out this army, one, Amīr, son of 'Abdullāh, applied for the post, but Hajjāj told him that both he and the astrologers had consulted their books and found out, also by the throwing of dice, that the country of Sind would fall to the sword of Āmīr Imādu-d-dīn Muhammad Qāsim, son of Ukail Sakifī (*Tuhfatu-l-Kirām*). He was the favourite nephew and son-in-law of Hajjāj, and this fact, no doubt, influenced Hajjāj in his choice more than his hazard with the dice. In this case, however, it was a happy selection, for, with the counsel of able men, with which, there is no doubt, Hajjāj took care to surround him, he did credit to his appointment. This new expedition set out in the year of the Hijrah 92 (A.D. 710), about the time the Moors were subjugating Spain.

It is now necessary to give the movements of Muḥammad Qāsim in some detail, as a proper grasp of the different accounts of these help us to identify some of the ancient sites of Sind, whose traces are now very few or are in great part obliterated. They centre chiefly round the old cities of Debal (or Dewal),

---

[1] These were set at liberty when Muḥammad Qāsim was advancing on Brahmanābād, after the fall of Dahlelah. It is also said they were set free when Debal was taken. The Arabs, spurred on by their new and aggressive faith, desire for the extension of Islam, and their cupidity and lust of conquest, after overrunning Persia, set their eyes and hearts upon the rich plains of India. The story of the captives from Ceylon may or may not have a foundation of truth, but the conquerors of 'Irāq needed no further excuse for their inroads into Sind.

[2] Bazīl must have reached Nīrūn by one of the mouths of the river other than that on which Debal stood, otherwise he would have been held up at that place in passing on to Nīrūn.

[3] Jāisimha. Also written Jebelah and Jaisisiah.

[4] From this onwards I shall call him Muḥammad Qāsim, by which abbreviation he is more generally known.

Nīrūn, Brahmanābād (more correctly Bahmanābād), Sīwistān (Sehwan) and Alor (or Aror). The difficulties in the identification of many places are increased by the copyists and translators of the original accounts, who often knew little or nothing of the topography of the country, omitting the diacritical marks or introducing wrong ones where so frequently omitted in the originals, and thus causing no end of confusion in the spelling and pronunciation of the names.[1]

Muḥammad Qāsim set out by way of Shīrāz, which place he made the grand rendezvous for the various bodies of troops that were to accompany him.[2] Here he loaded into boats all his war apparatus, such as battering-rams and catapults and coats of mail necessary for siege operations, and placed the whole flotilla in charge of Abū Mughairah and Hazūn. The sea-borne section of the expedition was to meet Muḥammad at Debal in Sind, while he proceeded with the main army by land through Armā'īl.[3]

Jaisiah was then at Nīrūn, and he lost no time in reporting to his father, Dahir, the arrival of the Arabs in the country, who advised him not to oppose them in the field. They arrived before Debal on Friday the 10th Muharram A.H. 93 (A.D. 711), and upon the same day the boats arrived. It is stated in the *Tuhfatu-l-Kirām* that Hajjāj established a service of fast runners between Baghdad and Sind, who covered the distance in seven days. Muḥammad immediately made preparations for the siege of the town. The great catapults were unloaded and set up, one of the largest being dedicated to the Commander of the Faithful, the Khalīfah, and called "the Wee Bride," which required a force of five hundred men to work it. These machines had been previously used by the Prophet in the siege of Tāif and had done effective service only a few years before at Damascus.[4] We are told that in the midst of Debal there was a very fine idol temple, surmounted by a dome and lofty spire, over which flew a green silken flag with four streamers. The total height of the temple is put at forty cubits. With the late disaster to Bazīl's army fresh in his memory, Hajjāj advised caution, and would not allow Muḥammad to attack the garrison troops which came out to meet him, until his own men had had a full week's rest.[5] As soon as the necessary permission arrived, Muḥammad attacked and drove the Hindu forces back within their walls. At this time a certain Brahman emerged from the fort, with a message for Muḥammad, to the effect that they had

---

[1] For instance, the lake near Rāwar, where the army crossed the river, is transcribed كوجري Gniri, كوچري Kuchri, and كنگري Kingri, where confusion has been made, not only with the dots but also with similar letters. It must be borne in mind that, often, places of the same name occur in different parts of Sind.

[2] In the fitting out of his expedition Bilāduri tells us that "He was provided with all he could require, without omitting even thread and needles." Elliot's *Hist.* 119.

[3] As exhibiting the great variety of ways in which some names are written, Elliot shows that this name is transcribed in no less than eighteen different ways. *Appdx. to Arabs in Sind*, 127.

[4] Elliot's *Appendix to the Arabs in Sind*, 27.

[5] It seems remarkable that Hajjāj should have required such details of the prosecution of the war to be constantly referred to him before they could be carried out, notwithstanding the council of advisors in attendance upon Muḥammad. His continual interference caused great loss of time and opportunities, and must have been more irritating than the meddling telegraph in modern times. Hajjāj, no doubt, felt conscious that Muḥammad Qāsim's appointment was more or less of a "job," and, with the Khalīfah's eyes upon him, his anxiety obliged him to support his protégé as much as he could with his personal advice. In the present case he advises to the smallest detail, as, for instance, that he should engage the enemy in such a manner as not to have the sun in his face.

found from their astrological calculations that Sind was destined to fall before the arms of Islām, but, he confided to Muḥammad, that so long as the spire and banner of the temple remained intact it would be impossible for him to take the town. Upon hearing this, Muḥammad summoned his chief military engineer, Jaubat Salmī, and promised him a great reward if he succeeded in bringing down the flag-staff and tower with missiles from his catapults. An agreement, approved by Hajjāj, was arranged whereby Jaubat, should he succeed, was to be paid ten thousand *dirams*, but should he fail, he was to lose both his hands.

On the ninth day after his arrival at Debal[1] Muhammad ordered a general attack on the fort, and had the "Wee Bride" brought to the front and set up for action. Five hundred strong pairs of arms, at the ends of the ropes, pulled back the mighty lever, which, when released, shot forth its huge projectile that carried away the proud banner from its staff as the war cry rang out from ten thousand throats "God is great, God is great." The second shot was no less successful, for it shattered the tower that carried the flag-staff. The superstitious garrison, seeing the prediction concerning their temple fulfilled, surrendered, when a great slaughter of the people ensued during the next three days. Jāhīn, who appears to have been the governor of the fort, escaped, and sent tidings of its fall to Dahir. Muḥammad raided the temple and captured seven hundred beautiful female attendants on the shrine, adorned with jewels and valuable ornaments and clothes.[2] He then marked out a quarter of the town for the Muḥammadan garrison, built a mosque, and left four thousand men.[3]

Jaisiah, who was then at Nīrūn, was instructed by Dāhir to cross the Mihrān and retire on Brahmanābād, which he did, leaving the Sāmānī governor of Nīrūn to defend that place. The battering-rams and other heavy *impedimenta* were re-embarked upon the boats and taken up the river to Nīrūn, or, as the *Chach Nāmah* puts it, "the boats were put under way in the lake, called the lake of Sangrāh,[4] while he himself went by way of Sīsam." Muḥammad

[1] This hardly gives time for all the communications to have been made between Muhammad and Hajjāj, so we must conclude many of these, and the long letters subsequently alleged to have been sent backward and forward, are but the product of the imagination of the historian

[2] The historian says they were under the protection of Budh, but it is likely that early Muhammadan writers were not very clear as to the difference between the Buddhists and the orthodox Hindus. Bilādurī calls the temple of the Sun at Multān by the same term, and tells us that, not only temples, but idols were called "Budh." Elliot's *Appendix to the Arabs in Sind*, 91.

[3] Elliot's *Hist* I, 120.

[4] It has been suggested that the lake mentioned is the Khinjar lake at the town of Helāī, but, as pointed out by Cunningham (*Ant Geo*), this lake never had any connection with the river, as a ridge of hills runs between them. Ibn Hauqal says "Between Mansūra and Makrān the waters from the Mihrān form lakes.' (Elliot's *Hist.* I, 40). The version as given in the *Tuhfatu-l-Kirām* is "Having placed his *Manjaniks* on boats he sent them to the fort of Nairūn, by way of the water of Sākūra." (Elliot's *Appendix to the Arabs in Sind*, 230). Elliot says: "We may consider the stream Sākura to correspond with the prolongation of the Gisrī or Ghārā creek, which at no very distant time must have communicated with the Indus above Thatta." (*Hist.* 398). Haig says: "Now we have seen there is strong evidence to support the belief that the present Ghāro is part of the channel—the great western branch—by which Alexander, and after him Nearchus, sailed down to the sea, and it is beyond question the channel which Ptolemy calls Sagapa. . . . . . . the correct and complete name was Sindu Sāgara" (*Indus Del. Country*, 50), and, a few pages further on, Haig quotes Idrisi as saying: "Nīrūn is half way between Debal and Mansūra, and people going from one town to the other here cross the river." Not the main stream, which then flowed *east* of Nīrūn, as it was also east of Debal, but the Ghara branch, which swept round north of Ṭhatḥah, which town was, no doubt, the position of Debal.

covered the twenty-five leagues between Debal (Ṭhathah) and Nīrūn (Haidarābād in six days, and encamped in a meadow called Balbār. As the floods of the Sehūn (Mihrān) had not then spread to that place, want of water was felt by the troops, but an opportune fall of rain, and the filling of the tanks, relieved the situation. They must therefore have encamped at some distance from the main river, yet it was up the main river their boats had gone to meet them. But as we hear no more about these boats or the famous catapults, they may, for some reason, have been abandoned before reaching the neighbourhood of Nīrūn.

In the absence of the Sāmānī governor, who had gone to consult with Dāhir, the gates of the city were closed against Muḥammad, but, on his return he opened them and submitted to the Arabs. When Muhammad took possession he erected a mosque in the place of the idol temple of Budh and appointed a crier to call the people to prayer.

After the downfall of Nīrūn, Muḥammad determined to march to Sīwistān (Sehwan), a fortified town to the west of the Mihrān, situated on the top of a hill, marching by way of a town called Maōj, about thirty leagues from Nīrūn.[1] In that town was a Sāmānī who was a man of influence among the people, the ruler being Bachehrā, son of Chandar and cousin of Dāhir. The priestly class, under the leadership of the Sāmānī, who were, like the modern Quakers, averse from war, were desirous of submitting to the invaders; Bachehrā, however, would not consent to this; but, when the place was besieged, and he saw there was no hope of defending it, he fled by night to Budhiyah, of which, at that time, Kākah, the son of Kotak (or Kotab) Sāmānī, was ruler. He resided in his fort of Sīsam, which was situated on the bank of the Kanbāh.[2] The Sāmānī party thereupon surrendered the fort After giving his troops a rest of some days, Muḥammad started off towards Sisām in pursuit of Bachehrā, who, with the army of Budhiyah, opposed him. The two armies met at a place called Budhan on the bank of the Kanbah, when Kakah surrendered without fighting. Muhammad then continued his march upon Sīsam itself.

About this time Muḥammad received instructions from Hajjāj to return to Nīrūn, cross the river and proceed against Dāhir.[3] In his letter to Hajjāj he promises to make a clean sweep of all idols and idolatry and to build mosques

---

[1] Haig thinks this may have been a suburb of Sehwān, where there was a Buddhist monastery (*I D. C.* 60) The *Tuhfatu-l-Kirām* says Maōj, ماوج was thirty *kos* (two miles to the *kos*) from Nīrūn. Raverty says others called this place Bharāj or Bahrāj, بهرج and this place is shown in the old native map, which he reproduces, opposite Mansūra, on the other side of the Mihrān main channel. But Bharāj, or Bharj, is mentioned in the *Chach Nāmah*, when Muhammad, after the settlement of Brahmanābād, appointed a governor to the place and established a garrison there

[2] The *Tuhfatu-l-Kirām* tells us that Bachehrā *fled to Budhiyah Chana, son of* Kakah, *son of* Kotak, who was ruler of Sīsam. Haig considers that the district of Budhiyah, which he transcribes Būdhīya, was to the west of the Indus, its southern limit being about 40 miles north of Sehwan (*I. D C.* 57) Elliot writes Sīm or Sīsam, which according to the *Tuhfatu-l-Kirām*, was in the province of Sēbī (Sīwistān) (*Appdx to Arabs in Sind,* 216). Haig thinks Sisām may be identified with Shāh Hasan, a place at the western end of Manchhar lake

[3] Mīr Ma'sūm's account runs; "When Muhammad Qāsim had accomplished the conquest of the province of Sīwistān, some people said that he should now go to Brahmanābād and that, after overcoming that fort, he should proceed to Alor. Muhammad Qāsim said it was better first to go to take Alor, and, after overthrowing Rāis Dāhir then to proceed to take other countries. All approved of this, and they crossed the river opposite to Tuluhter, and marched towards Alor." (Malet's *Mīr Ma'sūm*, 16). There is nothing here, or in the *Chach Nāmah*, about

in place of *kafirs'* temples. It would seem that from Nīrūn, after his return there or to its neighbourhood, he started for Alōr by way of the district of Rāwar and the town of Ishbha, which place he took He then continued his march until he reached a spot on the west side of the Mihrān opposite the fort of Rāwar,[1] where he encamped. There can be little doubt that this fort was situated upon the east bank of the Mihrān, some twenty to twenty-five miles to the west or west-by-south of Alōr, just below Kingrī, as marked upon the map. Here he was joined by Jāsen (or Jāhin), the ruler of Bet.[2] A certain prince Mōkah, son of Basāyeh, threw over his allegiance and went over to Muḥammad,

---

Hajjāj advising him to go to Brahmanābād first as Raverty says (*The Mihrān of Sind*, 240n.). This " Tuluhtee " is again mentioned by Mīr Ma'sūm as the crossing place of Jām Jūnah (Sammah), about the time that he succeeded to the throne of Sind (Circ. A.D. 1354), and when he marched against Bakhar (Malet's *Mir Ma'sūm*, 47). There is a Talti, or Tahlti تہلتی, about seven miles north of Sehwan, on the east side of the present river, which is possibly the same; but, as the main stream was at that time probably some twenty miles to the east of Sehwan, this place must have been on a smaller channel that ran into the main river. It evidently gave Muḥammad no trouble, and he was still on the west side of the main stream which he crossed very soon after at Rāwar, after great delay in his preparations for it, and not without very considerable trouble, as we shall see.

[1] It is necessary, here, to go into a little more detail with regard to the location of Rāwar, concerning which there has been a good deal of controversy. Haig (*I. D. C.*) places it about 70 miles to the south-east of Haidarābād somewhere in the vicinity of Wangab, on the far side of the delta from Debal, where it would have been on the edge of the Ran, or sea-shore, in those days. In this case Muḥammad would have been muddling about in the net-work of channels with which the delta must then, as now, have been covered. The almost insuperable difficulties of a march through this country would have been such that some notice would surely have been taken of it in the accounts of some of the chroniclers of the expedition, yet we hear of no difficulties until those which were confronted in the passage of the river near Rāwar. Raverty says: " What is surprising is, that these operations went on in the height of the hot season, when, at the present time, the rivers are in flood, and the country inundated, and yet no remark is made on the subject " (*Mihrān of Sind*, 239n.). Burnes, writing in 1831, says: " It would be impracticable to march a force through the delta, from the number of rivers; and it would be equally impossible to embark it in flat bottomed boats " (*Travels into Bokhara*, 221)." Pottinger writes, regarding crossing the delta from west to east: " In this opinion I entirely concur, and believe that no one who has not seen the delta, the state of the river's banks, and the violence of the current, can have an idea of what such an undertaking would be, more particularly with cavalry " (J. R. A. S. I, 199). We are told that, in connection with the operations of Sulṭān Fīruz Shāh in Sind, in A.D. 1361-62, in order to cross from the east side of the main river to Thaṭhah, he was obliged, owing to the great width of the stream and the great opposition of the Sindhis on the other side, to send his troops up to Bakhar (*Mihrān of Sind*, 272). So much for Haig's position. Raverty, who did not think there was any river of consequence between the old Hakṛāh and Sehwān, says, Rāwar lay on the west of Brahmanābād (*M. of S.*, 243), and, in order to place it upon the Mihrān, which he contends was the Hakṛāh or Eastern Nārā, he brings a branch of that river down to Brahmanābād, from a point about forty miles above that town. If this were the position of Rāwar, it would have been within ten miles or so of Brahmanābād. His mistake, in placing Nīrūn some eighteen miles south of Haidarābād, no doubt, caused him to bring Rāwar so far south.

[2] The word *beṭ* or *beṭu* बेटु means an island in Sindhi, and has the same meaning as the Persian word *jazirah* جزیرہ, and with that meaning only it is found used upon maps of Sind. Raverty, however, takes it to mean delta, but he does not give his authority for doing so; then he immediately says: "this Bet, it is stated, was situated on the east side of the Mihrān, on the margin of a stream" (*M. of S.* 236n.). The Arab writers seem to leave no doubt as to its meaning. It appears to have been a fort upon an island in the river and to have arrested Muḥammad's attention as an easy place to cross, there being the two smaller arms of the river instead of one wide main stream. The *Chach Nāmah* describes it as " the fortified town of Bet, to the east of the Mihrān [*i.e.* to the east of the main stream] on the bank of a rivulet [*i.e.*, the lesser branch going round the back of the island from him] in an island of the gulf [probably the *dhanḍh*, or expansion of the river, such as may be still seen on the map to the west of Rohri. Raverty renders this, "an island formed by the Kunbh river," and he has already placed the Kunbh or Kumbh considerably N. by W. of Brahmanābād.] of Khānlehat and is now called Basāmi Rāsal." Dāhir was upon the east side of the river and he " ordered Jāhīn Budh to post himself at the ferry landing, on the bank of the Mihrān opposite the fort of Bet, and to watch the enemy lest they should cross the river from there " (*Chach Nāmah*). So if Muḥammad on the west side, and Jahin on the east were each opposite Bet, the fort must have been in mid stream. In connection with Muḥammad's movements, up and down the west bank, to find a suitable crossing he is at one time, within the district of Jhim, and this name may possibly be perpetuated in Jhim Pīr, the name of the tomb upon the islet in the river opposite Rohri. Indeed, we might almost have identified the Beṭ of our story with the island of Bakhar did we not know for certain that the river did not flow in that bed in those days (see the section on the rivers of Sind), and Bakhar is also known as Beṭ.

to whom he was very useful in the crossing of the river, in return for which the Arab commander eventually gave him, in perpetuity, the whole of the district of Beṭ with all the villages attached to it. From his camp on the western bank of the Mihrān Muḥammad sent a challenge to Dāhir to come over and fight him. As was his custom, he consulted Hajjāj before making any further move, and so, as usual, loses much time, which he seems to have occupied in shifting his camp about from place to place. Hajjāj, even, asked him to send him a sketch map of the river, for some miles up and down stream, in order that he might be able to advise him as to his best point for crossing! Dāhir's inaction all this time, with the enemy almost at his gates, is surprising. It was finally settled that Muḥammad should take advantage of the island of Beṭ to cross by a bridge of boats where he would have two narrow streams instead of a single very wide one. The boats were lashed together along the side of the bank to the length of the width of the stream, and then, the lower end being made secure, the upper was let go and allowed to swing round until it came in contact with the opposite bank where it was fastened. The crossing was safely effected before Dāhir was aware of it, and Muḥammad entrenched himself against the enemy. Between himself and Rāwar, further down the river, was a lake called Gujrī.[1]

It is said that the Arab horsemen were "so covered with coats of mail that they appeared to be, as it were, drowned in iron." As Dāhir's army was somewhere in a south-easterly direction from this, Muḥammad moved towards the lake and arrived at the town of Jitor. He now had the lake between himself and a party of the enemy sent there by Dāhir to obstruct his progress and watch his movements. To make a long story short, it may be sufficient to record that after crossing the lake by a solitary boat which took thirty at a time,[2] and after sundry battles and skirmishes between the two armies, a great and final battle was fought in which Dāhir lost his life and his forces were dispersed. Jaisiah, with most of the stragglers, retreated to, and shut themselves up in the fort of Rāwar.[3] Dāhir had reigned thirty-three years, and the whole period of the Brahman dynasty was ninety-two years.[4] According

[1] This name گوجري Gūjrī, is also transcribed کوچري Kūchrī, but Raverty writes it کنجري Kinjri or کنگري Kingrī, in transcribing it from Mīr Ma'ṣūm, and locates it "about twenty miles west of the ruins of Alor," where there is still a place called Kingrī (*Mih. of Sind*, 240n.); and, perhaps, he is right, although he has located Rāwar more than a hundred and twenty miles south of this, and close to Brahhmanābād. Assuming the main river to have flowed, at that period, in a channel as shown on the map as its probable course, I would be inclined to place Rāwar on the eastern bank somewhere about the K in Khairpūr or even a little further south. North of this would come Kingrī lake, a straggling *dhandh* connected with the river at its lower end and extending away in a north-easterly direction. North of the lake again, and perhaps some distance east of the river, would be Jitor, close to or upon a stream, called Dohārah, running in a south-westerly direction into the main river. Further to the north still, on an island in the river, would be the fort of Beṭ. This arrangement lends itself to a better grasp of the movements of the opposing forces during the fights which followed. It is impossible to arrive at any certainty, however, on account of the sad want of agreement in the works of the different writers. As already stated, I follow chiefly the account as given in Fredunbeg's translation of the *Chach Namah*. Even the different authorities and eye-witnesses quoted in this work, do not always agree, which is, to some extent, a proof of the genuineness of the work.

[2] Not three at a time as Raverty quotes Mīr Ma'ṣūm as saying (*Mihrān of Sind*, 240n.).

[3] Mīr Ma'ṣūm says Alor, but this appears to be a mistake. He is rather a careless writer, and cannot always be depended upon.

[4] According to the *Tuhfatu-l-Kirām*.

to one account Muḥammad took Dāhir's wife, Lādī, to himself, but, according to another, she threw herself over the ramparts and was killed, on hearing of her husband's death.

Jaisiah, then, with his sister, Bāī, and the remnant of their forces, shut themselves up in the fort of Rāwar; but, upon the advice of the *Wazīr* Siyākar, Jaisiah betook himself to Brahmanābād, leaving queen Bāī, who was determined to defend the fort. When, however, she found there was no chance of holding out against the invader, she collected all her chief women, and, with them, committed herself to the flames. After this the fort fell to Muhammad Qāsim, who is said to have massacred some six thousand persons. There was, now, no immediate reason for going on to Alor, but rather to follow up Jaisiah to Brahmanābād before he could reassemble fresh forces, and this course Muḥammad took. Jaisiah invoked the aid of his own brother, Fōfī who seems to have been left in charge at Alor, or who had established himself there on the death of Dāhir, together with that of his nephew, Chach, son of Daharsiah, at Bātiah, and his cousin Dhal, son of Chandar, in the country of Budhiyah and Kīkāvān. On his way to Brahmanābād Muhammad attacked and took the two fortified towns of Bahrōr and Dahlelah which were situated between Rāwar and Brahmanābād, where he spent two months at each place before they fell into his hands. "Some say after taking Dahlelah, Muhammad Kasim called Banūnah, son of Dhāran [to whom he had given the governorship of Dahlelah], received homage from him and entrusted to him the work of collecting and superintending of the boats along the bank of the river from Dahlelah to a place called Wadhatiah.[1] The distance between that place and Brahmanābād was one league." Though nothing can be said for certain, it is quite likely that Muhammad crossed over to the Hakṛāh (Eastern Nārā) upon which Dahlelah stood, and, by a branch from it, running in the direction of Brahmanābād, brought much of his heavy stores on by boats.[2] He fixed his camp on the bank of the small stream Halwāi[3], to the east of Brahmanābād, where its old bed is perfectly distinct, for some distance up and down, to this day, and from here he summoned the town to surrender and pay tribute or become Muhammadans. There are said to have been some forty thousand fighting men in Brahmanābād, who daily issued forth and gave battle, and, in this way, they kept the invader at bay for six months. This was in the year A.D. 712. Jaisiah, taking some of the troops with him left the fort before Muhammad's arrival, and employed these in harrassing the Arab army, eventually retiring to the district of Jitor. When Brahmanābād was unable to hold out any longer, and Jaisiah continued to absent himself, certain of the leading men, after consulting among themselves, surrendered the fort to Muhammad Qāsim; and, to cover their treachery, they arranged with the Arabs that they should make a pretence of a sortie out of the Jarbaterī gate, and then retire, leaving the gate open so that the Arabs might enter upon

[1] Haig transcribes this name, from an India Office copy of the *Chach Nāmah*, as Duhātī and calls the governor of Dhalīl (Dahlelah) Nubah, son of Dhāran (*J. R. A. S* XVI, part 2).

[2] This may have been the river which Raverty brings down towards Brahmanābād from a point in the Hakṛān about forty miles to the north of that place.

[3] Haig calls this the Jalwālī, (*J. R. A. S.* XVI. Part 2)

their heels. Some accounts say that Lādī, Dāhir's widow, was then in Brahmanābād, and that she endeavoured to hold out to the last. Muḥammad is said to have executed 6,000 men, or, as some accounts have it, 16,000.

To the principal men who had surrendered the city Muḥammad gave over the government of the place, and honoured them, and he appointed tax gatherers for the towns and villages around. All Brahmans who had previously held offices were confirmed in these. Seeing that Muḥammad was so generous to the Brahmans, the keepers of the idol-houses and temples, who were out of pocket owing to the neglect of the people to carry on their worship, and who feared the Muḥammadans, presented this petition to him: "May the just Governor live long! We are monks and priests. We used to live long on the earnings of Budh temples. When you have shown so much mercy and kindness to the traders and other infidels, who have guaranteed to pay the fixed capitation tax and have become *zimmīs* (protected), we, your slaves, also entertain the same hope of your lordly kindness, and request that you will kindly intimate your permission to them to visit Budh temples, and to worship what they worshipped before." They further told him that all their temples were lying desolate and in ruins, and they had no opportunity of worshipping their idols, and asked that they should be permitted to repair their temples. Muḥammad referred this matter to Hajjāj who replied as follows: "I have received my dear cousin Muḥammad Qāsim's letter, and have become acquainted with its contents. With regard to the requests of the chiefs of Brahmanābād about the building of Budh temples, and toleration in religious matters, I do not see what further rights we have over them beyond the usual tax. Because, after they have become *zimmīs* we have no right whatever to interfere with their lives or their property. Do therefore permit them to build the temples of those they worship. No one is prohibited from, or punished for following his own religion, and let no one prevent them from doing so, so that they may live happy in their homes." Muḥammad therefore, allowed the people to follow their own customs in every way so long as the usual taxes were paid.[1]

From his camp, higher up the river and not far from Brahmanābād, Muḥammad, after he had settled all the affairs of that place, wrote an account thereof to Hajjāj, describing the conquest of Sind. Hajjāj advised him to quit Brahmanābād and establish his head-quarters at Alor or Multān, these being more important towns, and more convenient as a base of operations against the country further east, which Hajjāj was now anxious to bring under Arab rule. Therefore, after appointing governors over the principal districts of Sind, he left Brahmanābād on the third of the month of Muharram in A.H. 94 (A.D. 712) and arrived at a town called Musthal[2] in the vicinity of Sāwandī, where the residents were Sāmānīs, Bahzams (artizans ?), and merchants, encamping on the bank of the lake. Here he appointed two men to be their head-men — one a Sāmānī and

---

[1] In the early days of the khilāfat this practice was constantly followed.

[2] Haig writes this, Mathal (*J. R. A. S.* XVI, Part 2). On account of placing Rāwar in the south of Sind, he reverses Muḥammad's movements up to his arrival at Brahmanābād. More detailed notice of his movements round about Brahmanābād is given further on in the account of that place.

the other a Buddhist. Thence he marched to Bahrowar,[1] and from there proceeded to that part of the country where the Sammahs lived. Then he went on to the land of the Sahtahs, where he called for a list of all the stages and camping places on the way thence up to Alor. Continuing his journey, he arrived within a mile of Alor, where Fōfī, son of Rāi Dāhir, had been fortifying himself with the intention of resisting the Arab forces, and fixed his camp opposite the fort where he built a mosque. The people of Alor had been told that Dāhir was still alive and had gone to get assistance, and so, in expectation of his coming to their succour, they shut themselves up in the fort and prepared for defence. But Fōfī, being at length convinced of Dāhir's death, secretly left the fort and joined his brother Jaisiah at Jitor, upon which the people of the town opened the gates to Muhammad and submitted to him Within the town was a Budh-temple called Nōbhār or Nōwhār, (Naubahār or Nau Wihār) in which was an equestrian statue, made of marble or alabaster, with golden jewelled bracelets.

After he had settled the affairs of Alor, and had left Rawāh, son of Asad, there as governor, he marched to the fortified town of Bābiah on the southern bank of the Beas. Thence he crossed the river and proceeded to the fort of Gholkandah, which he reduced, and continued on to Sīkkah-Multān[2] on the banks of the Rāwī. He was over two months in besieging Multān after he had taken Sīkkah, and it only fell at last through treachery, one of the inhabitants having pointed out to him a weak part of the walls which he promptly breached, and sacked and destroyed the town. He was told that great treasure was buried beneath the idol in a temple on the eastern side of the city. This he visited, and "found an idol made of gold, with two eyes of red rubies in its face. It was so like a living man that Muḥammad Kāsim mistook it for one, and he drew his sword in order to strike it. The keeper of the idol said: "O just commander, this is only an idol, which has been made by Jaswīn, the king of Multān, who has buried his treasure here." Muḥammad then ordered the idol to be removed, and it was found to weigh 230 maunds of gold, and the treasure contained in the 40 jars, which were buried beneath the idol, was then brought out and weighed. It amounted to 1,320 maunds of gold. The idol, and the buried gold were removed to the treasury, and the town was looted of all other treasure, exposed or buried, that could be found.

At this time Muhammad received a letter from Hajjāj telling him that the money that he had sent to the Khalīfah had doubled the amount that had been originally advanced for the expedition, with 20,000 *dirams* over and above. He therefore exorted him to build mosques and set up pulpits in every town and village, and to strike coins in the name of the Khalīfah. Muḥammad, thereupon, fixed his head-quarters at Multān and built a large mosque there. All superfluous treasure he despatched to the Khalīfah's treasury, by way of Debal where it was transferred into sea-going ships.

---

[1] Probably Bahror, or Bahrūr, already mentioned, a fortified town between Rāwar and Brahmanābād, which he took on his way to the latter place. Raverty says: "Muhammad leaving a governor there (at Brahmanabad) moved toward Aror and Baghrūr." And later, after the fall of Multān, he says: "After this success, Muḥammad, son of Kāsim, returned to Alor or Aror and Baghrūr" *Mihran of Sind*, 241 and 254

[2] Sīkkah appears to have been on one side of the river and Multān on the other.

It only now remains to relate the tragedy of the death of the Conqueror of Sind—a born leader of men, though barely twenty, and a most faithful servant of the Khilāfat. Muḥammad set out upon a northerly excursion to demarcate the boundary of his newly acquired province quite unconscious of the terrible punishment that his outraged and angry master was preparing for him. While on a march to Udhāpūr[1] he received a letter from the Khalīfah charging him with having outraged the two daughters of Dahir before sending them on the Khalīfah's *zanānah.* The Khalīfah ordered him to have himself sewn up in a freshly skinned bullock's hide and sent back to him at Damascus. Muḥammad, faithful even unto such a cruel death, and without murmur, and conscious of his innocence, had the sentence carried out upon himself, and he died two or three days after being so treated.[2] The charge was made upon a pretended confession of the girls themselves who, when they knew that Muḥammad was dead, admitted that their confession was false, and that it had been made in order to bring disgrace and punishment upon the man who had brought such misery upon their own people. The Khalīfah, in great remorse for the death of Muḥammad, had the sisters put to an even more cruel death.[3] Muḥammad probably spent, altogether, about three and a quarter years in Sind. It is said that his tomb is still to be seen at Damascus.

This was the most notable invasion of Sind, carried out with a thoroughness that did not often characterize such campaigns. Whether the whole credit of its success is due to its young leader or not there are no means of telling; but, if it were due in part to his counsellers there is no mention of it, or of disputes among these persons, as one would expect there would be at times of divided counsels. He seems to have referred much to Hajjāj, whose advice he invariably followed, but this was more in connection with the larger issues; in smaller matters, though, at times, of vital importance, he more often had to fall back upon his own quick judgment and ready decision. There is no doubt that if Muḥammad Qāsim had not possessed wisdom and tact beyond his years, there would at some time have been trouble among his followers.

This concludes the story of the *Chach Nāmah*, which, of necessity, has been very much abridged in the telling. It is, however, full of interesting detail; and the reader who is more deeply interested in the history and traditions of Sind will find in it much to gratify his thirst for further knowledge. The outline of the continuation of its history is taken mostly from Mirza Kalichbeg Fredunbeg's second volume. The works from which he has compiled this are the *Tarikh Ma'ṣūmi*, the *Tuhfatu-l-Kirām*, the *Fath Nāmah*, and the *Frere Nāmah.*

---

[1] Raverty says this place Odih-pur is the Odipoor of the maps, 14 miles to the south of Alwānah on the Hakṛāh. (*Mihran of Sind,* 254n.).

[2] The *Futūhu-l-Buldān* states that Muḥammad Qāsim was seized, fettered, imprisoned and tortured by the Khalīfah's order (Elliot's *Appendix to the Arabs in Sind*, 312).

[3] Bilādurī, who ascribes his death to family and faction jealousy, gives a different story. Hajjāj, dying about this time "a new king arose which knew not Joseph"—Sālih, the new governor of 'Irāq. Between Hajjāj and Sālih there appears to have been a blood feud, so the latter sent Yazid to take charge in Sind, recalled Muḥammad and put him, and others of his family to death. The people of Hind wept for Muḥammad. (Elliot's *Hist.*, 1, 124).

Soon after Muḥammad's death things went wrong in the newly conquered province, for it is said that, two years after that event, of the whole country, save only that "from Debal to the salt sea," little remained in the hands of the agents of the Khalīfah. Many of the chiefs and feudatory princes of Sind revolted, and Jaisiah had regained possession of Brahmanābād, so that it became necessary to send fresh forces from 'Irāq against them. These punitive expeditions became frequent as time went on. For forty years (A.D. 711-750) the country was more or less under the Ummeide Khalīfahs when it passed into the hands of the 'Abbāsides. Of the thirty-seven Khalīfāhs of the 'Abbāside family Sind remained under the first twenty-five, when it passed into the hands of other rulers. The *Tuhfatu-l-Kirām* tells us that it was during the period of the Ummeide dynasty that Dalūrāi reigned at Alor, and Bhanbhōrāi at Bambhor in the delta, which place he is said to have founded and called after himself.[1] Dalūrāi was the king for whose misdeeds the punishment of heaven fell upon him and his people through the diversion of the river from Alor and the subsequent ruin of that town. The story is sometimes transferred to Brahmanābād, which, for his sins, was destroyed by an earthquake. This same story accounts for the ruins of many other towns in Sind and the Panjāb.[2] In A.D. 750 Abdullāh Saffāh, the first of the 'Abbāside Khalīfahs, sent an army into Sind which ousted the lieutenants of the Ummeides, and four years later the next Khalīfah, Manṣūr, also sent an expedition to Hind and Sind. Al Idrisi tells us that Manṣūra, the first Arab capital in Sind, was founded in the beginning of the reign of the latter (A.D. 753-774).[3] In the time of the fifth Khalīfah, Hārūn Al Rashīd, (786-808), Shaikh Abū Turāb seized upon the fortified town of Tharrah in the district of Sākōrah, Bakhar in northern Sind, and other places in the western parts. This man's tomb, together with those of other persons slain at the time, is still visited, and the dome over it bears the date 171 A.H. (A.D. 787). It is said to have been in this Shaikh's time that Bhambōr, and some other towns, are supposed to have been destroyed by an earthquake.[4] The tomb is situated about 8 miles south-west of Thaṭhah between Gūja and Kōrī. About the time of the Khalīfah Māmūn (A.D. 813-833) many Arab families residing at Sāmrah emigrated to Sind, together with Tamīm and his descendants, and permanently settled down in the country. From the colony from Sāmrah the tribe of Sūmrahs originated, and from the descendants of Tāmin sprang the Thahīms. When the power and influence of the Khalīfahs began to wane, towards the end of the ninth century or the beginning of the tenth, "the most distant provinces necessarily partook of the decline from which the heart of the empire was suffering; and Sind, neglected by the imperial government, came to be divided among several petty princes,

[1] It was while Bhanbhōrāi ruled at Bhambor that Sasūī was born, whose love for Punhūn forms the favourite subject of many Sindhi poems and legends, which are sung and told to the present day.

[2] This story of Dalūrāi is placed at a much later date further on in the *Tuhfat-l-Kirām*, where the events are said to have taken place in the reign of one of the Sūmrah princes. (Fredunbeg's *History of Sind*, Vol. II, pp. 28 and 37).

[3] It was this Manṣūr (Abū Ja'far Al Manṣur) who built the present city of Baghdād in A.H. 148 (A.D. 765) and made it the seat of the Khilāfat, having transferred it from Hāshimiya.

[4] Further details about these old cities will be found further on, in the accounts of their ruins.

who, though they transmitted no revenue and rendered no political allegiance to the Khalīf, were, like other more powerful chiefs who had assumed independence glad to fortify their position by acknowledging his spiritual supremacy, and flattering him by the occasional presentation of some rarity from the Kingdoms which they usurped..........The two principal kingdoms which were established in Sind a few years after this event [A.D. 871] were those of Multān and Manṣūra, both of which attained a high degree of power and prosperity."[1] The Amīrs of Multān and Manṣūra were independent of one another. The rule of the Arabs in Sind came to an end when Mahmud of Ghaznī sent an army under Wazīr 'Abdū-r-Razzāq (A.D. 1025), who carried his successful arms to the towns of Sehwān and Ṭhaṭhah, driving the Arabs out of the country. The governors of the 'Abbāside Khalīfahs are said to have ruled Sind for 283 years. The *Kāmilu-t-Tawārikh* places the capture of Manṣūra by Mahmud of Ghazni's troops in the year A.H. 416 (A.D. 1025),[2] on his return from the sack of Somnātha, when he placed a Muḥammadan prince on the throne of Manṣūra, from which it may be gathered that the prince there at that time had probably abjured his faith.[3]

"With regard to the Arab dominion in Sind, it is impossible for the traveller to wander through the land, without being struck with the absence of all record of their occupation. In language, architecture, arts, traditions, customs and manners, they have left but little impress upon the country or the people. We trace them, like the savage Sikhs, only in the ruins of their predecessors; and while Mahfūza, Baizā, and Manṣūra have so utterly vanished, that 'etiam periêre ruinæ,' the older sites of Bhambōra, Alōr, Multān, and Sehwān still survive to proclaim the barbarism and cruelty of their destroyers. It has, indeed, been observed, as a circumstance worthy of remark, that no people ever constructed so many edifices as the Arabs, who extracted fewer materials from the quarry—the buildings of the first settlers being everywhere raised from the wrecks of cities, castles and fortresses, which they had themselves destroyed."[4]

For the next 160 years Sind was, for the greater part, under the Sulṭāns of Ghaznī; after that, about A.D. 1187, it came under the kings of the house of Ghōr, which displaced the Ghaznī family and invaded India. Shāhābu-d-dīn Ghori appointed Quṭbu-d-dīn Ībak to lead an expedition against Sind, which he conquered, and where he left a governor in charge. Quṭbu-d-dīn became the first of the Slave Kings of Delhi, and, on his death, the empire was parcelled out into four parts, one of which comprised Uchh, Multān, and Sind which was governed by Nasru-d-dīn Kabā-Chah, son-in-law of Quṭbu-d-dīn. From the rule of the Slave Kings Sind passed under that of the Khiljīs, whose lieutenants were appointed governors of the country. During the reign of Ghiyāsu-d-dīn, the first of the Taghlaq kings, who followed the Khiljīs, the tribe of Sūmrahs assembled in the vicinity of Tharri or Tharrah, revolted, and took

[1] Elliot's *Appendix to the Arabs in Sind*, 50-55.
[2] Mīr Ma'ṣūm says A.H. 417.
[3] Elliot's *Appendix to the Arabs in Sind*, 59.
[4] Crichton's *Arabia and its people*, p. 426.

possession of Ṭhaṭhah, and, later on, during the reign of Firūz Shāh Taghlak (A.D. 1351-1389), they joined the rebel Tāghī, together with the tribes of Jārejahs and Sammahs, in revolt against Delhi, but were speedily subdued. Firūz Shāh, on this occasion, when on his return towards Delhi, visited the shrine of Shāhbaz Kalandar at Sehwān, and fixed some stipendiary allowances for the keepers of the shrine and other men connected with it.

During the Taghlak rule Sind was continually harrassed by the inroads of rival factions, until, on the approach of Āmīr Timūr, the Tartar prince, and the disturbance caused in upper India by this foreign invasion (about A.D. 1398), the rulers of Sind threw off their allegiance to the kings of Delhi and thereafter ruled their country independently. Foremost among these local rulers were the Sūmṛahs who, as already mentioned, are supposed to have come from the town of Sāmṛah some time in the ninth century of the Christian era, during the Khilāfat of Māmūn the 'Abbāssī. There were nineteen rulers in succession in this line, and they continued, as a power in Sind, until their fall at the hands of the Sammahs. They acquired supremacy in the district of Lār or Lower Sind, around Debal, about A.D. 874, and they were ousted by the Sammahs in A.D. 1337.[1] **The Sūmṛahs.**

Whatever the origin of the Sammahs may have been, who were at this time settled in Sind, it seems certain that they were of Rājput descent, and the Jarejahs of Kachh still derive their origin from them.[2] On clearing out the Sūmṛahs they set up one of their number, Unar as ruling chief, with the title of Jām (A.D. 1351).[3] One of his first acts was an attack upon Sehwan, where Malak Ratan, a Turk, was governor under Delhi. In this enterprise he was successful, Malak Ratan being killed in the action which followed. But falling into a profligate life, and losing proper control of his government, rebellions were fomented, especially by the friends of Malak Ratan, in one of which he lost his life. He was succeeded by his son Jām Jūnah[4] (A.D. 1354) who drove the Tartar forces from Bakhar. After a reign of thirteen years he was succeeded by his nephew Jām Tamāchī whose territory was invaded by Sulṭān Alāu-d-dīn, who carried him away a prisoner to Delhi. During his absence, his brother Bābīnah took over charge of the government in Sind until Khairu-d-dīn, son of Tamāchī, who had grown to man's estate during his exile, returned to Sind and became chief of the tribe. Khairu-d-dīn was followed on the *gadi* by his son Jām Bābīnah, who is credited with having built the town of Sāmuī,[5] but some say that the **The Sammahs.**

---

1 Raverty's *Mihrān of Sind*, p. 502n. The *Tuhfatu-l-Kirām* says their ascendancy extended over a period of 505 years. Elliot says they were expelled in A.D. 1251. *Appendix to the Arabs in Sind*, p. 194.

2 Burton's *Sind and the Races*, etc., 378.

3 Ferishtah (Briggs') gives a list of the kings of Sind, which purports to include only the Sammahs, Arghūns, and Tarkhāns, but it is defective in most cases, through the omission or the changing of the diacritical points and dots of the letters, *e.g.* he writes Chowbān for Jūnān—three dots instead of one dot under the initial letter, and the dot below instead of above the third letter.

4 Raverty gives the name as Jūnān. *Mihrān of Sind*, p. 329n.

5 Sāmuī lay just below the Makli hill, and quite close to Ṭhaṭhah. It is now represented by a small hamlet upon a mound.

foundation was laid by Jām Bābīnah the son of Unar. Jām Salāhu-d-dīn,[1] Jām Nizāmu-d-dīn and Jām Alīshar followed upon the throne. During this time there were constant invasions of the country by the Delhi troops, and local rebellions and outbreaks took place in the north of Sind. Tamāchī's other sons Sikandar and Karn conspired against Jām Alishar and killed him, when Jām Karn siezed upon the government, but was, in turn, assassinated and succeeded by his nephew Jām Faṭh Khān. Jām Taghlaq and Jām Sikandar followed. All through these reigns Sehwān and Bakhar figure as important governorships which, with the fortunes of war, frequently changed hands. Sāmuī appears to have been the capital during this period.

The government of Sind now passed into the hands of a family from Kachh Jām Rāidinah, who was now elected chief, had been living in that province, but his relationship to the late ruler is not clear. Within a year and a half of his accession he had brought the whole of Sind under his sway. He was, however, poisoned by one, Sanjar, one of his chief attachés, who usurped the throne and became the Jām of Sind. Under his rule Sind prospered more than it had ever done before. After a successful reign of eight years he died in A.D. 1490, and was followed by Jām Nizāmu-d-dīn, nicknamed Jām Nindo who was elected by the tribe to fill his place. According to the *Tuhfatu-l-Kirām* he was the son of Bābīnah, who was the son of Unar, who was the son of Salāhu-d-dīn, who was the son of Tamāchī. Jām Nindo's reign was a long and, on the whole, a peaceful one. It is variously given by different writers as, 43, 48, 63 and even 73 years. His tomb is one of the more conspicuous mausolea on the Makli hill above Ṭhaṭhah which is described further on in the account of that place (Plates XXXIII and XXXIV). He is said to have moved his seat of government from Sāmuī to Ṭhaṭhah, which he is supposed to have founded. He was a man of letters rather than of war, and was much in the company of learned men whom he delighted to honour. Mīr Ma'ṣūm, in writing of him, says: "It is said, that, at the commencement of his manhood, he sought after knowledge, spending much of his time in the college and cloister. His disposition was modest and happy; he was celebrated for his good affectionate temper; he offered much prayer to God, doing great abstinence. His excellences are beyond what little I can write." The date of his death is variously given, the *Tuhfatu-l-Kirām* placing it in A.D. 1508 and the Tarikh *Ma'sūmi* in A.D. 1510. His son, Jām Firuz, followed him on the throne, but being a minor, an officer of the court, and adopted son of Jām Nindo, Darya Khān, was constituted regent, and managed all public affairs. He had such power in the state, since the Jām, as he grew up, preferred to pass his time in his *harīm*, seldom appearing in public, that Firuz began to get uneasy and entertain secret fears of him. As a precautionary measure, he enlisted in his service Kībak Arghūn, and a large number of Mughals, who, during this and the previous reign, had come into the country with Shāhbeg from Kandhār. Jām Firuz gave them a special quarter in the town of Ṭhaṭhah, which was called the Mughal

[1] The author of the *Hadikatu-l-Aulia* states that Jām Jūnāh, Jām Tamāchī and his son Jām Salahud-d-in occupied the throne of Sind in succession.

Wārah. Though he flattered himself that he had checkmated Darya Khān by this move, he little dreamed of what trouble these same men were destined to bring upon him, for it was through some of these that Shāhbeg Arghūn was induced to push home his conquest of Sind in A.D. 1519 and displace the Sammah dynasty. The Sammahs appear to have been either Hindus or Buddhists who subsequently became proselytes to Islām.

The Arghūns

When Shāhbeg advanced against Ṭhaṭhah, he passed through the Lakī hills, and came to within about six miles of the capital, where he halted and encamped on the bank of the Khānwāh (A.D. 1519). Here he fought a successful battle with Darya Khān, who led the troops of Firuz, and killed him. The Jām, abandoning all hope of a successful resistance, surrendered to him; but Shāhbeg was magnanimous enough to reinstate him in the government of Ṭhaṭhah and its immediate dependencies, retaining the northern half of Sind for himself. When this settlement was ratified, Shāhbeg left Ṭhaṭhah and marched out on his return journey.

Jām Firuz then settled down to rule his diminished province, but it was not long before Jām Salāhu-d-dīn, who had some time previously rebelled against him, and had retreated to Gujarāt, once more invaded Ṭhaṭhah with an army of ten thousand men provided by Sulṭān Muzaffar. Salāhu-d-dīn was defeated and slain and his army was scattered. One of the leaders in this battle was Mīrzā 'Isā Tarkhān who, later on, became the founder of the Tarkhān dynasty of Sind. Shāhbeg, about this time, went to Sehwān and inspected the new fort, and erected buildings in the fort of Bakhar. The ancient site of Alor and the old town of Bakhar were denuded of their materials in order to repair the fort of Bakhar and provide it with housing accommodation for his troops. After appointing Muḥammad Tarkhān as governor of Bakhar, Shāhbeg set out upon the conquest of Gujarāt, by way of Sehwān and Ṭhaṭhah, but died upon the road (A. D. 1521).[1] Before starting, however, he promised Jām Firuz, that, should he conquer that province, he would restore the whole of Sind to the Jām. Mīrzā Shāh Hasan was proclaimed his father's successor, and he publicly assumed control in the town of Naṣrpūr. Shāhbeg's remains were sent to Makka, where they were buried.

Mīrzā Shāh Ḥasan, hearing that Jām Firuz contemplated throwing off his allegiance, now that Shāhbeg was dead, returned to Ṭhaṭhah, when the Jām took to flight at his approach and fled to Kachh in order to get assistance from the Rāi. Obtaining this he opposed Shāh Ḥasan in a general engagement, but was defeated, whereupon he fled to Gujarāt where he remained until his death. Mīrzā Shāh Ḥasan now took possession of the whole of Sind.

After several minor punitive expeditions against local offenders, Mīrzā Shāh Ḥasan determined upon the reduction of Multān; but, before carrying out this enterprise, he paid homage to the emperor Bābar, who was then marching into Hindustān, and between them a matrimonial alliance was concluded. Shāh Ḥasan continued his march upon Multān in the following year (A.D. 1524).

[1] The *Tarkhān Nāmah* states that Shāhbeg died in A.H. 926 (A.D. 1519), but Ferishtah puts it in A.H. 93 (A.D. 1523).

taking certain forts and towns on the way. He reached the city without further opposition, and coming to terms with the ruler, fixed the river Ghārō as the boundary between their respective provinces. After reducing the fort of Dilāwar where much treasure was said to be buried, Shāh Ḥasan returned to Bakhar. Fresh trouble at Multān took him back there again the next year, when he attacked and took the place and once more returned to Bakhar.

The Mīrzā's next enterprise was an attack upon Rāi Khangār of Kachh in his own country, who had challenged him to battle for having killed his brother, Āmīr Amrānī, in a fight which took place between Shāhbeg's forces and Darya Khān's sons on the river near Taltī.[1] Rai Khangār was defeated.

During Shāh Ḥasan's reign, the emperor Humāyūn, who had succeeded Bābār on the throne of Delhi, was driven forth from his capital by Sher Shāh Sūrī Afghān. With his following, he made his way towards Sind and camped at Bakhar. It was during his wanderings about Sind and Rājputānā that Akbar, his son, was born at Umarkoṭ in A.D. 1542. We are told that Bābarlo, or Bāburlo, a place six miles from Bakhar "with its four celebrated gardens was decorated, its buildings adorned and its fort repaired, in order to be fit for the residence and protection of the Emperor Humāyūn and his family," as it was a very pleasant spot.

Towards the end of his reign Mirzā Shāh Ḥasan was attacked with paralysis, and he then allowed his administrative work to fall into the hands of strangers, while he, it is said, took a strange fancy to sailing up and down the Indus between Ṭhaṭhah and Bakhar; so it came about that in A.D. 1554 the Arghūns and Tarkhāns made common cause, and taking Mīrzā 'Īsā Tarkhān as their leader, openly caused a revolt. A division of the province was agreed upon, but it was deferred until Mīrzā Shāh Ḥasan's death, which, it was then considered, could not be far off. Shortly after, in the same year, he died on his way to Sehwān. It was arranged to take his body to Makka for burial, but it was at first taken to Ṭhaṭhah where it was temporarily interred in the enclosure of Mīr Aḥmad Walī, on the bank of the river. Within three months a mausoleum was built upon the Makli hill, whence, after two years, it was removed to Makka where it was buried beside his father's remains. Mīrzā Shāh Ḥasan reigned thirty-four years.

The Tarkhāns.

On the death of Mīrzā Shāh Ḥasan, Ṭhaṭhah was seized by Mīrzā 'Īsā Tarkhān while Sultān Maḥmud Khān established himself at Bakhar, Sehwān becoming a bone of contention between them and other nobles, and finally falling into the hands of the Mīrzā. He married Māh Bēgam the widow of the late ruler, Mīrzā Shāh Ḥasan's only son died in infancy.

From his youth Mīrzā 'Īsā Khān had been a companion of Shāhbeg Arghūn, and subsequently became one of his principal lieutenants. Early in his reign he

[1] Taltī seems to have been a favourite crossing place on the river, and it is no doubt the same place as shown upon modern maps six or seven miles north of Sehwān. Shāhbeg had just crossed before this action took place; nor was this the only time he used this crossing. Mīr Ma'ṣūm, forgetting that the main river, at that time, was very much further away from Sehwān, makes Muḥammad Qāsim cross it at Taltī on his way to Alor after the fall of Nīrūn and Sīwastān. Raverty, who spells it Tahlti, says it is "on the east side of the river which we call the 'Western Nāra', whose channel in former times, was, no doubt, a branch of the Sindhu or Āb-i-Sind, and at that period, it may have been known as the Kumbh or Kunbh, or river of the Kumbh or Kunbh." (*Mihrān of Sind*, p. 240n.).

quarrelled with Sulṭān Maḥmud K͟hān and attacked him at Bakhar; and it is at this juncture that we first hear of Europeans in Sind. About the year A.D. 1555[1] the Mīrzā sent an embassy to the Portuguese at Bassein to ask their assistance against Sulṭān Maḥmud of Bakhar, with whom he was fighting. This request was complied with, and a force of 700 men sailed under the command of Pedro Barreto Rolim. On their arrival at Ṭhaṭhah they found that their services were no longer required, and they were refused the payment of their expenses by the governor of Ṭhaṭhah in the absence of Mīrzā 'Īsā K͟hān, who was still in the field. Exasperated by this treatment, and finding the city unprotected and defenceless, the Portuguese fell upon it and sacked it. "Barreto landed his men, entered the city, and in the fury killed above 8,000 persons and destroyed by fire the value of above two millions of gold, after loading the vessels with one of the richest booties that had been taken in Asia."[2]

Internecine quarrels and fights were constantly taking place during the reign of 'Īsā K͟hān, especially between his sons, and between him and Sulṭān Maḥmud Khān of Bakhar. In A.H. 980 (A.D. 1572) Mīrzā 'Īsā K͟hān died, and he was buried upon the Makli hill. He was succeeded by his son Mīrzā Muḥammad Bāqī.

Mīrzā Muḥammad Bāqī Tarkhān began his reign with a wholesale massacre of the Arghūns and their families who were at that time in the capital. Assisted by certain Arghūn chiefs, his brother, Mīrzā Jān Bābā, attacked him, but was defeated and obliged to retire. The attempt was repeated, when Mīrzā Muḥammad narrowly escaped with his life, being surprised when off his guard. This happened about A.D. 1568(?), and soon after Mīrzā Jān Bābā was murdered.

About this time the emperor Akbar was marching towards Multān with the professed object of visiting the shrines of the saints at that place. Upon hearing of this, Muḥammad Bāqī, in order to stand well with him, sent him his daughter in marriage, accompanied with a large retinue and presents. The Mīrzā now seems to have become possessed of a devil, and to have taken leave of his senses, for he started upon a course of wholesale assassination for which his name is still held in execration, and this ended in his taking his own life by falling upon his sword (A.D. 1584). He was buried upon the Makli hill.

After Mīrzā Muḥammad's excesses, his grandson, Mīrzā Jānī Beg's succession came as a relief to everybody, for he was a man of a kindly and considerate disposition.[3] One of his first acts was to crush a rebellion started by his uncle, Mīrzā Muzaffar, at Badīn. He encouraged commerce throughout his territory and made some important changes in the weights and measures and the coinage of the realm. It is said that, before that time, no gold coins were used except the *ashrafīs* bearing the French mark or impression. Mīrzā 'Īsā Tarkhān had introduced certain copper money that was called *'Isāī*.

[1] *History of Goa*, by J. N. Fonseca, (1878). Elliot puts the date at A.D. 1585. *History of India*, I, 276. The *Chach Namah* gives A.D. 1555.

[2] This probably accounts for a quantity of Sind tile decoration found in the church of the Jesuits at Bassein, see the Progress Report of the Archæol. Survey of Western India for the year ending 30th June, 1898, p. 6.

[3] Mīrzā Muḥammad Baqi's eldest son, the father of Jānī Beg, was Pāindah, but he was set aside as being, more or less, insane.

The emperor ot Delhi now began to interfere in the affairs of Sind, and the fort of Bakhar comes more prominently to the front in connection with the events which followed. This fort, and the country around, had for some time been governed by Sulṭān Maḥmud Khān, who, off and on, had been opposed in arms to the ruler of Ṭhaṭhah, their constant quarrels being as often patched up for the time being. The Sulṭān was of Persian descent on his father's side, his mother having been an Afghān. In A.D. 1543 the Persian king Tahmāsp bestowed upon him the title of Khān, and six years later the *parganahs* of Uchh, Āmin, and some others were given him as a *jāgīr*. In 1571 he received the title of Khān Khānan. Under Shāhbeg he followed his father, Mīr Fāzil Kōkaltāsh, as governor of Bakhar, in which post he was subsequently confirmed by the emperor Akbar, and in 1574 he died from an attack of dropsy. He was one of the most powerful and important local governors of Sind. Subsequent governors were appointed to Bakhar, in succession, by the emperor of Delhi, one of them being Nawāb Muḥammad Sādik Khān who took over charge of his office in A.D. 1585 with express instructions from the emperor to reduce Ṭhaṭhah. He encountered Mīrzā Jānī Beg's troops at Pāt where he defeated them, and again upon the river, where a battle was fought in boats. The Nawāb then turned his attention to Sehwān, but, meeting with a reverse there, fell back upon Bakhar. The Mīrzā received a letter from the emperor requiring him to pay him homage as he had previously done, and to use the imperial coins and have the emperor's name mentioned in the public orations. To this Jānī Beg sent a conciliatory reply, but it was not long before he again provoked the emperor's wrath by assuming an equality with him. A battle of boats took place upon the river in which the imperial general, Nawāb Khān Khānām, defeated Jāni Beg's troops.[1] Subsequently peace was arranged between them, but not before Jāni had written to his father, Mīrzā Pāindah Beg, and his son, Mīrzā Abul Fath, instructing them to destroy Ṭhaṭhah, probably with the intention of preventing it from falling into the hands of the enemy, and to remove their families and the people to Kalyān Koṭ, which he had already built as a fort of refuge. The destruction of the city could not have been very complete, since some part of it, at any rate, was in sufficiently good condition to accommodate Khān Khānām and his retinue when he afterwards visited it as the guest of Mīrzā Jānī Beg. Following upon this reconciliation, they both went together on a visit to the emperor (A.D. 1591). From this year the Tarkhān family surrendered the last vestige of their independence and became vassals of Delhi.

After confirming Mīrzā Jānī Beg as governor of Sehwān, Ṭhaṭhah, and the seaport Lāhori, the emperor invited him to make a long stay at his court, which lasted some eight years, during which time Mīrzā Ghāzī Beg, his son, was installed in charge of lower Sind. The latter being a minor, a council of regency was appointed. Jānī Beg's daughter was married to Akbar's son Khusro. In A.D. 1599 Mīrzā Jānī Beg died of apoplexy, and, under the emperor's orders

[1] Mīr Ma'ṣūm Shāh, the author of the *Tarikh Ma'ṣumi*, was at this time in Bakhar, and received from the emperor the *parganahs* of Darbelah, Kākri and Chāndikō.

his body was sent to Ṭhathah and buried upon the Maklī hill in the mausoleum, or *rānk*, which still stands, though in a sad state of disrepair.

Upon his father's death Mīrzā Ghāzī Beg was confirmed as governor of Ṭhathah and its dependencies. He began his term of governorship by asserting his independence of the council of regency, and made and unmade appointments as the whim seized him. For instance, he is said to have raised one, Shāhbāzī, the keeper of his pigeons and dogs, to a high post with the title of Khān. As he dismissed most of the old officers, putting new ones in their places, his conduct, naturally, very soon caused general discontent, which culminated in the rebellion of Abū-l-Qāsim Sultān, the officer in charge of Nasrpur, who openly defied his authority. But this officer, after being reconciled to his chief, and having apparently been again received into favour, was treacherously seized and blinded.

The Jām of Kakrālah now gave him trouble by encroaching upon his frontiers, but Mīrzā Ghāzī Beg marched against him and drove him off.

The emperor summoned him to court; but, soon after his departure for Delhi, the blinded Abū-l-Qāsim succeeded in making his escape only to be recaptured in the hills by Darya Khān and thrown into prison once more. On Ghāzī Beg's arrival at Agra (A.D. 1604) he was received by the emperor with marked distinction and was confirmed as governor of the *Subah* of Sind. Akbar dying, Ghāzī Beg secretly left the capital and returned to Ṭhaṭhah whence, however, he was immediately summoned back again by Jahāngīr, who professed to value his counsel in difficulties. He then appointed him to the governorship of Kandhār in addition to Ṭhaṭhah, Sehwān, and part of Multān. About this time the Mīrzā sent an embassy to Shāh Ābbās, king of Persia, with rich presents.

On learning that Khusro Khān, whom he had left in charge at Ṭhaṭhah, had been misappropriating the public money, he sent Rāi Khōriāh, with the title of Hindu Khān, to Ṭhaṭhah to examine the accounts. Khusro Khān, after some opposition, was arrested and taken back to Kandhār where Mīrzā Ghāzī Beg was at the time; but the Mīrzā being murdered just about that time, Khūsro Khān, taking advantage of the confusion which ensued, effected his escape and hurried back to Ṭhathah. Ghāzī Beg's body was brought to Ṭhaṭhah and was buried in a mausoleum in the neighbourhood of that of his father. He was the last of the rulers of Sind to be buried upon the Makli hill.

The Kalhōrahs.

The Tarkhān dynasty was succeeded by that of the Kalhōrahs. With the rise to power of this family we come to comparatively recent times, but, as their tombs, with those of the Talpūrs, who came after them, bulk largely among the monumental remains in Sind, it is necessary to notice them briefly here. They claimed descent from Ābbās, a paternal uncle of the Prophet, and, on that account, are sometimes called 'Abbāssīs. A more immediate progenitor was Ādam Shāh, whose tomb conspicuously crowns one of the hills at Sakhar, a religious leader who was killed by the ruler of Multān and thus became a *shāhīd* or martyr. It was at his own dying request that he was buried at Sakhar. His successors gained power and influence in the north of Sind, and, by degrees, gathered such a formidable following that Miān[1] Naṣīr Muḥammad, who succeeded to the chiefship of the clan in 1696, founded the town of Khārī and made it his headquarters. They are at this time spoken of as the "Sirāīs," as they came from Sirah or the upper Sind frontier. They were also known as the "*Faqīrs.*"

Miān Naṣīr Muḥammad was succeeded by his son Miān Dīn Muḥammad, who spent the latter years of his life at Multān. The Dāudpōtahs, a rival clan, who had taken up their headquarters at Shikārpūr, fought with the Sirāīs for supremacy and gave them much trouble; but they were eventually suppressed by Yār Muḥammad, the brother of Miān Dīn Muḥammad, who forged his way to the head of affairs, and seems to have usurped the ruling power. He died in A.D. 1718, and was buried in his great mausoleum at old Khudābād near Dādū. He was succeeded by his son Miān Nūr Muḥammad, who took the title of "Khudāyār Khān." He carried his arms into the surrounding districts and greatly extended his borders. Up to this time the Kalhōrahs had confined their influence and operations to upper Sind, but, in A.D. 1736, the Bakhar district fell to their lot, Sehwān having already been brought into their possession. In the next year the emperor of Delhi handed over to them the city of Ṭhaṭhah with its dependencies.

About this time Nādir Shāh, who had usurped the throne of Persia, and had taken Kandhār, meditated an invasion of India. Miān Nūr Muḥammad having been apprised of his intention of passing through Sind, sent envoys to meet him with the purpose of making friends as he was not able to meet him as an enemy. On the approach of Nādir Shāh, however, panic spread throughout the country and the Miān and his son fled to Umarkōt, whither Nādir Shāh followed and took them prisoners. For a substantial financial consideration Nūr Muḥammad was able to secure his reinstatement, but his two sons, Ghulām Shāh and Muḥammad Murādyāb, and subsequently Atur Khān, were taken away as hostages. Siwī (Sibī) was left in the hands of the Afghāns, and Shikārpūr with the Dāudpōtahs as of old. It is said that Nādir Shāh had ordered ships to be built, for his use, at Surat. Nūr Muḥammad was confirmed in his governorship by Ahmad Shāh Dūrānī, who had succeeded Nādir Shāh, and, in A.D. 1749, the Miān's sons were released and returned from Persia. His third son, Murādyāb, who had proceeded to Maskat, returned, and was appointed to take entire charge of the financial business of the state, with his headquarters at Khudābād.[2]

Miān Nūr Muḥammad died in A.D. 1755, and was succeeded by his son Muḥammad Murādyāb Khān. It was from about this time that the emperor of Delhi began to be styled "King," the empire having become much broken up, and his power and influence curtailed.

Muḥammad Murādyāb Khān was confirmed in his office by the king of Delhi, when much rejoicing took place at Naṣrpūr, near which place he founded a new town called Murādābād.

---

[1] The Kalhōrah rulers always used the prefix "Miān" to their names, which carried the meaning of spiritual guide rather than temporal chief.

[2] This Khudābād, which I call old Khudābād, about seven miles south of Dādū, must not be confused with the place of the same name near Hāla, which was, for a time, the capital of the Tālpūrs, and where there are still the tombs of some of that family.

In the fourth year of his reign, his nobles, owing to his oppression of them and his other subjects, conspired to dethrone him, and, having arrested him, they placed his brother Ghulām Shāh upon the *gadi*. Owing to his head-quarters being surrounded by the floods from the river, he abandoned it, and built another town near his father's Muḥammadābād and called it Allahābād. Atur Khān, who was, at this time, a hostage with the king, pleaded his cause with the latter so successfully that he was appointed governor of Sind and Ghulām Shāh was obliged to retire. But Atur Khān soon began to oppress the country, and, his nobles, becoming disgusted with him, espoused the cause of Ghulām Shāh who, after defeating his brother in the field, was replaced upon the throne. In due course he was confirmed by royal decree (A.D. 1758).

Atur Khān, having obtained the assistance of the Khān of Kalāt, returned to Sind and encountered Ghulām Shāh near Shāhbandar. The upshot of the engagement that followed was an arrangement whereby Ghulām Shāh was to hold all the country from Shāhgarh[1] to Naṣrpūr, including Ṭhaṭhah, while the rest was given to Atur Khān and his brother Ahmadyār Khān. Discontent between the two brothers, and the incapacity of Atur Khān as a ruler, enabled Ghulām Shāh in the end to appropriate their share of the country. Atur Khān, however, assisted this time by certain Dāudpōtah chiefs, made yet another attempt to regain his lost possessions, but he eventually gave up the struggle and surrendered himself to Ghulām Shāh who received him with kindness. In 1768 Ghulām Shāh commenced to build a strong fort at Nīrūnkōt, with the view of turning that place into his future capital, which he named Haidarābād. He died suddenly in A.D. 1772 of paralysis. He was the son of Miān Nūr Muḥammad by a dancing girl, and it is said that Nūr Muḥammad obtained that son through the blessings of a contemporary saint, Shāh 'Abdūl-Latīf Bhitāī. He is said to have been quite illiterate. His imposing mausoleum, the dome of which has fallen, stands upon the rocky plateau to the north of the town of Haidarābād.

He was succeeded by his son Miān Muḥammad Sarafrāz Khān, who was confirmed in the position by Taimūr Shāh who had succeeded Aḥmad Shāh Dūrānī. During his own and his father's time, the Derahs (Derah Ghāzī Khān and Derah 'Ismāīl Khān) were added to the government of Sind.

It was during the reign of Sarafrāz Khān that the Tālpūr Mīrs came to the front, who were destined to supplant the Kalhōrahs in the government of the land, and to hold the reins of government until they in turn were overthrown by the British. It seems he was much attached to the members of that family, but jealousy caused one, Rājāh Līkhī, to poison the mind of the Miān against them, more especially against Mīr Bāhrām. Thus it happened that, in spite of the advice of the faithful old *Diwān*, Gidūmal, the Miān treacherously had Mīr Bāhrām assassinated in his presence, which was immediately followed by that of the son, Mīr Sōbdār (A.D. 1774), the other son, Mīr Bijār, being away at the time on a pilgrimage. Mīr Sōbdār left four sons—Fath 'Alī Khān, Ghulām 'Alī Khān, Karam 'Alī Khān and Murād 'Alī Khān.

---

[1] Shāhgarh was the village of Kūjah which Ghulām Shāh rebuilt as his temporary headquarters. In its vicinity he founded a new fort which he called Shahbandar.

Mīr Fath Khān collected a number of Balūchis and surprised Sarafrāz Khān in his fort at Khudābād, when the latter fled by river to Haidarābād, where he was followed up and obliged to submit. The keys of the fort were tendered to Fath Khān who declined to receive them as a ruler, saying that he fought on behalf of Mīr Bijār, who, being his uncle and brother of Mīr Sōbdār, had a prior claim. Mīr Fath Khān's *derah* or head-quarters were at Shāhdādpūr. Rājāh Līkhī, who had transferred his allegiance to Mīr Fath Khān, took matters into his own hands and placed Miān Ghulām Nabī, son of Miān Nūr Muhammad upon the *gadi* (A.D. 1777). Sarafrāz Khān is said to have set his face against the English factories at Thathah, which had been established there in A.D. 1758, and they were eventually withdrawn in A.D. 1775.

About this time Mīr Bijār returned from his pilgrimage to Makka, and, as soon as Rājāh Līkhī heard of his arrival, and fearing his vengeance, he committed suicide. Miān Nabī Khān, who had become a tool in the hands of Tājāh Līkhī, the son of Rājāh Līkhī, and his party, was prevailed upon, against his wish, to oppose Mīr Bijār. In an action which followed between the two sides he sent confidential messengers to Mīr Bijār, throwing himself upon his mercy; but this, coming to the ears of Tājāh Līkhī, he assassinated him. He gave Miān Nabī a costly funeral and sent his body to Haidarābād for interment, where it now reposes in its mausoleum in the vicinity of that of Ghulām Shāh. ʿAbdu-n-Nabī Khān, brother of Miān Ghulām Nabī, had charge of Sarafrāz Khān, and other claimants to the throne, in the fort of Haidarābād, where, in order to secure the succession to himself, he had them all put to death.

Mīr Bijār, who had taken up his residence at the new town of Khudābād, seeing that there was no other Kalhorah chief, summoned ʿAbdu-n-Nabī from Haidarābād and placed him upon the throne, the turban of rulership being placed upon his head at the shrine of Makhdūm Nūh, whence he was escorted with great pomp to Khudābād and lodged in the palace of Sarafrāz Khān. Mīr Bijār constituted himself his chief minister and counseller, and affairs of state were properly managed. Tājāh Līkhī fell into the hands of ʿAbdu-n-Nabī and was sentenced to death, but Mīr Bijāh interceded for him and his life was spared.

The Sind revenues having seriously declined since the time of Sarafrāz, the yearly tribute could not be paid to the Kābul treasury, whereupon the king despatched an army under Izzatyār Khān, whom he appointed ruler of Sind in place of ʿAbdu-n-Nabī, but he was defeated by Mīr Bijār at Shikārpūr (A.D. 1781). King Taimūr then set out himself with an army against Sind, but, instead of opposing him, Mīr Bijār had a boat bridge made for his convenience at Rōhrī, and himself set out to meet the king. Having explained matters, and finding that his enemies had slandered him, the king forgave him and confirmed ʿAbdu-n-Nabī in the governorship of Sind. Soon after this Mīr Bijār was murdered by two Hindū Rājpūts at the instigation of ʿAbdu-n-Nabi, but he succeeded in cutting down his assailants before himself succumbing to their daggers. "Thus died the wisest, bravest and most pious nobleman, that Sind had ever produced." He was succeeded, as head of the Balūch tribe, by his son Mīr ʿAbdullah. The head-quarters of the Mīrs was now at Shāhdādpūr.

'Abdu-n-Nabī, fearing revenge at the hands of 'Abdullah, fled, with a few adherents, to Kalāt; and, as he refused to return, the latter placed a *faqīr*,[1] Sādik 'Alī Khān, on the throne, he being a distant relation of the late ruler, whom he discovered at Khāt on the river.

As Mīān Sādik 'Alī Khān was a religious devotee he did not interest himself in the affairs of state, and left that entirely to 'Abdullah Khān. 'Abdu-n-Nabī, assisted first by the Khān of Kalāt, and then by the chief of Bahāwalpūr, made unsuccessful attempts to regain his lost throne. He now sought to be reconciled with Mīr 'Abdullah, and the latter, believing in his sincerity, was thrown off his guard, with the result that one day 'Abdu-n-Nabī, getting him and his relation Mīr Fath Khān at a disadvantage, had them both assassinated together with their adherents. The Mīr's friends and relations, however, collecting a force around them, once again compelled 'Abdu-n-Nabī to flee for safety to his friend of Kalāt. In an engagement that took place Tājāh Līkhī was killed (A.D. 1782) Mīr Fath Khān, who had been elected, on the death of 'Abdullah, as chief of the Balūchi clans, was in command of the forces in this action, which was fought near the village of Hālānī Mīān 'Abdu-n-Nabī for the third time sought the assistance of the chief of Kalāt, with the result that the Brohī army, that was placed at his disposal, deserted him on arriving at the Indus, and returned home (1783). He now appears to have retired from the struggle; but, hearing that there were quarrels and factions between the Tālpūr chiefs, he determined upon one more throw of the die and petitioned Taimūr Shāh for help, telling him he had been invited to return, by Mīr Suhrāb. An Afghān force was sent to his assistance while, at the same time, he obtained additional help from the Khān of Kalāt; but, in a battle that ensued, these forces were defeated and dispersed (1787) Taimūr then marched to Sind in person only to return immediately on hearing of trouble in the far-away provinces of his own dominions. But he eventually resumed his expedition to Sind, when Mīr Fath 'Alī Khān appeasing his wrath, a treaty was made whereby the latter engaged to pay certain enhanced tribute

The Tālpūrs.

About this time Mīr Fath 'Alī Khān moved his head-quarters from Khudābād (near Hālā) to Haidarābād which became the capital of the Tālpūrs from this time onwards, and here he erected additional accommodation within the fort for the residence of himself and brothers. He divided Sind into seven shares, of which he retained three for himself. Two he apportioned to Mīr Suhrāb Khān, who was the ancestor of the Mīrs of Khairpūr, one to his own relations, and one to Mīr Thārah Khān, who became the head of the Mīrs of Mīrpūr (Mīrpur-Khās) Later, on the death of Mīr Murād 'Alī Khān, these shares were further subdivided. In this manner the whole of Sind was divided into small shares, each being retained by a young Mīr, who considered himself independent of every other. But Mīr Nūr Muhammad Khān, the eldest of the Mīrs at Haidarābād, came to be

[1] The word *faqīr*, Fredunbeg tells us, was a respectable term or title for a courtier or a follower of the Kalhōrah chiefs, who were looked upon as spiritual guides. On the tombs of the old Tālpūrs and Mīrs, the word is inscribed instead of Mīr, as on the tombs near Shāhpūr in the Sakrand *tālukah*.

acknowledged as the chief ruling prince in Sind. Of these separate states only one—that of Khairpūr—survives, as such, to the present day.

Taimūr Shāh died in A.D. 1793, and was succeeded, on the throne of Kābul, by his son Zamān Shāh, who confirmed the Mīr in his government of Sind. Mīr Fath 'Alī Khān died in A.D. 1802, when his body was taken to Khudābād (near Hālā) and buried near his relations.[1]

During the struggles between 'Abdu-n-Nabī and the Mīr, and the rebellion of certain of the Tālpūris, the country suffered terribly from the depredations of the troops, both home and foreign, who ravaged the land most unmercifully. Foreign armies, brought in to aid one side or the other, seem to have had no other object than plunder.

The British. The Tālpūrs held the country from this time onward until at the battle of Miānī when it passed into the hands of the British. The government of the country—what there was of it—was carried on in a very free and easy manner by these chiefs, who spent most of their time and means in hunting, a pastime of which they were inordinately fond. Most of the land, and that of the best, chiefly along the river, was set apart and enclosed as *shikārgarhs* or hunting preserves, where the country people were chiefly occupied in beating up game for their masters; and these *shikārgarhs* were most jealously cared for to the general neglect of the rest of the country.

It is needless to go into further details regarding the doings of the Tālpūr chiefs. They lived in indolent ease and rude luxury, and built themselves gaudy but shoddy mausolea in two great groups near the Kalhōrah tombs at Haidarābād and Khudābād, which they bedecked plentifully with brightly coloured enamelled tiles. By degrees, British influence had begun to make itself felt in the province, and in A.D. 1799 a commercial mission was opened up, but for some time the presence of European merchants or officials was not very favourably received. English factories were, in time, established, and, of course, these required troops to guard their interests. A Resident at the court of Haidarābād, and commercial and political treaties followed naturally, until the final rupture which ended in the battle of Miānī (A.D. 1843) and the downfall of Balūchi rule in Sind. In the meantime the Kābul ruler still asserted his suzerainty, and compelled the Mīrs to pay up substantial tribute. During most of this time the rupees used in Sind were those coined by the Kābul government. It was not until the time of Mīr Murād 'Alī Khān that coins were struck in his own name at Haidarābād.

[1] Mīr Karam 'Alī Khān was the first of the Tālpūr rulers to be buried at Haidarābād, in A.D. 1828.

PREHISTORIC REMAINS AND RUDE STONE MONUMENTS.

OF the prehistoric and rude stone monuments of Sind, traces of which have been found in the valley of the Indus, and in the wilder country among the hills that separate Sind from Balūchistān, we know very little as yet. To undertake the study of these remains satisfactorily, requires a considerable initial general knowledge of the subject to start with, if false and hasty deductions, from superficial examination, are to be avoided. With prehistoric monuments, especially, the " Bill-Stumps-his-mark " trap is ever set for the unwary. Hence it is not surprising that so very few among local officials, who have the best opportunities of coming across them, have attempted to explore them in any methodical manner. Casual accounts have been written of a few of these remains, but they generally lack more definite details, measurements and photographs.[1]

Among the earliest prehistoric remains are the " cores " and " flakes " of the Neolithic inhabitants found in the valley of the Indus, chiefly in the vicinity of Rōhrī and Sakhar, which are of flint from the nummulitic limestone. The following notice of these is taken from the lately published *Catalogue Raisonné of the Prehistoric Antiquities in the Indian Museum at Calcutta* : " In Sind, on the hills near Sukkur and Rohri, quantities of imperfect flakes and cores are found made from the flint which abounds in the nummulitic limestone. Many of the cores are from 3 to 4 inches long. Some smaller but very perfectly and regularly shaped cores of the same material have also been found in the bed of the Indus at Sakhar."[2] The early finds, from the bed of the river, have been described by Sir John Evans,[3] while later examples are recorded by W. T. Blanford who writes : " There can be little doubt about the late age of these cores. They are by far the most carefully formed of any hitherto found in India, and are so far superior to all ordinary forms made of the same material, that, as was pointed out by Mr. Evans in the Geological Magazine, they rather resemble those of obsidian which are found in Mexico and in some other places. Mr. Fedden noticed a peculiarity in many of the cores, which I do not recollect having seen before ; this is that several of them, at the base, present the appearance

---

[1] Mr. G. E. L. Carter, of the Indian Civil Service, has taken up this subject, as far as he is able in the intervals between his official duties, and the accounts and photographs he has sent me give promise of further interesting results of his research.

[2] See *Manual of the Geology of India*, Pt. I, p. 442.

[3] *Geological Magazine*, 1866, pp. 433-434, with plates.

of a flat surface ground by artificial means. The material is in all cases nummulitic flint.

"I am much disposed to believe that the cores found in the Indus were made by a different people from those who chipped their flakes on the hills around. This may be due to the more civilized flake-makers having established themselves on the river bank, while their less expert contemporaries roamed among the neighbouring hills or visited them for the purpose of obtaining a stock of cutting implements; or the former may have lived later, when the art of flint chipping had been brought to greater perfection. There is a possibility that the best flints were selected and carried home to the dwellings on the bank of the river, in order that cutting flakes might be obtained from them by pressure, while less perfect materials were utilized and thrown away at once.[1] However it may have happened, it is certain that all the specimens I have yet seen from the river bed are singularly well formed, shewing as a rule no trace of a flaw, and although an occasional well-shaped core may be found on the hills, the majority are broken or imperfect."

Lieutenant Twemlow, R.E., who found these, discovered them three feet below the rock in the bed of the river. The specimens were from "a mass of flints, packed together, in layers of from one and a half to two feet in thickness," resting on limestone which proved to be true nummulitic limestone, full of *N. lævigata*, and covered by recent silt deposit.

Most of what we know about prehistoric monuments in Sind is contained in an article by the late Sir Bartle Frere, when he was Commissioner of Sind, who visited some of these about 1851, in which he quotes communications from Captain Preedy, Collector of Karachi, and other local officers, and contributed an account to the Journal of the Bombay Branch of the Royal Asiatic Society for 1851 (Vol. V, p. 349). He tells us that cairns and cromlechs, such as described by Captain Meadows Taylor, are common on the road to Shāh Billāwal, in Balūchistān, and also on the direct road from Karāchi to Kotrī. They are generally known as "Kaffirs' graves."

There are numerous stone enclosures, the three principal ones being: one near Karachi, a second near Dunrāj, on the direct road to Sehwān, and a third in the valley of the Hab, near the village of "Oomed Alli Chootah," about a hundred miles north of Karāchi. The whole of these enclosures face east and west, and are constructed from large unhewn stones, piled together without cement; they are in the shape of a parallelogram, and are usually divided by transverse walls into several apartments. They vary in dimensions, that near Karāchi being 112 paces in length by 15 in breadth, the one near Dunrāj about half that size, and the third being still smaller.

Cromlechs are not numerous, only one having been noticed, a few yards in front of the stone enclosure near Dunrāj.

Cairns, met with, are piles of unhewn stones, varying from 6 to 10 feet in height. They are very numerous and are supposed to be comparatively modern.

[1] The writer seems not to have been aware of, or overlooked the fact, that the Indus did not flow in the Sakhar-Rohri bed, or near it, until long ages after this period. H. C.

Graves and barrows are frequently met with, either singly or collectively, and are always spoken of by the Sindhis as the graves of former Kaffir inhabitants. They are found most numerous in the vicinity of hot springs, and are usually covered with large stones, and are about two feet high, eight or nine in breadth and from fifteen to twenty in length. None of these seem to have been opened. The graves are most numerous in the valley of "Naing," where Mr. Frere also found "a rude kind of tope" which stood on the top of a small limestone hill, in which the spring that waters the valley has its source. It is constructed of large unhewn stones, put together without cement, and is said by the inhabitants to be over the remains of some of their tribe who were slain in battle with Delhi troops. Captain Preedy thought it far older. The dimensions he gives are, height of lower storey 7 feet, of second 6 feet, and the third 3 feet. Each storey is circular and apparently solid, the lower being 12 feet, the second 6 feet and the third 3 feet in diameter. A flight of steps on the eastern face lead up to the top of the first storey. Nūr Muḥammad Kalhorah intended to have fortified the neighbouring hills, where the spring has its source, but, beyond collecting heaps of stones for this purpose, nothing further was done.

Not far from the spring head in the valley of "Kehm," are to be found several rude caves hewn out of the rock, which have evidently been used as human habitations, though now used as cattle sheds. There is a small cave between the town of Sehwān and the *bandar*, called the "Ek Thamb" or One Pillared cave, which was visited by Dr. Wilson and is noticed in his *Memoir on the Cave Temples, etc., of Western India*. There are also several rude caves in the rock near the springs at "Kahee."

With reference to the stone graves, Captain Preedy wrote: "The stone graves alluded to by Mr. Macleod are found in great numbers throughout the hilly district which extends along our western frontier. They are usually met with in elevated positions, and consist of three or four large stones set on edge, with a flat stone placed horizontally on the top. There would appear to have been no uniform rule observed as to the direction in which these graves were placed, as in the groups I have met with they are found in all directions. I had the pleasure of pointing out one of these groups to you [Mr. Frere] a few days ago, on the hills near Waghodur, and I think we both agreed that, with the exception of the hole in one of the side stones or walls,[1] the graves exactly resemble those described by Captains Taylor and Congreve, and we are, I think, justified in regarding both as the remains of the same Scythic Druidical race."

Mr. J. Macleod, writing to Mr. Frere, said: "In the hill country west of the Indus, graveyards far from human habitations are frequent. They are the burial grounds of particular tribes and families, to which the dead are brought at times from a considerable distance. In such places certain graves are pointed out as those of Kaffirs; they are generally well defined, with large stones set on edge, and are easily distinguished from the more modern graves of the Muḥammadans.

[1] Dolmens, with a hole in one of the side stones, are found in the south, such as those on the hill at Aihole in the Bijāpūr district. See my *Châlukyan Architecture of the Kanarese Districts*, under "Aihole. H. C.

"Similar graves are found in sequestered spots, without admixture of Muḥammadan graves, one spot being a small valley between 'Run Pittana' and 'Moulmacharee' in the direct road between Haidarābād and Karāchi.

"Scattered over the hill country in every direction, enclosures of stone, called by the natives "Kaffir Kote," are to be found....... They are of too small a size for dwellings. Some of these may be seen on the right bank of the Gugger river.

"Near the village of Truck, on the direct road from Kurrachee to Sehwan, is a remarkable erection, not, I think, of modern date. It is composed of a double row of upright stones, and is in the form of a cross, the arms being in the direction of the cardinal points. The top is yet [1851] in part covered with large stones, the length of which may range from 6 to 9 feet."

Mr. Carter, I.C.S., has recently discovered several remains of this class in the Mol valley, about twenty miles from Karāchi, amongst them being one pile which he calls an altar. It looks like a great stack of dressed stone left by some builder or contractor (See Plate III). But the rude carvings upon it look like old work, and yet it is possible, however improbable it may be, that the rough outlines of a horse and a camel may be the handiwork of some nomadic camel-men whiling away the time whilst their animals were browsing. Still, if this were so, who stacked the stones there? The rosettes in the circles, upon these stones, are exactly like those upon the Sonda tomb (See Plate XCVI), and the horseman has its counterpart upon one at Pīr Paṭho (See Fig. 27); so that, whatever age the pile may be, I doubt whether the carvings are any older than the Balūch tombs which I have described further on. But the presence of other remains such as stone circles, cromlechs and dolmens in the neighbourhood supports the claim for the antiquity of this pile. As will be seen in the photograph, there are some letters scrawled on either side of the horse, as if intended to be the name of the horseman. Looked at sideways they look very like Persian or Arabic characters, but, if they were carved upon the stones after they were set up, then it would seem that they should be read downwards vertically. I must say that I am strongly inclined to accept them as Persian letters. The absence of dots, or other diacritical marks, makes it difficult to make sense out of it. Mr. Carter says: "On the strength of one piece of carved stone which, unfortunately, I did not take away with me, and of the general circumstances, I believe this is a Eurasian-Greek altar of about B.C. 150." It is not easy to form any definite judgment upon one or two small photographs, so I refrain from saying more about it. Mr. Carter, in his further investigations, may be able yet to verify or modify his views. He says that, in the Mol valley, there was a large stone age settlement where he made a considerable collection of stone age implements. He has traced the stone age men as far as Unārpūr, where he found five little megalithic altars. At the Tharro[1] near Gujo, between Ghāro and Thaṭhah, where there is a wonderful walled

[1] Tharro or Tharri is a name frequently met with. Mr. Carter tells me that strings of Tharros run across Sind like Dak Bungalows (rest houses). Helāi lies between two, one behind Jarak and one just north of Ṭhaṭhah.

neolithic city, he made a fine collection of flints. He also found some at Budhke Tahar on the other side of the river opposite Jarak, upon two tumuli of brick debris, which look like the remains of Buddhist buildings, possibly *stūpas*.

BRAHMANĀBĀD-MANSŪRA-MAHFŪZAH.

NO ancient site in western India has given rise to more controversy, or has been more harried by the excavator, than that which has been known as Brahmanābād or Bahmanābād, situated in the hitherto deserted plains which stretch away to the east of the Indus, eight miles south-east of the railway station of Shāhdādpūr, and forty-three miles north-east of Haidarābād. The suggested sites for the famous city of Tagara, of the Greek writers, have also, from time to time, evoked considerable discussion, but the uncertainty of its ever-shifting positions, coupled with its meagre superficial remains, if any, have hitherto prevented its further investigation with the pick and the shovel. Not so Brahmanābād, which has served as a great bran pie to many an amateur explorer and curio hunter, who, with no further purpose in view than the turning up of some object of intrinsic value or uncommon character, has dug and raked about over its site in what seemed to him the most likely corners. But, beyond broken shell bangles, pottery sherds, occasional beads and much corroded copper coins, they have rarely found any object to repay them for their trouble. There is the spirit of gambling in it—each fresh visitor hopes to be lucky where others have failed.[1] In a more systematic manner, a series of excavations were carried out by Messrs. Bellasis and Richardson in 1854, the results of whose investigations were published in the Journal of the Bombay Branch of the Royal Asiatic Society and the Illustrated London News of the 21st February, 1857, while some of the objects unearthed were deposited in the British Museum, and others in the museum of the Bombay Society. Amongst these there was nothing of any special interest or value. But far more disastrous to the site than the work of all the relic-hunters together has been the havoc wrought by the people of the villages round about, both far and near, who, like the present Egyptian, having discovered the fertilizing properties of the earth upon old sites, impregnated, as it is, with certain salts, the result of many centuries of human occupation, carry it away in great quantities to their fields. This annual process of denudation of the site has, long ago, almost obliterated all signs of the plan of the city, which the fallen ruined heaps still afforded, or of any of its buildings that once jostled one another for room on its crowded area. The hoe of the cultivator is now very surely wiping out every trace of the lower courses of the walls, which up to now have been protected within the mounds (Plates IV—XVIII and Figs. 4—8).

[1] For a diverting account of an imaginary exploration at Brahmanābād, and an unexpected meeting, not with the traditional serpent, but with a real live trooper of Alexander the Great—a local Rip Van Winkle—see Mr. Cox's article in *East and West* for March and April, 1908.

Until the great Jāmrāo canal was constructed, which, with its network of branches, is transforming a waste wilderness into smiling corn fields, the site lay on an extensive arid plain, in many places scored with the beds of ancient streams, each of which, in turn, has dried up as the main river has shifted its course westwards. The general plan of the site resembles, in shape, an old top-boot with the sole presented to the north-west and the leg stretching towards the south-east, and the whole of it is covered with rolling mounds of brick debris, cut up into irregular blocks by a network of furrows which indicate the alignment of its former roads and streets (Plates IV-VI). Beyond the stump of an occasional wall, no structure now stands, save in one place, about the centre of the ruins towards the eastern side, where the tower-like remains of what may possibly have been a *stūpa*, by its very loneliness, accentuates the utter desolation around. Like Babylon of old, this once renowned city has been most thoroughly "swept with the besom of destruction." There is a total absence of stone masonry of any kind, but lumps of charred wood, scattered throughout the debris, indicate the former presence of woodwork of some description[1].

Before considering the question of the identification of the site, I shall describe, shortly, the results of my own investigations on the spot. Generally, any deep excavation through the mounds reveals two distinct periods of occupation at least. In the upper crust are found the foundations of walls built of bricks of the small size and shapes usually associated with Muḥammadan work. In some cases there is a mixture of these with a small percentage of the very large Hindū bricks such as were in use before the advent of the Arabs into Sind. But, far deeper in the excavation, with generally a thick layer of earth, potsherds, ashes and other debris between, are found portions of walls built *entirely* of the larger bricks. As will be seen in the photographs, walls have been built upon walls, crossing one another in all directions, which shew very clearly that in these sections we have evidence of two or more successive occupations of the ground. In the north-west corner of the city are a number of great pits from which earth has been carried away, showing interesting sections through some of the higher mounds. Upon the top of one of these we unearthed the foundation walls of a large building with its many small rooms, the whole being planted upon the mound. It was in the sections here that great numbers of buried earthen bowls of large size were found (Plate VII).

It is in the upper layer that are found most of the beads and coins, especially the later Muḥammadan coins; but there is an absence of anything of value. Corroded copper coins are plentiful, silver exceedingly rare, and gold not as yet found. Nor are there any domestic utensils of any value, though there surely must have been such in metal. There is little but broken pottery, and even this of the very commonest kind. There can be little doubt that each layer was thoroughly exploited and ransacked, both for treasure and building material, by the settlers of each successive period

[1] A preliminary account of this site was published in the Progress Reports of the Archæological Survey of India, Western Circle, for the years 1895-96, 1896-97 and 1908-09, and also in the Annual Report of the Archæological Survey of India for the years 1903-04 and 1908-09.

Along one street alone, and upon the surface, we cleared the foundations of three mosques, with their buttressed *miḥrābs,* all placed in their usual positions, that is, directed towards Makka; and this position the builders seem to have got exactly, the direction being a trifle south of west. There is no mistaking the foundation and plan of a mosque when found, for it is almost invariably constructed with three walls forming three sides of a rectangle, the fourth side, or entrance, being open towards the east. When, with this arrangement, are found the projecting buttresses on the outside, indicating the *miḥrābs,* or prayer niches within, as in this case, one of which is always in the centre of the back wall, there can be no doubt of the religious nature of the building (Plate VIII). Excavations, that were made at a spot about a furlong to the west of the *ṭhul,* or tower, disclosed what may possibly have been the foundation of a very large mosque. Being at a much lower level than those just mentioned, it was probably a much older building, and, possibly, the first mosque erected by the Arabs after taking the city. We were not able, with our limited time and funds to uncover the whole area. Placed in six regular rows, seven to eight feet apart, twelve rectangular blocks of brick masonry, each measuring seven feet by three, were laid bare, with other fragments of masonry as of a wall surrounding them on the north and west (Plates VIII and IX). These blocks are four feet six inches apart in their rows; and, if they formed the foundations for double or linked pillars of a mosque, as are often found in such buildings, in this case of wood, it would require, at least, sixty such to complete the building and preserve its proper proportions. This would mean a building measuring about 114 feet by 73 feet. Eleven of these foundations were uncovered, namely, the whole row of five in the north end and three in each of the next two rows, the rows running from front to back of the building. What lends colour to the supposition that this may have been a mosque was the discovery, in one place, among these foundations, of about two basketsful of the sherds of large earthenware pots with Arabic writing upon them, in black ink, covering both the outsides and the insides of the fragments. This writing seemed to consist largely of names repeated over and over again and, like talismanic cups, so much used by Muḥammadans, may have been intended to contain water rendered specially efficacious in certain circumstances, as a healing agent, by being brought into contact with the name of some revered local saint. Most of the pottery, shewn in the coloured illustration, in red and buff ware, was obtained in this excavation. Upon one fragment is painted, in black, a two-humped camel, not now seen in Sind so far as I am aware (Plate X).

These foundations, as may be seen in the illustrations, are considerably below the ruined walls upon the surface, but they are, themselves, built immediately upon older work. The latter, so far as we uncovered it, appears to be a large brick drain to which are attached, at intervals, flat earthenware oval slabs which look like libation slabs. They are connected with a main drain by short lengths of earthen piping. That this drain has no connection with the great brick foundations is evident from the fact that the latter are built over it in places, and the drain runs diagonally across the end of the plan and has no symmetrical arrangement with it. It is constructed entirely of the very large old Hindū bricks, and it is likely that it was from some large Hindū building, that stood here, that the Arabs obtained the bricks with which they built these foundations. They were easily removed from the older work as the only cementing material in those days was mud. Found in this lower layer were several unmistakable Hindū objects such as an image of Gaṇapati, another of Śiva and Parvatī, and a head, possibly, of Sūrya. There were also found a small bronze lamp, a small glass bottle, and the broken-off and well carved *kīrtimukha* of a stone libation slab (Plate IX), and, in addition to these, an earthenware trough.

In the upper ruins, several broken arches were met with in which the flat Muḥammadan bricks, forming the radiating voussoirs, are set edge to edge in their different rings, instead of flat side to flat side as might have been expected. This method was used in the construction of the *ṭhūl*, and the same arrangement was found in the *stūpa* at Mīrpūr-Khās. The largest size of brick used in the oldest and deepest work was 16¼×10½×2½. In the great brick foundations the bricks, for the most part, measure 14¾×9½×2 inches.

Fig. 4.—Narrow wells at Brahmanābād.

A great number of deep narrow wells were found all over the site. Within the limited area of the brick foundations, just described, there were found no less than seven, so, if they are as numerous over the whole city site they must exist in thousands. Probably most houses had their own private wells (Plate VIII and Fig. 4). That they belonged to the latest occupation is shown by the fact that they start from the upper surface and are, in many cases, carried down through the masonry of the lower walls to the sand below the alluvial deposit underneath the lower strata of masonry. In sinking one of these wells they had cut through a six-inch water pipe. These narrow wells are about two feet in diameter, and are formed of deep earthenware rings or short cylinders, placed one upon the other, thus forming great vertical pipes. Each of these rings, or sections, has a flange top and bottom in order that, when placed one upon the other, they may not telescope into each other. I found wells, rather larger in diameter than these, still being made of earthenware at Pattan in North Gujarāt, but, in this case, the rings were made in sections. These narrow wells remind one of modern cast-iron tubular pillars where the flanges are riveted together.[1] The wide distribution of these over the site seems to point to the drying up or change in the course of the river that flowed past Brahmanābād during the last occupation. Two large wells were found, one on the site excavated near the *thūl* and another, about eight feet in diameter, on the plain to the east of the city, across the river bed, the bricks being large and carefully moulded to the curve of the well. Until the Jāmrāo canal was brought along the west side of the city site, the only water, immediately available, was obtained from a deep well in the little hamlet to the east of the *thūl* and almost in the river bed.

The loose objects found during excavation embrace pottery of various kinds, clay balls and toys, shells, and bangles made from them, stone and glass beads, glassware in fragments, mutilated Hindū images, coins and coin moulds in baked clay, rusted masses of iron, which were once sword blades and sword hilts, fragments of turned ivory and other odds and ends. Such articles are usually found on ancient sites, especially in northern India.

The earthen pot having been in so great demand for domestic use in every household throughout the brick and pottery districts of the Panjāb and Sind, and being so fragile and often replaced, it is no wonder that the heaps of debris which cover the ground should consist largely of accumulations of potsherds (Plate X and Figure 5). Fragments, and very rarely a whole specimen, of four distinct kinds are found, namely, a common red which is most abundant; common black, or rather dark grey, both plain and decorated; plain buff ware, of a harder material, not so common; and buff ware glazed both inside and out, which is rare. The last two kinds were probably imported by the Arabs, and were not made in Sind. Amongst the first, or common red kind, are the pots which were used for the storage of water and other ordinary domestic purposes, some of them with spouts and lids.[2] There were also found small plates and saucers with little handless cups in shape like a diminutive flower pot, and little lipped vessels for *batties* or oil lamps. At Depār Ghāngro, the site about six miles to the north-west, we dug up in the open plain the fragments of at least four pots or goblets of different patterns, of one of which we recovered sufficient pieces to fit one half together by joining up the pieces upon a lump

---

[1] Similar wells have been found on the ancient site of Sravasti. Annual Report of the Archæological Survey of India for 1907-08, 110.

[2] Pots with spouts, similar in shape to these, are found figured on the ancient Padan rock in the Thana district (Thana Gazetteer, Part III, appendix). This has always been a favourite shape of drinking pot with the Muhammadans. Spouted vessels were dug up at Besnagar (Archæological Survey Annual, 1913-14, Pl. LXI).

of clay This is shown in the illustration (Fig. 5), the back of it being non-existent The ornament is raised, having been applied after the pot was made, and a piece of a mould for stamping out this ornament was found, it being shaped to the curve of the pot. Somewhat similar decorated vessels are still being made at Haidarābād Broken handles and necks, of the plain buff variety, show that they were chiefly water goblets holding a pint to a quart while the fragments of the glazed ware indicate very large jars, from a foot to two and a half feet in diameter. The colours of the glazes are blue, green and white, the inside generally being of a lighter tint than the outside.

FIG 5 —Vase unearthed at Depāi Ghāngro

The largest articles in the pottery line are the great bowls, already noticed as being found in the north-west quarter of the city. Here they are found embedded below the surface and are underneath the foundations of the upper walls, the latter, in some cases, cutting through them, they all occur in an upright position, and often telescoped one within the other (Plate VII) They are bowl-shaped, and measure three to three feet six inches across the top, and are about two feet six inches deep. They have no flat bottom to stand upon, the bottom being round with a projecting protuberance—the excess of the lump of clay out of which they were turned—hence they were not intended to stand upright upon a flat surface, but to be wholly or partly set in the earth. They now contain nothing but earth, brickbats and ash, washed into them in the course of ages Just such jars, though better made, were seen by us in the Chāndā district of the Central Provinces, placed beside wells for holding water for cattle. These, then, were probably used for the same purpose, possibly in connection with the state stables. There would be a constant breakage going on, and new ones would be planted within the broken ones, just as we find them, in such great numbers

Other objects of baked earthenware are balls of various sizes, measuring from two to six inches in diameter (Plate XI). They are found in great quantities, embedded in the earth, on the other side of the river, to the east of the city; and, in the absence of stone, which is not found in this neighbourhood, they were no doubt used as missiles for slings and catapults. The people of the village call this spot, on that account, the *tōp-khānā* or arsenal, and, curiously enough, it was here that we unearthed the basketful of rusted fragments of old swords. The great jars, just described, are again found here.

Both here and at Depār Ghāngro are found abundance of small shells of many shapes and sizes. They are scattered over the whole place, some of them being very small, reminding one of the seashore; while, in some places, large areas are quite white from the quantities crushed and pulverised upon the surface (Plate XII). Out of some of the excavations were obtained several old conch shells—the Hindū *śankha*—some quite decayed, and great quantities of shell bangles made from these, the shell being cut across in sections and joined together with wire exactly as we find them still made and worn by the women of the Brinjāri tribe. In many cases ornamental designs were incised upon them, and, as they have somewhat the appearance of ivory when polished, Mr. Bellasis and others have mistaken them for such. Some of these shells were found cut away to the core, the outer wall of the shell being alone used. Similar fragments to these are found on the site of Charsada, and, indeed upon most old sites in the north.[1] We did find ivory in a room in one place, and from it being in lumps and partly turned, we judged the place to have been that of an ivory turner. The ivory is more or less disintegrated, whereas the shell seldom seemed to have suffered in the same way.

Beads are found scattered about through the ruins, but, excepting in one case, they were not found in any quantities together. In the exceptional case we found about a pound of glass beads, much like the common old-fashioned English glass bead, made by breaking up glass tubing into short sections. In plate XIII eight of these are seen in the row of glass beads to the right of the centre. They are very much decayed, and have, of course, lost their polished surfaces. But, far more common than these glass ones, are the beads made from the precious stones such as cornelian, chalcedony, amethystine quartz, hæmatite or bloodstone, rock crystal, lapis lazuli and onyx. In the case of these stones, each bead had to be cut, polished, and drilled separately, and this, alone, would show how cheap labour must have been in those far off days, for the beads are very plentiful. The drilling was done half from one end and half from the other, and, with the transparent stones, it is seen that the holes seldom met truly; indeed, some do not meet at all. These were made locally, for at Depār Ghāngro we came across the sites of several lapidaries' houses where we scraped together several basketsful of chips of all these kinds of stones, and, among them, many undrilled and unfinished beads. They are made of all sizes and shapes, depending entirely upon the size and shape of the rough pieces, from an eighth of an inch to an inch and a half in length—round, flat, oblong, barrelled-shaped and cylindrical. Many of the cornelian beads, which vary in colour from a pale pinkish straw colour to a deep red, are figured on the surface with some white pigment which appears to have been burnt in, and cannot be moved by scraping with a penknife. The designs drawn are very simple, being, for the most part, plain lines, little circles or zigzags. No letters or writing appear upon any of these, but we found one little cornelian seal with Kufic of Arabic letters engraved upon the surface. Mr. Bellasis also found

[1] Annual Report of the Archæological Survey of India for 1902-3, p. 152.

similar ones, and one with *devanāgarī* letters. Of these he writes : " Among the curiosities found at Brahmanābād, showing an advanced state of art, are some beautiful engravings on cornelians and agate. Many of them are perfect gems of art, and, like the intaglios of Rome, are polished on the inside of the device —an art, I believe, now lost. Some that were found had upon them a bull, and others a lion ; some merely a name in Arabic, and some in characters resembling the Devanāgri or Sanskrit : most of these appeared cut in ovals and circles." From this we may gather that the art was an ancient one continued through the period of the Arab occupation

In connection with the cornelian beads, with designs upon them traced in white, Mr. Bellasis writes : " Respecting the cornelian ornaments found figured with patterns in white lines, on a perfectly smooth surface, and which I thought so curious in my first paper, I have made further enquiry : and while at Sehwan, in upper Sind, an old city famed for cornelian engravers, I found some stones figured in exactly a similar manner. On examination it was ascertained that the chief ingredients used were potash, whitelead, and the juice of the Kirar bush (Capparis aphylla), made into a thick liquid, and applied with a pen on the cornelian, which, on being exposed to red heat in charcoal, rendered the device indelible."[1]

Glassware is rarely found, and, as might be expected, it is, as a rule, in fragments. The surfaces of the pieces that are found are, almost always, decomposed and weathered into fine laminæ which produce those beautiful iridescent colours of the rainbow. The only whole object in glass, that we were fortunate enough to find, is a dainty little bowl of blue glass which seems to have been overlaid with white or cream enamel, possibly with the same mixture that was used on the cornelian beads. It is remarkably like many a small flower bowl made at the present day, but its decomposed state, and the iridescent colours of its surface save it from the suspicion of having been bought in a modern fancy goods shop.

At one spot were found a great many fragments of Hindū stone images, one of which was the frame which surrounded an image, most elaborately carved with rings of little gods around the top and down the sides (Plate XIV). Occupying the principal position on the frame, immediately above the place where the head of the image would have been, is Sūrya, with the lotus in either hand and wearing his long boots. To accentuate his importance the more, he is repeated on either side and above. On his right is Brahmā, showing three of his faces, while, upon his left, is Śiva with trident and snake. Above Sūrya is a little goddess, and Gaṇapati figures frequently. The frame, in all probability, encircled an image of Sūrya, whose worship was prevalent in this part of India. Multān was famous for its great temple of Sūrya, which was destroyed by the Muḥammadans about the tenth century, and was converted into a mosque. Hiuen Tsiang tells us that there were, in his time, at Multān, eight temples of the Brahmanical

[1] For further illustrations of these beads see the article and plates, some of them coloured, by Mrs. Rivett Carnac in the Journal of Indian Art, Vol. IX, p. 5. Anglo-Saxon beads, similar to these, with white figured designs upon them, have been found in Dover hill, also glass tubular ones, and may be seen in the Folkestone Museum.

gods, and the temple of the Sun-god, Āditya, was very magnificent. Kāthiawād, on the other side of Sind, was full of Sūrya worship about this time. We also found fragments of other images, amongst them pieces of at least two large-sized Gaṇapatis.

Copper coins are plentiful, being found scattered all over the site, but so corroded with verdigris that it is not often that they can be cleaned with any success. Nevertheless, the corrosion having, in many instances, gone on equally all over the coin, the impression is often quite distinct, though there may not be a grain of pure copper left. These coins are of two types (Plate CII.). One is very thin, and is beautifully impressed with Arabic writing, part within a central circle and part around the rim. These seem to belong to the Eastern Khalīfahs, and, though some bear the names of governors of Manṣūra,[1] they were, judging from their style and execution, coined in the Khalīfah's own mint and not in Sind. The other type, squat and dumpy, are very much smaller in area, and are represented by the two rows of silver coins at the top of plate CII, and rows 6, 7, 8 and 10 among the copper ones. There can be little doubt that these were coined in Sind, their clumsiness and coarseness of execution stamp them as the output of unskilled workmen.

In one particular spot, near the *ṭhūl*, which was supposed to be the site of the citadel, were found heaps of honeycombed baked clay slabs, all broken up into fragments. These slabs or cakes vary from about a half to three-quarters of an inch in thickness, upon one side of which are impressed rows of little cup-like hollows forming a regular honeycomb pattern, while the lower sides have been subjected to great heat and are vitrified (Plate XV). These hollows are of three different guages, the largest being about seven-sixteenths and the smallest barely three-sixteenths of an inch in diameter. We found them, first, on the ruined site of Bhambōr in the delta, upon a small heap at one corner; but, on finding near them, both at that place and at Brahmanābād, not only copper coins, but little pellets of copper which fitted into the little cells or hollows, the real use of these curious slabs became apparent. Further confirmation of this is found in the fact that the honeycombed surface of many of these clay cakes had lumps of verdigris (subacetate of copper) adhering to the edges of the cells. They were, no doubt, connected with the coining apparatus of the Arabs. The slabs, after being impressed with the requisite hollows, would be heated over a fire to take the chill off, when molten copper would be poured over and allowed to settle in them, all surplus metal running off; when cold, each hollow would contain a little pellet of uniform weight and size. These, one by one, would then be placed between the dies, and a heavy blow from a sledge hammer would do the rest. This mode of manufacture would account for the dumpy shape of the coins; not being all of the same thickness, often thicker at one side than the other, depending upon the angle at which the hammer fell; and frequently burst at the edge when too heavy a blow was given. The small silver coins would seem to have been made in the same way. The heating of the moulds vitrified the under sides of the slabs; and, being easily

[1] See Thomas' *Prinsep*, Vol. II, pp. 119-124, and the section on Sind Coins in this volume, at the end.

broken and easily replaced, the heaps of fragments were left as we find them. The thin Khalīfah coins were, no doubt, stamped out of thin sheet metal.

So far as they can be deciphered, these coins show an unmistakable connection with Mansūra, the Arab capital, and the copper ones are found, as already stated, lying all about the place in the shape of lumps of verdigris. Beside these, but in very much smaller numbers, are found little thin copper coins, more or less square, as if cut from very thin sheet copper, which are certainly Hindū, for they have sundry old *devanāgri* letters stamped upon them. They are seen in the last line but one on the plate.

In four or five places were found immense heaps of ashes and bones, in which were mixed quantities of potsherds and fragments of charcoal. It is possible these were spots where the Hindū dead were cremated. Cremation is generally carried out on a river bank, but after the city came under Muhammadan rule, this practice was, perhaps, forbidden, as interfering with the water for drinking purposes. Potsherds and charcoal would, of course, be found upon a cremation site.[1]

The *thūl*[2] is close to the village on the east side of the ruins, and is the loftiest pile still standing, being about 36 feet high above the general ground level around (Plates XIV and XVI). This tower-like mass has puzzled every one who has seen it. It has been supposed to be the site of King Dalur's palace,[3] but an examination of the mound shows that it was no part of a palace at all, nor was it a tower or bastion of a citadel, which I at first thought probable. An examination of the mound with pick and shovel, much the most satisfactory method of procedure, disclosed, right in the middle and heart of it, on the east side of the standing masonry, a square well in the solid brickwork seven feet square, which had been partly filled in with debris from the fallen walls. The so-called tower is but a portion of the mass of masonry that surrounded the well. We excavated the south side of the mound, out of which it rises, and came upon a heavy square basement, also of brick, 50 feet square, below ground level. The corners of this were found, and, on plotting it and the well on paper to scale, it was found that the well exactly occupied the centre of the square plotted upon the side of the basement unearthed. The plan on Plate XVI will explain this. Upon the west side of the tower is a small portion of the original brick facing, showing a few lines of vertical offsets and recesses. There seems to have been a passage or entrance, from the north side, into the building which passed up a ramp or stair on the west side of the central well, winding up spirally round it, as shown by the arrows on the plan, and returning over the entrance passage by a brick arch,

[1] For similar mounds elsewhere read Archæological Survey Annual for 1912-13, p. 145, the Journal of the Anthropological Institute, XVI, p. 74; and the Journal of the Royal Asiatic Society, 1899, p. 1, where Mr. Sewell tells us there is a large number of cinder mounds in the Bellary district which appear to have been enormous funeral pyres of dead soldiers, etc.

[2] Raverty says the word is not *thūl*, a tower or bastion, as Bellasis supposed, but the Arabic word *tāll*, a heap, a mound, such as in Tall-al-Kabir in Egypt (*Mihrān of Sind*, 201 n). I prefer to keep the word *thūl* (Sindhi, ठुलु a tower or bastion). The Sindi knows nothing of the origin of these erections, and, without doubt, looked upon them as ruined towers. Moreover, the Sindhi *stūpa* was always, in shape, a tower, and not a hemispherical "heap" or "mound" as were the very earliest *stūpas*. Cunningham writes it both *thul* and *tul* (*Ant. Geo.* 273). Burton calls it a "*burj* or thul," *burj* meaning a bastion, tower or turret.

[3] Or Dalū Rāi. This story is also told of Alor, and the change of the river at that place, and that for his wickedness, the city was destroyed. The story is given elsewhere.

continuing to rise over itself as it doubled round the well-shaft, but as a wooden staircase whose beam ends were let into the wall. Mr. Bellasis says: "In the time of the Kaloras, so much [of the tower] remained that the reigning Prince ordered the demolition of the steps leading to the top, for the purpose of frustrating the designs of robbers, who used the tower as a place of observation, from which to watch travellers as a preliminary to plundering them. A large portion of the tower, without the steps, was standing till about thirty-five [now close on a hundred] years ago, when it fell, and has since remained in much the same state as it is now—a mere fragment."

Upon excavating the debris from the inside of the well we came upon a layer of fragments of carved bricks (some of which are shewn upon the accompanying drawing) laid loosely together, with no attempt at any special arrangement. These were the only decorative bricks found in or about the *ṭhūl*, and are of a material superior to the rest of the masonry. Immediately beneath these were found four beams of wood, or what once was wood, for we found it in a state of powder, except where the butt-ends were better preserved in the side walls. These crossed the corners of the square well forming another square within and diagonally to it. The inner square, thus formed between the beams and the four triangular corner spaces, were filled in with brickwork, while beneath this was solid brickwork set in mud.

The carved bricks were such as are usually found decorating Buddhist *stūpas*, in Sind, and the presence of these, coupled with the general plan of the ruin, as revealed by our excavation, leads me to believe it to be the remains of a *stūpa*, but of a comparatively late date—possibly the re-construction of an older one, to which the carved bricks may have belonged. Convinced that this was a Buddhist *stūpa*, and thinking that the relics, if any, might possibly have been buried in the heart of the masonry, on or below the floor of the chamber, I excavated down through the solid brickwork 26 feet to virgin soil but without result. It is possible that the relic was kept within the well-chamber above the wooden cross beams, and that access to it for worship was obtained through the passage leading up from the north. The object of the cross beams it is difficult to guess, unless to support a floor.

Running under the south-west corner of the basement of the *ṭhūl* is a deep brick drain, or, perhaps, old water conduit to or from the river, most carefully constructed of very old bricks of the largest size. It is 2 feet 2 inches deep inside by one foot broad and is closed in on the top by the bricks being corbelled forward to meet. This covering is further protected and strengthened by a transverse arching of bricks (see drain A on plan). If the *ṭhūl* were a late construction, as I think, it would account for this, the conduit by that time being in disuse, and the deviation in the style of the building from that of earlier *stūpas*. Another thing which indicates late work is the masonry of the basement, below ground level, which is built of brick and white lime mortar. We know that the earlier *stūpas*, at the time of the Arab invasion, were more or less ruined and in need of repairs. Hiuen Tsiang says that worship of Buddha had then (A.D. 641) almost disappeared at Multān, and the monasteries were in ruins.

The bricks taken out of the bottom of the excavated well measured $17'' \times 10\frac{1}{2}'' \times 2\frac{1}{2}''$, the largest found at Brahmanābād, and larger than those used in the tower above. It is thus possible that the core and foundation of the older building were retained. A further clearance of the mound is very desirable.

Six miles to the north-east of the great site of Brahmanābād is the site of a smaller place now known as Depār Ghāngro, or Dībal Kāngara as Captain McMurdo calls it.[1] A glance at the map (Plate V) will show the exceedingly small area covered by the ruins. Apart from the area covered with potsherds, shown by the dotted portion, and which are not brick ruins, the site does not cover a tenth of the area of Brahmanābād. The part where there have been buildings are in black, the shaded portions are mostly covered with brickbats scattered around from the buildings. The great mound we found to be the remains of a Buddhist *stūpa* which was built of good, large-sized burnt brick set in mud, with a core of sun-dried bricks. A cutting was carried through into what was judged to be the centre, but nothing of special note was found, and the time at our disposal did not allow of further investigation. We may not have struck the centre, for we had little to guide us to it; it would be necessary to unearth some portions of the basement to obtain a basis to work from, and I have little doubt some parts of the basement and the foundation are still intact in the mound. During our digging we found several fragments of terra-cotta ornament similar to that found at Mirpūr-Khās and Ṭhūl Mīr Rukhan, and so very like the work at those places that they might be supposed to have been turned out by the same hands. The same moulded, or carved brick was found by General Cunningham at Shorkōt in the Panjāb, and this he likens to the work on the Yusufzāi remains.[2] He found letters and writing on some of the bricks which he ascribed to the first or second century of our era. We picked up two fragments at Ṭhūl Mīr Rukhan with parts of letters upon them, but not sufficient to be clearly legible.

General Haig says that Sāwandī, which I identify with Depār Ghāngro, is mentioned in the legends of the *Mujmalu-t-Tawārikh* as having been built by the king of Kaśmīr during an expedition to Sind.[3] The known *stūpas* in Sind, namely, that near Tāndo Muḥammad Khān, and those at Jarak, Mīrpūr Khās, and Depār Ghāngro, and the Ṭhūl Mīr Rukhān, form a string up the valley of the Indus, beyond which is the Sue Vihār, near Bahāwalpūr, where an inscription of the time of Kanishka (possibly the king of Kaśmīr referred to) was found, and others that have been reported in that State. *Stūpas* in the Panjāb take up the running, such as that at Shorkōt, and link up with the remains of Yusufzāi and Kaśmīr. With reference to the *stūpa* at Depār Ghāngro, we have already noticed that Chach, about the middle of the seventh century, paid a visit to a Buddhist devotee at a celebrated shrine (? *stūpa*) in the vicinity of

---

[1] *Journ. R. A. S.*, Vol. I, Haig says it is, more correctly, Depāl Gāngrah. *J. R. A. S.*, Vol. XVI, Part 2.

[2] Archæological Reports, Vol. V, p. 101, and Plates XXX and XXXI. Compare these, allowing for their bad drawing, with Plate XI, in this volume.

[3] Journal of the Royal Asiatic Society, Vol. XVI, Part 2, p. 292

Brahmanābād, when the latter complained that some parts of the structure had, owing to the vicissitudes of time, become ruinous, and asked him to do a good deed by rebuilding them.

What few other ruins there are at Depār Ghāngro partake of the nature of those at Brahmanābād, except that the larger old Hindū bricks are not so common Coins, beads, fragments of shell bangles, with pieces of glass, are found about the place, and, as already mentioned, old rusty sword hilts and a quantity of chips from some lapidaries' shops As may be seen on the plan, a number of small buildings lined the river banks for some distance along its course. The river bed is very clearly marked here, not only by its depression, but by the ruins and scattered potsherds which end abruptly at the margin on both sides. There are no signs, whatever, of any fortifications, walls, or gates as at Brahmanābād.

On the site of Brahmanābād were found the same variety of objects by Messrs. Bellasis and Richardson, and some of these are seen in plate XVIII. Amongst these are some articles which Mr. Bellasis looked upon as ivory chessmen. He describes them thus: "In this house we were further repaid by finding nearly a complete set of ivory chessmen, one set white, the other black. The Kings and Queens are about three inches high, and the pawns about one, the other pieces of different heights. All have been made for use on a board with holes, for each piece has a peg in it, similar to chessmen used nowadays on board ship, to prevent the pieces being easily knocked down and the game disturbed The ivory of these, too, is in a very decayed state, and very brittle, every particle of animal matter seemed completely exhausted, and the ivory reduced to a substance not unlike lime or chalk. Dice were also found,—some square cubes of ivory, numbered exactly as dice used at the present day; others, the long dice, used by natives to play the game of Punchweshee. The discovery of these chessmen is a curious fact; they are probably the oldest known set in existence, and tend to confirm Sir William Jones' assertion that chess was a game of Brahminical origin."

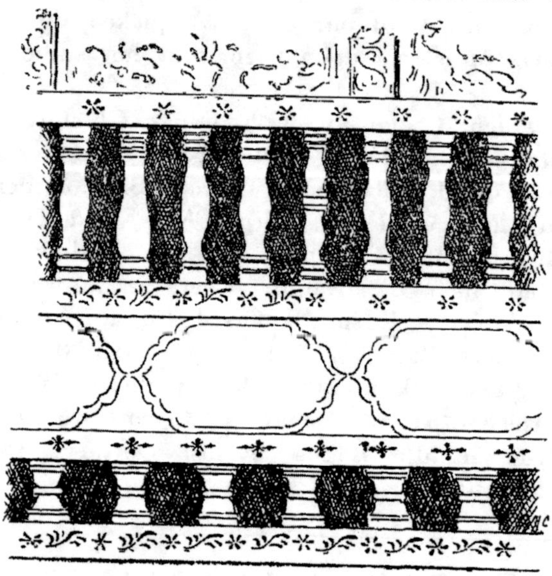

FIG 6.—Modern furniture balusters.

Without entering into the question of the origin of chess, of which I know nothing, I must take exception to his identification of these objects as chessmen. They are, as I will show, nothing more than the little balusters or spindles of furniture rails. I have reproduced two illustrations (Plate XVIII) from the *Illustrated London News* of the 21st February, 1857, with the kind permission of that paper, in one of which are shewn these same articles, on the left and right. Had they been chessmen, with pegs to keep them steady, the pegs would not have been required at *both top and bottom* of the pieces; what would have been the necessity of pegged chessmen where there was neither sea nor frequent earthquake to disturb them? If we examine the two upper pieces on the right side of the illustration, we find that one has a hole in the *top* for a peg, while the other has a peg in the top and a hole in the bottom for another peg, and both the upper pieces on the left have holes in the *tops* for pegs. I examined these pieces, which now repose under false colours in the British Museum, and the use of them became so obvious that I wonder how Mr. Bellasis overlooked it. In figure 6 I have copied a piece of a similar ivory rail adorning the back of an old settee in the palace at Maisur,[1] and have given a conjectural restoration of his "chessmen" in figure 7 which shows the style of rail the pieces were used in, the "pawns" being nothing but little knobs or finials along the top, with a larger one at the corners. In these little balusters or spindles, pegs were required *both top and bottom* to fix them into the rails. A use is also shown for the flat pieces beside the "chessmen" on the left, namely, as portions of rails, but which were supposed to be parts of the chessboard. When last in Sind I purchased at Haidarābād an ornamental Sindhī chair, all the work of turners, with just such spindles used in the back rails and the arms, only that the "pawns" hang as drops from beneath the lower rail.

FIG 7.—Mr Bellasis' "chessmen" as balusters.

I cannot so easily dispose of his dice, not having noticed them in the collection at the British Museum. In his illustration he shows but one piece, with little circles carved upon it. In figure 8 I give similarly marked pieces of ivory or bone which I found on the site, which are not dice but portions of a necklace, the pieces being drilled for a cord to pass through, and the little circles being mere ornament.

FIG 8.—Dice-like neck ornaments.

Mr. Bellasis, at his second visit, found carved stone slabs with four feet, raised about five inches off the ground, and varying in size from two to two and a half feet square. "I found many other slabs of the same kind, but none so richly carved; they were all found buried very deep in the ruins, and near the lower floors. Their use was evidently connected with religious worship. They may have been used by the Hindūs of Brahmanābād to place their idols upon,

[1] *Technical Art Series*, 1903, Plate XIX.

when performing the ceremonies of their ablutions."[1] Other objects found by him were impressions of seals in clay, with sometimes fifteen to twenty impressions on one lump of clay[2]; carved figures in ivory; the remains of an inlaid tortoise-shell or ebony box; pottery, glass and glazed ware; copper coins, cornelians, onyxes, agates, beads, women's bangles of glass, of ivory (? shell) and brass; bones and teeth, both of men and animals, and a few engraved seals.

Unless the following story be true, the origin of the famous city of Brahmanābād is lost in the mists of antiquity. Little, indeed, is known of it before the time of the Arab invasion, and that little has been rescued from oblivion by the inquiring mind of an Arab, who set down what he could glean from "the oldest inhabitant," some time soon after the Arab conquest, and his account, subsequently translated into Persian, became known as the *Chach Nāmah*. Whether Alor was first or Brahmanābād we do not know, but it is not unlikely that Brahmanābād preceded Alor. According to the *Mujmalu-t-Tawārīkh*, it is said that in the lifetime of Gustasf, king of Persia, "Bahman led an army to Hindustan and took a portion of it; as to the other parts every one (that could) seized a corner. No one of the family (of Sunāgh) retained any power. Bahman founded a city between the confines of the Hindūs and the Turks, to which he gave the name Kandābīl [Kanda'il],[3] and in another place, which they call Budha,[4] he founded a city which he called Brahmanābād. According to one account this is Mansura; but God knows."[5] Elliot doubts this story but Raverty records it as a fact. Bahman, who became King of Persia, was Ārdishīr Darāzdast, the Artaxerxes Longimanus of the Greeks. He succeeded his grandfather, Gastasp, in B C. 464.[6] Raverty, after translating the same account from the *Zainu-l-Akbar* of the Gardaizī, written in the reign of Sultān Farrukhzād of Ghazni, about A. D. 1053, observes: "We also know from Aṭ-Ṭabarī, as well as from many others, that Nūshīrwān, the Just, held extensive tracts of territory in the direction of Sind, if not in Sind itself. The author of the Muj-mal-ul-Tawārīkh, in his 'Kafand,' a Hindū King contemporary with Alexander, the Macedonian, says:—'It is stated that he, Kafand, sent a Brāhman to Sāmīd, his brother, directing him to go to Mansūriyah,[7] expel the Ī-rānīs from the places which Bahman had conquered, and erect idol temples in the place of fire temples'"[8] In his article on *The Periplus of the Erythræan Sea*,[9] M. Reinand says: "Persian and Arab writers who come later do not speak of Darius, and attribute the conquest of

[1] The pear-shaped libation slabs, already mentioned as having been found under the great brick foundations, were for the same use, I should think, but are probably far older than these stone ones. H.C.

[2] We are not told what became of these.

[3] This place has, by some, been identified with Gandāva; in any case it could not have been far from it. H.C.

[4] Fredunbeg writes it Budhia, Haig, Būdhīya. This district, at the time of Muhammad Qāsim, apparently lay to the west of the Mihrān towards Sehwān and Lārkhāna. H C

[5] Elliot's *History of India*, I, 106.

[6] Beale's *Oriental Biographical Dictionary*, 1894 Edition.

[7] The author does not mean that this city was then called Manṣūryiah, but Brahmanābād, which was then called Mansūriyah when he wrote. (*Mihrān of Sind*, 198.)

[8] Figure 1, in the text, shows six gold Sassanian coins found near Lārkhāna in upper Sind, having the king's head on one side and the fire altar on the other.

[9] *Ind. Ant*, VII. 336.

India to a King called Gustasp. They add that Gustasp gave the government of the Indus valley to one of his grandsons named Bahman surnamed Deraz-Dest or Longimanus. During his government Bahman founded in the north of the delta of the Indus, a city which he called Bahmanābād, or city of Bahman. After the death of his grandfather, Bahman returned to Persia, and mounted the throne; but, at his death he left the crown to his daughter, Humai, in preference to his son Sassan, and the latter retired discontented to Bahmanābād, where he had a family. From one of his children descended Sassan, the father of Ardeshir, founder of the dynasty of the Sassanian kings." He goes on to show that the capital of Sind of the Chinese pilgrim, Pi-chen-pho-pu-lo or Vijanvapura is the same as Bahmapura or Bahmanābād. Cunningham identifies Brahmanābād with the city of Brahmans described by Alexander's historians. "After Ptolemy's time we know nothing of Brahmanābād until the Muḥammadan conquest, a period of nearly six centuries."[1]

So much for the origin of Brahmanābād. If this account be correct its name should be Bahmanābād, but I retain the name by which it is best known in the province. Different writers have almost as many different names for it, such as Bahmanu (Biruni), Bāmīwān in the *Ashkalu-l-Bilād*, Tāmīrāmān (Ibn Haukal: Gildemeister), Mamiwan (Ibn Haukal: Major Anderson), Mirman (obviously a blunder, by Idrīsī), Bāīnwāh or Bānbanwāh (*Chach Nāmah*, the latter of which Fredunbeg says is the present name of the place), Pāīnwāh (in the *Tārīkh-i-Tāhri*), and probably the Bhāmbarāwāh of the *Tuḥfatu-l-Kirām*.[2] McMurdo calls it Bāhmana, Bāhbina and Bahnbanā;[3] Briggs, Bamunwasy, and Raverty, Bahmano or Bahman-nih. Elliot thinks Bahmanābād merely an abbreviation of Brahmanābād, and locates it at Haidarābād.[4] Brahmanābād was the head-quarters of one of the four governors of the Hindū King Sahiras, son of Sāhasī Rāi, who had divided his kingdom into four divisions, he, himself, governing at Alor. In the time of Chach all the country between that place and Debal, or the sea, was dependent on it. In the *Ā'īn-i-Akbarī* we are told that Brahmanābād was a very populous city, that the fort had 1,400 bastions, and at the time that that work was written there were still considerable vestiges of the fortification. The city had four principal gates which were, according to the *Chach Nāmah*, the Jarbaṭṭerī or Bahār, the Sātia, the Manōrah, and the Sālbah. Raverty makes five gates thus: the Jariṭarī, the Bhārand or Bhārind, the Sātiyā, the Manorah and the Salāh,[5] making the first two separate gates, and not two names for the same gate.

With regard to the foundation of Mansūra, the Arab capital, we are on surer ground. It was not, however, their first settlement: that was Maḥfūzah. Al Bilādurī tells us that Ḥakam, Āmīr of Sind, built Maḥfūẓah about the year

[1] Ancient Geography of India, 268—270.

[2] Elliot's *History of India*, I, 369.

[3] Journal Royal Asiatic Society, I, 27.

[4] Elliot's *History of India*, I, 370.

[5] *Mihrān of Sind*, 242. It will be seen by those conversant with the Persian letters that many of the differences in these names are due to their being written in the different copies without diacritical marks, or with wrong ones, put in according to the copyists' fancy, or arbitrarily supplied by the translator. Elliot, when he transcribes names in his footnotes to his history, writes the characters as be found them without dots

A. H. 120 (A. D. 738), and that 'Umaro ('Umar), son of Muhammad Qāsim, who served under Hakam, founded Mansūriyah. Al Idrisi, says, on the contrary, that Mansūriyah was founded in the beginning of the Khilāfat of Al Mansūr (Abu-Ja'far-al-Mansūr), the 'Abbāsī, the second Khalīfah of that family, who did not succeed to the Khilāfat until A H 136 (A D. 754), some sixteen years after the time of Ḥakam and 'Umaro, and some four years after the overthrow of Mansūr, son of Jamhūr, the last Amīr Raverty thinks that it would appear from this, if all three writers are correct, that Mansūra was founded in Ḥakam's time, finished in the time of Mansūr, son of Jamhūr, and the name merely continued by Abū-Ja'far-al-Mansūr [1]

Ibn Hauqal and Al Idrisi tell us that Mansūra was surrounded by a branch of the Mihrān, at a distance from it, and that it was on the west of the branch. It was therefore to the east of the Mihrān itself. Idrisi then goes on to describe the climate and fruits in almost the same words as Ibn Hauqal, and says it was named after Al Mansūr of the 'Abbāside family This prince gave his name, "The Victorious," to four different cities, namely, Baghdād in 'Irāq, Mansūra in Sind, Al Masīsa, on the Mediterranean, and that of Mesopotamia [2] "That of which we are now speaking is great, populous, rich and commercial. Its environs are fertile The buildings are constructed of bricks, tiles and plaster It is a place of recreation and of pleasure. Trade flourishes The bazars are filled with people, and well stocked with goods The lower classes wear the Persian costume, but the Princes wear tunics, and allow their hair to grow long like the Princes of India[3] . . . . Fish is plentiful, meat is cheap, and foreign and native fruits abound. The name of the city, in Indian, is Mirmān."[4] The *Masālik wa Mamālik* of Ibn Khurdadba, which agrees very closely with Ibn Hauqal, says: "Mansuriyah which they call Sindiyah, is a city of Sind, about a mile long and a mile broad, and is surrounded by a branch of the Mihran. It is like an island. The people of Mansuriyah are Ḳureshīs, the descendants of Habbār, son of Al Aswad, who seized upon it, and, up to this time, it is in the hands of his descendants . . . The people, in their dress and habits are like the people of 'Irāk, but their Bādshāhs are like Hindus in appearance, and have rings in their ears.[5] Al Berūnī tells us that Muhammad, the son of Qāsim, marched from the side of Sijistān into Sind and subdued Bahmano بہمنو to which he gave the name of Mansūriyah, and to Multan, Ma'muriyah."[6] This, of course, is quite wrong, for Muhammad Qāsim died before Mansūra was founded, but it shows the persistent idea in the minds of these early writers that Brahmanābād and Mansūra were one, or, at least, that they occupied the same site Zakarīyā, the Kazwīnī, says: "Mansūriyah, so called after the second 'Abbāsī Khalīfah, is also styled Mansūriyah-i-Sānī, or the second Manṣūriyah, and

---

[1] *Mihrān of Sind*, 196.

[2] According to Ibn Al Wardī-al-Karshī, the other three were Baghdād in 'Irāq, Al Maṣīsat on the sea of Shām (Syria) and Al Rāfiqat in the Diyār-i-Muzar. (*Mihrān of Sind*, 205) There is also a Manṣūrah in Central Asia, in the neighbourhood of Khiva (*J R A S*, 1902, 742)

[3] See the long hair and curls of the image of a noble or prince found in the *stūpa* at Mirpur-Khas, Fig 14

[4] Elliot's *History of India*, Part I, p 78

[5] The Mirpūr statue has them. See Fig. 11.

[6] *Mihrān of Sind*, 196.

a branch of the Mihran encircles it. It is very hot and has many fleas, but it is a place of considerable size, and has good and sweet water." Abu Muslim, the 'Abbāside Khalīfah, appointed Mūsa, son of Ka'bu-t-Tammīnī, to Sind, who repaired the city of Manṣūra, and enlarged its mosque. Previous to this, Manṣūr, son of Jamhūr Al Kalbī, with his brother Manzur, had rebelled against the Khalīfah, and was driven out by Mūsa. Coins of this Manṣūr, and of other Sind rulers, have been found on the site of Brahmanābād.[1]

Al Mas'ūdī visited Manṣūra after the year A. H. 300 (A. D. 912-3), and he mentions several persons then living there.[2] Haig says: "It [Manṣūra] is spoken of by Yāqūt, who wrote his great geographical work in the second decade of the thirteenth century, as if it was still flourishing; but Ebu'l Fidā, writing in the first half of the fourteenth century, says that the city, with three others of the same name in different parts of the East, was in ruins. If both writers were correct, it is probably to be inferred that a great change in the course of the Indus took place at some time between the middle of the thirteenth and the early years of the fourteenth century, and caused the ruin of Manṣūra."[3] Maḥmud of Ghaznī is said to have appointed a Muḥammadan governor to Manṣūra.[4]

The fort of Maḥfūẓah was built in the neighbourhood of Manṣūra. Al Bilāduri says: "Junaid was succeeded by Tamīn, son of Zaid al 'Utbī, who squandered eighteen millions of Tārtarīya dirhams, which he found in the treasury of Sind. He was succeeded by Ḥakim [or Ḥakam], son of 'Awān al Kalbī. By this time the people of Sind had returned to idolatry excepting those of Kassa, and the Musalmans had no place of security in which they could take refuge, so he built a town on the other side of the lake facing India [that is, on the India side], and called it Al Mahfūza, 'the Secure,' and this he made a place of refuge and security for them, and their chief town. . . . . 'Amrū, son of Muḥammad, son of Kasim, was with Ḥakim, and the latter advised him, trusted him with many important matters, and sent him out of Al Mahfūza on a warlike expedition. He was victorious in his commission and was made an amīr. He founded a city on this side of the lake [he probably means northwards of the lake, he being in that direction when writing] which he called Manṣūra, in which city the governors now dwell."[5] From this it is plain that Maḥfuẓah was built before Manṣūra, and the ruins of Brahmanābād constituted the quarry for both. M. Reinaud says that "Mafuza was built in the neighbourhood of the capital (Brahmanābād) on the other side of a lake fed by the waters of the Indus."[6] "The Balazārī states that Manṣūriyah was founded on one side of the eastuary or lake facing Hind, and Maḥfūẓah on the opposite side."[7]

The conclusions I draw from the evidence available, both as contained in these accounts, allowing for inaccuracies, and from my own investigations on

---

1 Thomas' *Prinsep*, Vol. II, p. 119, and Elliot's *History of India*, Part I, pp. 126-127.
2 Raverty's *Mihrān of Sind*, 189.
3 *Indus Delta Country*, 72.
4 Cunningham's *Ancient Geography of India*, 276.
5 Elliot's *History of India*, I. 126.
6 Elliot's *History of India*. 371.
7 Raverty's *Mihran of Sind*, 474n.

the spot, above and below ground, are that Manṣūra was built upon the ruins of Brahmanābād, that the ruins at Depār Ghāngro may be those of the Buddhist colony of Sāwandī, and that the detached block of ruins to the south-east of Brahmanābād is the site of the fort of Maḥfuẓah (see plates IV and V).

After disposing of the greatest mass of ruins as those of Brahmanābād, Mr. Bellasis continues: " Besides Brahmanābād, at a distance of about a mile and a half is the distinct and ruined city of Dolora [Dalūr, the ruins which I take to be Maḥfuẓah; it is only half a mile from the edge of one to that of the other], the residence of its last King, and five miles in another direction is the ruined city of Depār, the residence of his prime minister (wuzeer); and between these cities are the ruins of suburbs extending for miles far and wide into the open country."[1] From various articles which he discovered in his excavations, and, more especially, some carved stone slabs decorated with unmutilated figures, he contends that Brahmanābād could never have been occupied by Muḥammadans. General Haig, on the other hand, identifies the same site as that of Manṣūra, the Muḥammadan capital, while he considers the ruins at Depār Ghāngro to be those of Brahmanābād.[2] Modern writers seem to have got rather mixed up with these sites. Elliot writes: " When we consider the space which is always covered by the sites of old Indian towns, from the straggling mode of their erection, we are authorized to conclude that *a large portion of Brahmanābād was included in Manṣūra, and that, in point of fact, the two sites are identical*,"[3] and this, after mentioning what Bilāpurī says about the two places being 2 *parasangs* apart. But Elliot, in another place, has also said that he considered Manṣūra to be represented by Haidarābād![4]

Cunningham identifies the great site, which he calls Bambhra-ka-Thul, with Manṣūra, while " Brahmanābād must therefore be looked for in the neighbouring mound of ruins now called Dilura,[5] which is only one and a half miles distant from the larger mound."[6] But he also says that Manṣūra must have been founded on the site of Brahmanābād.[7] Dr. J. Burnes, Sir A. Burnes, and Mr. Crow all considered " Kullan Kot," near Ṭhaṭhah, and even Ṭhaṭhah itself, to have been Brahmanābād.[8] Tod speaks of " Bekker " (Bakhar) as Manṣūra, and he further mixes it up with Alor by saying " On the final conquest of Sinde the name of its capital, Arore, was changed to Manṣūra."[9] He was probably following the *'A'in-i-Akbari* in which Abū-l-Faẓ says Bakhar was Manṣūra.[10]

---

[1] Journ. *Bom. Br. R. A. S.*, V, 413. The country is full of large areas covered with potsherds, which Mr. Bellasis and others have mistaken for the ruins and sites of buildings. This is not so; they are rather the sites of the encampments of armies on the march, and are generally found along the banks of old river beds. They are the remains of countless waterpots which were used by the troops, and were probably requisitioned from the neighbouring villages in advance.

[2] *Journ. R. A. S.*, XVI, Part 2.

[3] *Appendix to the Arabs in Sind*, 237, and *History of India*, I, 371.

[4] *History of India*, I, 400.

[5] Or " Dolora," simply because it is within the lands of the present village of Dalūr, close beside the site.

[6] *Ancient Geography*, 273.

[7] Raverty's *Mihrān of Sind*, 202n.

[8] Raverty's *Mihrān of Sind*, 203n, and Burnes' *Travels into Bokhara*, 2nd Ed., 1835 28.

[9] Raverty's *Mihrān of Sind*, 203n and 204. Also, Tod's *Rajasthān*, Vol. II, 229.

[10] Raverty's *Mihrān of Sind*, 201n.

I have already shown that there were at least two cities, or two distinct occupations of the site called Brahmanābād. That the one was an ancient Hindu city is clear from the great size of the bricks, which were never made so big after the advent of the Muhammadans; from the Hindu coins and images found; and from the historical records which clearly tell us that there was such a large city in the neighbourhood, called Brahmanābād or by some variation of that name. There are no other known ruins in this locality of anything like the same extent that could pass for those of such a city. They would have been found long before now if only by the cultivators who, in swarms, year after year, harry those of our present site for the fertilizing earth which is always found upon the sites of ancient cities. That the uppermost one was a Muhammadan city is seen by the smaller thin bricks which are of the regular Muḥammadan type; the ruins of the three mosques discovered within the very small area examined; the abundance of copper coins with Arabic legends, some of which connect them with the Arab governors of Manṣūra; lime plaster on the upper walls of houses, and the pottery ware which looks more Muhammadan than Hindū, especially the pots with spouts. Writing of Brahmanābād General Haig says: "Its name, linked to that of the neighbouring Arab fortress, long survived the ruins of the ancient city, and even at last extinguished the proud title given by the conquerors to their capital. Bamanah-Manṣūrah, in process of time, became Bamanah only, and at this day no native of Sindh has any notion where Manṣūrah stood."[1] The linking of the names together is very significant, and is what we might expect where two cities had occupied the same site within so short a period.[2] It was for so short a time, comparatively, the Arab capital that the name Manṣūra was the more easily forgotten. Brahmanābād was taken, but not destroyed, by Muhammad Qāsim in A. D. 712, and Manṣūra was founded some twenty-five to thirty years afterwards; it is thus probable that Brahmanābād was destroyed when the Muhammadans again got the upper hand after the temporary revolt of the Hindu chiefs. Its sudden disappearance from history is easily explained by the fact of Mansūra being built out of its ruins. General Haig says: "From this time nothing more is heard of Brahmanābād." Ibn Hauqal speaks of "Manṣūra, which, in the Sind language, is called Bāmīwan."[3] Al Bilāduri, however, says: "Then Muḥammad, son of Qāsim, went to old Brahmanābād, two *parasangs* from Manṣūra, which town, indeed, did not then exist, its site being a forest. . . . The place is now in ruins."[4] Biladuri does not, himself, seem ever to have visited Sind, but writes from the accounts of others.

The Arab geographers describe Manṣūra as being encircled by a channel or branch from the Mihrān, so as to make the land, in which it stood, an island.[5] If, then, the main river at that time flowed in or near the old Lohāno Dhoro bed, then the loop branch from it, which left it at some distance to the north-

---

[1] *Indus Delta Country.*

[2] Rashīdu-d-dīn speaks of "Bahmanū-Mansūra" (Elliot's *History of India*, I, 61).

[3] Elliot's *History of India*, I, 35.

[4] Elliot's *History of India*, I, 122, and Elphinstone's *History of India*, I, 506.

[5] See inset map on the general map of Sind accompanying this volume (Plate CIII).

west of the great site, and joined it again three *farsangs* south of the capital, and ran in the bed on the east side of the site, was, no doubt, the Ḥalwā of Fredunbeg and the Jalwāli, Jalwālik or Jalwāti (he writes it in these different ways) of Haig.[1] In his map he places a stream, which he calls by these names, on the *east* side of the Depār Ghāngro site to fill the requirements of the narrative, since he assumes this to be the site of Brahmanābād. There is a stream bed, already referred to, on the *west* side of this site, shewn in my map, but I was unable to find any traces of one on the east.

For locating these two cities General Haig relied in great measure upon the movements of Muḥammad Qāsim, the Arab conqueror of Sind. He writes: "After relating the capture of the fort of Dhalil, the last of the strong places taken by the Arab army before reaching Brahmanābād, the historian [he is quoting his own version of the *Chach Nāmah*] says: 'Some relate that when Dhalil was captured, Muḥammad Qāsim called for Nūbah, son of Dhāran, and after giving him strict injunctions, entrusted to him the charge of the business of the boats, along the bank of the river, from that point to a place called Duhati,[2] and from that place to Brahmanābād there was a space of one *farsang*.' There is no place in the neighbourhood of Brahmanābād called Dūhāti, but there is a township named Dūfāni, and this I have no doubt is the name intended." Then he shows how easily the mistake might have been made by very similar Persian letters being substituted one for the other. He goes on to say: "The township of Dūfāni [which is really a small hamlet] is two miles and a half from Brahmanābād [that is, from Depār Ghāngro, his Brahmanābād], and by writers who never employ a fraction this distance would be called a *farsang*. Now the Arabs were advancing from south to north, and while it would be intelligible that the commander should assign to one of his officers the duty of watching the communication by river up to Dūfāni, if that place were *short* of—that is, south of—Brahmanābād, it would have been a useless and absurd proceeding on his part if Dūfāni had been some way *beyond* the great fortress, held, as we are told it was, by a strong garrison. Dūfāni is four miles north-west of the place popularly supposed to be the site of Brahmanābād [it is on the road between that place and Depār Ghāngro], but which I believe to be Manṣūra." But this argument is altogether wrong in view of the fact that the Arab army was not proceeding from south to north, but, as I have shown in the Historical Outline, from *north to south*. He has made his whole argument hang upon this initial mistake in the important matter of the location of the fort of Rāwar, which he places some 70 miles to the south-east of Haidarābād instead of away north in the vicinity of Alor. My own ideas with regard to this, though they may not be strictly correct, I have already set out in full. Thus it happens that

---

[1] The Persian characters for ḥ and j are identical, save for the dots.

[2] There is a great difference between these names as translated by General Haig and Mīrzā Kalichbeg Fredunbeg. Duhati is rendered Wadhatiah, and Nubah is Banunah in the latter's account. The د and و and the ز and ر are easily confused in badly written manuscripts or where diacritical marks have been omitted or displaced. I prefer to follow the Mīrzā who had collected some seven or eight copies of the work from different sources. so that one often supplied the deficiencies of the others.

Bellasis and Haig were both right in their identification of the great site, but the one only needed to be linked to the other.

Muḥammad Qāsim approached Brahmanābād from the north, or, more correctly, the north-east. His boats proceeding down the stream past Depār Ghāngro[1] to Dūfāni or its neighbourhood [2] (that is, if Dūfāni is the same as Duhati). The *Chach Nāmah* tells us that he now moved on until he came to the bank of the small channel of Halwāī (Haig's Jalwāli) to the east of Brahmanābād, where he fixed his camp, and whence he called upon the garrison to surrender. This spot is shown, on the accompanying map, as covered with brick debris and potsherds in a fine state of comminution. It is here that so many burnt clay balls are found scattered about, which were, no doubt, made for use with catapults during some siege of the city; and this must have been the scene of many a conflict. Bones, which have come to the surface, by the shifting of the sands, are found scattered about, and in one spot I saw the complete bones of an arm and fingers embedded in the surface. Here, too, were found a quantity of iron slag and masses of rusted swords.

As already stated, there are, upon either side of the river bed at Depār Ghāngro, very extensive areas of broken pottery, the sites of encampments, much of it reduced to very fine powder, which is being gradually covered by the sand. There is more of it near Dūfāni and close to Shāh 'Alī Mutalo, nearly four miles north of Brahmanābād,[3] along what was probably the course of the stream Halwāī. This last site corresponds with the position of Muḥammad Qāsim's camp when he quitted Brahmanābād, and a short march on the first day would be natural for an army starting on a fresh excursion. In writing an account of that place to Ḥajjāj, he said that he was writing from his camp higher up the river of Halwāī, near Brahmanābād. The *Chach Nāmah* records that he marched out of Bānbanwāh (Brahmanābād) on Thursday, the third of the month of Muḥarram of the year A. H. 94 (A. D. 712), and alighted at a town called Musthal, in the vicinity of Sāwandī and close to a beautiful lake with a pleasant meadow, called Wikarbhā, and on the bank of this *ḍhanḍh* he made his camp. Haig calls this place Mathal; Raverty has Muthal, which in one MS is Munhal, the Muthalo of the Sindhis.[4] This lake may have been an expansion of the Halwāī. We do not know what direction that stream took after rounding Muthalo.

Bilādurī states that Manṣūra was built on this, the west, side of the *buhairah*, and that Maḥfudah (or Mahfuẓah) was built on the far side of the

---

[1] It is possible that he used the Hakṛāh (Eastern Nārā) on his march, from Rāwar and Bahrōr, for his heavy impediments, as far as it served, and, perhaps, left it by a branch channel trending in the direction of Brahmanābād. This point of departure from the main river may have been Dhālil (or Dāhlelah, as Fredunbeg transcribes it), and as this transference of the boats from the main stream to the smaller channel required special supervision, he entrusted to Nubah, or Banūnah "the work of collecting and superintending the boats along the bank, [that is, they were towed along the bank of the smaller channel] of the river from Dāhlelah to a place called Wadhatiah. The distance between that place and Brahmanābād was one league" (Fredunbeg).

[2] Dūfāni may not have been always where it is now. There is a patch of brick ruins, as large as the present village, a mile and a quarter nearer Brahmanābād.

[3] Not two and a half miles as Haig says.

[4] *Mihrān of Sind*, 243n. In "Munhal" one dot has been placed above the letter, ن, instead two, ت

same. General Haig says *buhairah* is properly a lake, and he thinks it probable that the lake, beside which Muḥammad Qāsim encamped, was the same as referred to by Bilāduri. But this will not do. This would carry Manṣūra away beyond Depār Ghāngro, and ten miles, at least, to the north-east of the great site which he has already identified as Manṣūra, for his Jalwāli, on his map, trends away north-east from Depār Ghāngro.[1]

Before I knew that the native writers had mentioned a lake between those two places, I had written the following in my notebook on the spot: "The detached block, seen on the plan to the south-east of Brahmanābād or Manṣūra proper, is but a part of the great site, and appears to have been separated from the latter by an artificial tank, whose water was retained by a dam connecting the two groups of ruins, and which seems to have cut off a stream which ran between the two into the main river. This lesser block appears to have had its own engirdling walls, which are seen in several places, especially where they cross the fields on the west of the site and are shown on the map by a thick black line across the white ground". This is what Mr. Bellasis calls "Dolora," the residence of the last king. This sheet of water must have been half a mile square, and might well be the *buhairah*, and this smaller site that of Maḥfuẓah.

As to the fate of Manṣūra, or the last town upon this great site, I feel that I cannot agree with either Mr. Bellasis or General Haig. Brahmanābād, there can be no doubt, was overthrown by the Arabs, and it must have been, more or less, a ruin when Ḥakam was so much distressed about having no place of security wherein to establish his head-quarters. He would hardly have built the temporary fort of Maḥfuẓah in such close proximity to the old city if that place was at all habitable. It was probably only available as a quarry for material for the fort; and, selecting his new site as near as possible to it, saved the further carriage of the material. The small fort of Maḥfuẓah was eventually found too small, and the rebuilding of Brahmanābād as Manṣūrah was decided upon and entrusted to 'Umar, the son of the Conqueror. The idea of its destruction by an earthquake or desertion, on account of the failure of the river to supply it with water, appears to me to be untenable. The great quantity of wells all over the site, already described, show that the river, indeed, must have dried up, but, there being plenty of water in the subsoil the sinking of wells obviated the necessity of abandoning the site on that account. That the subsoil water did not fail is clearly seen by its presence to the present day in the village well on the site, and good water it is. A desertion of the place for this cause would have been a gradual affair, in which case we should hardly find the great quantities of copper coins left scattered about the site.

The earthquake theory, a convenient tradition which has attached itself to many of the oldest ruined towns all over the country, was entertained by Mr. Bellasis after his superficial inspection of the ruins. He says: "The destruction is too complete to have been the work of time . . . Had the city been destroyed by an invading army, the destruction would hardly have been so

[1] See the map which accompanies his article on Brahmanābād in the *Journ. R. A. S.*, XVI, Part 2.

complete . . Had the city been regularly deserted, the inhabitants would surely have carried their valuables with them,—money in particular and ornaments." Save corroded copper, and a very few silver coins, no valuables, that I know of, have been found on the site: Mr. Bellasis does not mention any among his finds. They were evidently removed: by whom? Mr. Richardson, who was with Mr. Bellasis, says in his notes: "We found no remains of wood, which might have been used in the construction of the buildings; and, save on the floors, and there only in small quantities, no charcoal or remains of burnt wood; so we may fairly conclude the city was not burnt."[1]

For my own part, I would rather believe that the city was sacked by an enemy, and the inhabitants were put to the sword. A disastrous defeat of the Muḥammadan arms, especially at the hands of Hindūs, was very likely to have been conveniently forgotten by Muḥammadan historians, upon whom alone we have to rely for any history at all. They would have been ashamed to record the downfall of their proud capital at the hands of idolaters. Amongst the ruins we find great quantities of human bones, in and about the houses, and broken shell bangles in great abundance. No articles in the precious metals have been met with; nor anything, save an occasional fragment, in copper or brass. Even in the general sacking of a city some things would be overlooked. The small copper coins, that are found, are scattered everywhere, not where persons would have left them intentionally, but where they fell in the general scrimmage and scramble, when the more desirable precious metals were especially sought for. Then, again, the total and complete destruction of the walls of the houses is easily accounted for, for the woodwork, being a valuable commodity in that part of Sind, was afterwards pilfered and carried away. Walls were thrown down in order to get at the door and window frames and roof timbers; and, being brick cemented with mud, were easily overturned with this rough treatment. We are told that the materials of the old city of Alor were carried away to help in the building of residences in Bakhar fort by S̲h̲āhbeg; and, further, materials were carried away from the loot of Uchh for the same purpose. Mr. Bellasis says he found skeletons huddled up in the corners of rooms and prone across the doorsteps; but this is just what might be expected after a general massacre. In connection with the sack of the place there may have been a few fires, but no general conflagration, else the bones and fragments of shell bangles, not to speak of the abundance of small shells which thickly litter the site, would have been calcined to powder. Ibn Hauqal, speaking of the town of Bilha (? Bania) says it was the residence of 'Umar, son of 'Abdul-l-Aziz Habbari, of the tribe of Kureish, and the ancestor of those who reduced Manṣūra.[2]

[1] Cunningham combines the two theories, and attributes the destruction to some earthquake before the beginning of the 11th century, and the failure of the river prevented any thought of rebuilding (*Ancient Geography* 276).

[2] Elliot's *History of India*, I, 37.

THE RUINED SITE OF VIJNŌṬ.

VIJNŌṬ[1] is situated in a flat barren plain about 5 miles south of Rētī railway station, and some 63 miles west-by-north of Rōhrī; and the ruins rise from it like an island from the sea, the margin around being so sharply defined. The area is covered with heaps of brick debris which have much the same appearance as those at Brahmanābād. The place is now totally deserted, and the only signs of life, if I may so put it, are freshly-made graves to the south-west of the ruins, a spot that seems to have been a favourite Muḥammadan burying place for some time back. At the time of my only visit to the ruins, in the cold weather of 1896, there was but one small insignificant ruined building, in part standing, which looked like a small Muḥammadan tomb of no great antiquity. I was only able to give the place a cursory examination, but, from what I saw, I think a thorough exploration would be of great interest. I must, therefore, fall back upon Colonel Branfill's account as given in the *Indian Antiquary* for January, 1882. He and Mr. F. E. Robertson, of the Indus Valley State Railway, whom he quotes, appear to have spent some time in their examination of the ruins.

" On approaching the place one notices a great number of dark-coloured ridges and mounds rising to a height of from 16 to 20 feet above the flat ground at their base; and on reaching them, they are found to consist of heaps of broken bricks, both in small sharp-edged pieces, and in pulverised fragments, mixed with loose salt soil and a large amount of charred wood in extremely small pieces. It is the presence of this comminuted charcoal chiefly that gives the dark colour to the mounds of debris; but on examination a considerable portion of the brick fragments is seen to be composed of semi-vitrified brick of a dark colour. An entire brick, or a large piece of one, is not to be seen on the surface of any of the undisturbed mounds, the whole having been reduced to small sharp-edged irregular fragments, apparently by the action of the saltpetre present. Recent excavations were made to provide metal ballasting for the Indus Valley State Railway, but the old site has probably been a quarry, for centuries, for any one who wanted a few stones or burnt bricks, in that part of the country. Bricks of the Vijnōṭ pattern are to be seen on Muslim graves for many miles around and far into the desert to the south-

[1] Written also " Wingrote " and " Vinjrote," but the people of the neighbourhood only know it as " Vijnōṭ."

east. The bricks in the foundations underground are in perfect preservation when first taken out, and measure usually 15 inches long, 10 inches wide, and $2\frac{1}{2}$ inches thick; but a few were found as large as 18″×12″×4″. They are roughly moulded but well burnt generally and of a good deep red colour. The bricks seem to have been well laid and bonded in mud; and no lime was noticed unless in the form of whitewash on the walls and pillars when first unearthed.

"The circuit of the mounds measures a mile and a half, the extreme length being over half a mile east and west, and the breadth from north to south nearly a quarter of a mile, beside a suburb of mounds at the south-west corner, now occupied by a Muḥammadan graveyard, and some outlying ruins at a short distance from the old city in various directions.

"Across the centre of the ruins runs a large open area or 'square' from 200 to 300 yards long north and south, and about one-third as wide.

"The west side of the 'square' is occupied by the principal mounds of debris, which were probably the houses of the chief persons of the place, and in their centre was the temple, the ruins of which have been excavated more completely than the rest; for not only was the temple more solidly built, but from the pieces of stone still lying about, it appears to have been faced with carved stones brought across the desert from Jesalmēr."

From the drawings of some of the stones accompanying the article, it is seen that the sculptures are of the same type, and no doubt of the same age, as the temple or temples whose material was used in the building of Aḥmad Shāh's mosque in the Bhadr at Aḥmadābād (*Samvat* 1307, A. D. 1251). It was, therefore, of a comparatively late period compared with that of the older brick-work.

"Altogether there may have been a score or so of stones remaining scattered about, all more or less shaped and dressed, and mostly slabs, not exceeding 4 feet in length, and less than a foot in thickness and height. That so little stone remains is perhaps due to the fact of the temple, in which only it was used, being but a small one, and that all of it which was not buried deeply in the ruins, has long since been carried off by any one who wanted it, for use or ornament. Many such instances were heard of. One finely carved block has been set up in the arched opening over the door of the little masjid at Rētī.

"Amongst the objects picked up on the site were the following:—

"*Coins*—principally copper, corroded beyond recognition, measuring about half an inch in diameter and one-tenth of an inch in thickness (weights 30 to 40 grains): these were the commonest, but there were others a little smaller weighing 17 to 22 grains. A few little rude silver coins were also found, about three-tenths of an inch in diameter and one-fourteenth of an inch thick, weighing six to seven grains each. They are also very corroded, but have plainly had an impression on one or both sides: and what remains gives the idea of the human figure, or a couple, rather than of a legend with symbols.

"*Beads*—round, flat, and oval, mostly of carnelian apparently—one of the flat ones had a pattern marked on it in white (enamel ?). A very similar one was picked up at Sirwāhi with the same pattern apparently, only rather more clearly marked and alike on both sides. Carnelian beads and ornaments of this description with almost identical markings in white have been taken out of the stone-circle graves in Central and Southern India. A few specimens of glass, green, blue, and white, were found, the latter iridescent and in a state of flaky decay; and some pieces of plain (glass ?) bangle, like those worn to the present day.

"Many little fragments of copper or brass ornaments turned up, and amongst them a complete (though corroded) little anklet bell (*ghangri*), with a ram's-head pattern on it.

"Besides the above many pieces of shells, and amongst them a few *cowries*, some marbles of stone and of earthenware, and some burnt clay figures of animals, probably children's toys.

"At a few feet or less below the surface, bones were found in the last stage of decay, and, here and there, well preserved pieces, with charred fragments in close proximity, a few of them undoubtedly human.

"Amongst the debris not far from the surface of the mounds, iron spikes such as may have been used in fastening the roof and flooring timbers were found. One or two pebble stones were picked up of an elongated or pointed shape, suggesting the idea that they may have been used as domestic Mahādeva or linga symbols. Two or three slight excavations were made in the mounds, which disclosed several layers of charred debris, apparently undisturbed since the burning.[1]

"The appearances generally were as if the town had been destroyed by a tornado, or an earthquake; and that the ruins, composed principally of mud or sun-dried bricks mixed with masses of inflammable materials such as timber and thatch, had then caught fire. Or perhaps an unusually high flood may have overthrown the houses, and the fire may have occurred afterwards. The marks of a great conflagration are unmistakeable over the entire site, whilst it is equally certain that some of the bones and things found below the surface shew no signs of having been burnt. The age and long occupation of Vijnōṭ is attested by the height of the mounds of ruins and the extraordinary amount of saltpetre about them, whilst the surrounding country is comparatively free from it."

In Mr. Robertson's account of his discoveries on the site, dated 7th July, 1873, he tells us that about 150,000 cubic feet of brick-bats were taken from the ruins to ballast the Indus Valley State Railway, and that the workmen stole all the valuables found and decamped. "One man was caught with 28 tolas weight (11·5 oz.) of gold of which some parts of the ingots were missing. The gold was in rough ingots without any mark." As at Brahmanābād, great quantities of broken pottery were found and of the same class of vessels. "Several very large waterspout pipes or tubular drainage tiles were found, one of them nearly entire, about 30 inches long and 6 to 8 inches in diameter." The coins found here are described in the section on coinage.

[1] It will be seen that the various objects found are of the same nature as those found at Brahmanābād. H. C.

Raverty says the correct name of the place is "Wanjh-rūṭ," "It stood, in ancient times, before the Hakṛā or Wahindah ceased to flow, on the east side of that branch of the great river which passed Aror on the east. Its situation was in the *do-ābah* or delta, between that branch and the main channel, about forty miles below the junction of the rivers. The changes in the river caused it to go to decay centuries since."[1] He then proceeds to give a description of the site very similar to Robertson's.

---

[1] *Mihrān of Sind*, 497.

ALŌR.

ABOUT five miles south by east of Rōhrī, and close to the Eastern Nārā supply channel, is the present small village of Alōr or Arōr,[1] of a few hundred inhabitants which stands upon part of the site of the old capital of Sind of more than a thousand years ago. The country here, as at Rōhrī, is very hilly, and the old city was built, for most part, upon high rocky ground, the old fort or citadal occupying the highest part Hindū bricks, of the very large and ancient kind, are to be seen in the foundations, and are being dug out of extensive pits in the very bed of what is said to have been the old river channel, a few feet only above the very lowest present level (not of the canal bed) at the old bridge. Speaking of the latter, Mr. Eastwick says that to the old bridge an undue antiquity has been ascribed by some, and that there is no reason to suppose it older than about two centuries.[2] It is a very small Muhammadan structure of one principal span, with a pointed arch. It certainly does not look a very ancient structure, and was probably built about the time the adjacent ruined mosque of Ālamgīr was erected. Two hundred years ago there could thus have been but a very small stream as a residue of the great Mihrān or Hakrāh river that once flowed past the town. There is no stream there now save a little branch canal which, for convenience, has been led under the bridge, and naturally follows the low level of the old bed. In a description of the ancient Alōr,[3] given in the *Chach Nāmah*, we are told: "It was a town adorned with various kinds of royal buildings, villas, gardens, fountains, streams, meadows and trees and was situated on the bank of the river Mehrān.[4] In this beautiful and splendid city, there lived a King whose name was Sahiras, son of Sāhasi Rai. This King had innumerable riches and immense buried treasures. His justice was well known in the world, and his liberality and bravery were widely spread. The limits of his dominions extended on the east to the boundary of Kashmir, on the west to Makran, on the south to the coast of the sea and Debal, and

[1] The name is written in various ways by different native writers. Al Rūr, Al-Rūz, Dūr, Alrūd, Aldaur, and Al Dūr are some of the variations. Elliot thinks the real name is Rūr, and that it survives in the name Rōhrī, which he spells Rori (*History of India*, 363). Raverty speaks of it as Aror, also written Aldor. "The '*al*' in this word as here written, and by all the old geographers, is not, and must not be mistaken for, the 'Arabic article *al* because the name Alor or Aror was the Hindī name centuries before the Musalmans had any acquaintance with it, and it may be, and is written and styled Aror, with '*ar*' as well as with '*al*'" (*Mihrān of Sind*, 209n).

[2] Journ. *Bom. Br. R. A. S.*, Vol. I (1843), p. 208.

[3] Mīr Ma'ṣūm gives a similar account, probably copied from this.

[4] According to the *Tārikh-i-Tāhirī* and the *Tuhfatu-l-Kirām*, it was navigable to the sea.

on the north to the mountains of Kurdan and Kīkānān. He had appointed four Governors (Maliks) in his kingdom: one at Brahminābād; and the fort of Nerun and Debal, Luhānah, Lākhah, Sammah and the river were left under his management; another at the town of Siwistān; and Ludhia, Chingān, and the skirts of the hills of Rojhān up to the boundary of Makrān, were given into his charge; the third at the fort of Iskandah; and Bābiah, Siwārah, Jajhōr, and the supplementary territories of Dhanōd were given in his possession; and the fourth at the town of Multān; and the towns of Sikkah, Karad, Ishthar and Kīh up to the boundary of Kashmir were entrusted to him. The King himself had his headquarters in the city of Alōr, retaining Kurdān, Kīkānān, and Barhamas directly under his sway. Each of these Governors was called upon by the king to keep in readiness troops and arms, and accoutrements for horses. He ordered them to protect the interests of the country and the people, to look after the repairs of the (state) buildings, and to keep the feudal assignees and estate-holders happy. In his whole dominion, there was not a single refractory or rebellious head who perversely opposed the measures passed by him or (transgressed) the boundaries fixed by him."[1] From this we gather that Alōr was, at this time no mean city. In the reign of Jām Fatḥ Khān (predecessor of Jām Tughlaq Shāh, son of Sikandar) Alōr was a *parganah* which had been given to one Sayyid 'Abdu-l-Ghais.[2]

Bilāḍurī, speaking of Muḥammad Qāsim's march northwards, after the fall of Brahmanābād says: "At last he reached Alrūr, one of the cities of Sind. It is situated on a hill." Muḥammad Qāsim seems not to have interfered with the temples, for "the temples," he said, "shall be unto us, like as the churches of the Christians, the synagogues of the Jews, and the fire temples of the Magians." He imposed, however, a tribute upon the inhabitants, and built a mosque in the city.[3] Istakhri tells us that "Al Rur approaches Multan in size. It has two walls, is situated near the Mihran, and is on the borders of Mansura."[4] Ibn Hauqal says the country [? city] of Al Rūr is as extensive as Multān, etc., just copying Istakhri. Idrisi says: "Dur [Alōr] is situated on the banks of the Mihran, which runs to the west of the town. It is a pleasant place, and worthy of comparison with Multan as regards size."[5] Just a paraphrase of Istakhri again. Haig says Alōr is not heard of after the middle of the 10th century.

Save for the insignificant little village, the site is now a wilderness. After mentioning two or three ruined buildings of the Musalmān period, Burton thus describes the rest: "Thence ascending the left bank [of the dried up river bed] and turning to the right, or away from the modern village, we front what appears to have been an acropolis, built to command the stream. The enceinte is an irregular oval, with a long diameter of, perhaps, 150 yards. On the eastern crest two piles of good brick-work, one tall and the other much eaten away

[1] Fredunbeg's translation of the *Chach Nāmah*, pp. 11 and 12.

[2] The *Tārikh-i-Sind*, by Mīr Ma'ṣūm, as translated by Mallet.

[3] Elliot's *History of India*, I, 122.

[4] Elliot's *History of India*, I, 28.

[5] *Ib.* 79.

by time, appear to denote the main gate: The surface of the mound is cut and tumbled as if the treasure-seeker had been busy; and the base of adobe and tamped clay bears baked bricks, some scorched to blackness, and heaps of sandstone and unworked limestone flints. Here, after rain, the people still pick up coins, which are said to be mere bits of metal; I could not hear of any Hindu finds dating before the days of the Moslem conquest."[1]

Captain Wood thus describes the place as he found it in 1837: "The ruins of Arore lie three miles and a half from Rorī. They occupy a rocky ledge, overlooking what appears to be the deserted arm of the Indus. From the existence of a substantial causeway connecting Arore with the Rorī side, it would seem that this bed, up to a very late date, was submerged by the waters of inundation. The causeway [the bridge already mentioned] is 480 yards long, fifteen feet wide in the centre, and ten towards the ends. It has a central arch of fifteen feet span, besides five other small ones. The height of the former is ten feet. Arore is also known to the Sindīs by the names of Kumun and Jatrī. While here I heard of the ruins of a place called Mulala on the east bank of the river, fifty miles to the north of Rorī."[2]

At a short distance below the hill on the south-west of the village, lying upon one side of the valley which runs into a *cul de sac* among the hills, is a large block of stone bearing a very much weatherworn Persian inscription. Mr. Eastwick says: "I could discover nothing else in Alōr worthy of notice except two stones in the bed of the river bearing an inscription to the effect that they were set up by Muḥammad Maäsum to mark the ancient course of the stream."[3] The one inscribed stone which I found is difficult to read, owing to the partial obliteration of some of the letters, but so far as I have been able to get it deciphered, there seems to be no reference to the stream: it appears to be a short exhortation to shun the world and follow the godly path, and records the fact that Āmīr Muḥammad Ma'ṣūm ordered the inscription to be engraved in the year A. H. 1008 (A. D. 1599). It possibly commemorates the retirement of his *murshid* or spiritual guide, and there may have been more of the inscription which has been lost. Mr. Yazdani thus translates it: "March like (experienced) travellers, place thy foot in the wilderness (*i.e.*, the world) like (courageous) men. Written by order of the refuge of Sayyids, Amīr Muḥammad Ma'ṣūm. A. H. 1008 (A. D. 1599)." The inscribed stone, for I could find but one, the other stone being but a rough uninscribed block lying a short distance from it, seems to have fallen from the crest of the hill above, where the stone was inscribed as part of the rock before it became detached. The block is not dressed, except the sunk flat surface, which is engraved. The rock of the hill is stratified, but it is only at the top that the strata correspond in thickness to the stone; the strata of the rest of the rock, lower down, being very much thinner. Another reason for supposing that it rolled down from the top to the foot of the slope is that it is resting with the inscription upside

[1] *Sind Revisited*, Chap. XXIX, pp. 269-275.
[2] *A Journey to the Source of the River Oxus*, New Ed., 1872, p. 26.
[3] Article on *Allore and Rohri*, *Journ. Bom. Br. R. A. S.*, Vol. I, April (1843), p. 200.

down. The inscription was thus, I believe, engraved upon the projecting face of the upper layer or rock, whence a large fragment fell carrying the inscription with it, the hammering, when chiselling the letters, having, perhaps, loosened it. The foot of the slope is covered with smaller but similar fragments. However, Mr. Eastwick's two stones may not be these: I could find no others. Concerning these stones Raverty writes: "I am unaware whether the two stones set up by Mīr Ma'ṣūm of Bahkar in the bed of the diverted branch of the river, are still in existence, or whether if they are, any inscription is legible; for he is said to have cut an inscription on them. If we could find an inscription we might obtain further information on this interesting subject."[1]

On the north side of the village, upon a knoll, and near the old bridge, are the remains of an old brick *masjid*, with fragments of tile work, mostly of a coarse star pattern, in blue and white, like some of that on the Sātbhāin at Rōhrī. There are also the tombs of two *Sayyids*, Shakar Ganj Shāh and Khatālu-d-dīn, or Quṭb Shāh.

---

[1] *The Mihrān of Sind*, 486n.

BHAMBŌR.

THE ruined site of Bhambōr lies upon the right bank of the Ghāro creek, about 33 miles east of Karachi, but 40 by boat from that place, and is about 3 miles west of the village of Gharo.[1] Some writers have supposed these ruins to be those of the ancient delta city of Debal or Deval, about the location of which there has been more discussion than about any other site in Sind. But the most casual inspection of the place is sufficient to dispel this idea, for it is too insignificant a site to have been that of the city which for some time defied the forces of the Arab invaders in the eighth century.[2] The ruins are situated upon a small patch of ground which forms the extreme end of a low range of hills running seaward, and a break in the continuity of the range isolates the site from the rest. The whole area measures but 600 by 400 yards, and the outline is sharply defined, the site being contained within the periphery of the hill top itself. The place could not very well have extended beyond these limits, without being in danger of being flooded in those early days when the sea was not so far from it as now, and when the river flowed in considerable volume past it. Nothing now remains but the foundations of walls, and these are loosely built of the very coarsest unhewn rubble, not a sign of cut-stone being visible. An outer wall, 8 to 10 feet wide, of the same material, engirdled the whole place, and was strengthened at intervals with bastions. Little of interest was to be found beyond a number of corroded copper coins, like those smaller ones found at Brahmanābād, which were picked up, for the most part, on the sands immediately below the edge of the mounds on the creek face, whither they had been washed or had rolled from the ruins above. Shells of different sizes and shapes were found scattered about in abundance, and fragments of glazed pottery, glass, and clay coin moulds were just as were found at Brahmanābād.

Bhambōr was, I should think, nothing more than an outpost guarding the creek, or a small port regulating the shipping admitted into the open waterway leading to Dewal and the interior, where sea-going ships discharged their cargo into river craft, and where customs dues were levied. When the creek became disconnected with the Indus, the place was most likely then abandoned and fell into ruin.

---

[1] The name is spelt in many ways, such as Bhambōra, Bhambūr, Bhambūra, Bhambhūra and Bhambharāwā.

[2] Moreover, the *Tuhfatu-l-Kirām*, in enumerating certain cities which lay within the land of Sākūra, mentions both Debal and Bhambōr as two different places (Elliot's *History of India*, I, 398).

General Haig, in commenting upon Elliot's and Cunningham's identification of Bhambōr with Barbarikon, the chief port of the delta at the time of the *Periplus*, thought Barbarikon was probably in the vicinity of the modern S͟hāh Bandar.[1] Cunningham thought Bhambōr was probably deserted about A. D. 1250, and says that about the tenth century it was the capital of a chief named Bhambo Rāja, and, according to the traditions of the people, the most westerly branch of the Indus once flowed past Bhambura.[2] Elliot says: " Bhambūra, or Bhambūr is not named in our oldest works on Sind but it is mentioned in a modern native historian as having been captured during the K͟hilafat of Hārūn-ur-Rashīd. It is the scene of many legendary stories of Sind; and, according to one of them owes its destruction, in a single night, to the divine wrath which its ruler's sins drew down upon it."[3] Natives of Sind consider it the oldest port in the province, and its position, and the course of the river at that time, so far as we are able to locate it, make it probable that there was a port in this position at the time of Alexander's expedition into India, though there is nothing now above ground earlier than the Arab invasion. The story of its destruction is mixed up with the story of King Dalū Rāi given elsewhere. It has been connected with the loves of Sassūi and Punhūn—a favourite story still told in the homes of Sind, which has been well recounted by Burton in his *Sind Revisited.* It is thus also called Sassūi-jo-Takar.

[1] *Indus Delta Country*, 31.
[2] *Ancient Geography*, 294 and 295.
[3] Elliot's *History of India*, I, 368.

BUDDHIST STŪPA AT MĪRPŪR-KHĀS.

MĪRPŪR-KHĀS, the head-quarters of the district of Thar and Pārkar, is upon the line of rail connecting Haidarābād with Mārwār Junction, and is 42 miles east of the former place. It is a town of comparatively modern date, having been built in 1806 by Mīr 'Alī Murād Tālpūr. The place came into the hands of the Manikānī Mīrs about 1793, when the country was divided up between the different members of the Tālpūr family. It was the chief town of Mīr Sher Muḥammad Khān Tālpūr, whose army was totally defeated at Dabba, near by, by Sir Charles Napier in 1843. About half a mile to the north of the town there is an ancient site, extending over about thirty acres, covered with mounds, over the surface of which brickbats and potsherds are thickly scattered. Very little excavation is sufficient to show that these mounds represent the sites and ruined foundations of very old buildings of sorts; and the occurrence of very large bricks of an early pattern and make, together with numerous fragments of *htis* [1] of small *dāgobas*, make it pretty certain that the site was that of a Buddhist establishment. The place is now known as Kahu-jo-Daro

When I examined this site in 1909, I found that one of the larger mounds, at the north end, was undoubtedly the remains of a Buddhist *stūpa*, as some portion of the core of the tower, of sun-dried bricks, protruded from the top; and the quantity of carved brick lying about it, which was not observed to any extent elsewhere on the site, in patterns found so plentifully about many of the ruined *stūpas* of the Panjab and the north, as well as on that of Mīr Rukān, near Moro in Sind, which is still standing, declared its character. My excavation of the mound was carried out in the following year. I was not, however, the first to be attracted to it and to probe its contents. General John Jacob, when acting Commissioner in Sind, made an excavation here, but, we are told, that nothing of interest was discovered. Probably his excavation did not get beyond the surrounding heap of fallen debris. Then it was examined by the Honourable James Gibbs, who thus described his search in the ruins: "On the 27th January 1859, we pitched at Mīrpūr-Khās, in the Hyderabad Collectorate, and at about 1½ miles to the north, or north-west, we found the remains of a brick 'Thūl'; it was very dilapidated, and, if my memory serves, not above 6 feet of the round portion was left. It was soft and easily worked; after some little clearing we came upon a hollow chamber, in which was a vase of fine

---

[1] The "Tee" tops of *dāgobas*, under the umbrella.

earthenware which contained some pieces of crystal and amethyst, with what appeared to be bits of bark. No remnant of bone could be found. The vase is, I believe now in the Kurrachee Museum. Further researches produced nothing but bricks, some ornamented, until the third day, when a head in a greenish stone and of an Egyptian type, was found. This was also, I believe, placed by Sir Bartle Frere in the museum at Kurrachee."[1] When Mr. Woodburn, I.C.S., was Collector of Hyderabad, about 1894, he rescued from the depredations of the railway contractors, who had been using up all the ornamental brick they could lay hands on for ballast, a large terra-cotta seated image of the Buddha, and a head and aureole of another.[2] These, it will be seen, on comparison with those which we unearthed, were evidently taken out of the very walls of the *stūpa*, and are the only ones which I found missing. It is strange that the wall, from which they were taken, was not noticed, though it contained other statues, uncovered during my excavation [3] (Plates XVII--XXVII).

I found the mound in such a ruined and dilapidated state, being, apparently nothing but a heap of mud debris, that, when I commenced my excavations, I had little hope of recovering any of its original walling (Plate XXII). Should there have been no walls standing in the mound, I thought it likely that, at least, the lower courses of the basement would still be there, so I made cuttings from the outside ground level straight into the middle of the south and east sides. At the same time, having located the centre of the mound, as near as I could guess, I began sinking a ten-foot well down the middle through the firm sun-dried brickwork. I saw that what remained of the core of the mound had not been disturbed, so, if it were a relic mound, the relics were probably still within it. In these first two cuttings we soon came upon the broken upper edges of the burnt-brick walls of the platform upon which the tower of the *stūpa* stood, and this was opened out to right and left along the walls. We next uncovered three of the corners of the platform, the walls of burnt brick being only a few bricks thick.

Around the circular core of the *stūpa* of sun-dried bricks, which projected from the top of the mound, was a kind of rough platform, which was the remains of the flat terrace originally surrounding the base of the circular tower. This was deep in loose debris, and, on starting to clear this on the south side, the head of a Buddha rolled away when the few inches of earth covering it was removed.[4] An examination of the spot showed us that we had struck the

[1] This note was written in 1877, from memory. Miscl. Memorandum of the Archæol. Survey of Western India, No. 8, p. 33. The vase and other objects were not to be found in the Museum in 1910, and no one knew anything about them.

[2] *Journ. Bom. Br. R. A. S*, XIX, 44.

[3] Sir James Campbell made the following note on Mr. Woodburn's find: "The commonest of the brick towers noted by Mr. Woodburn recalls Hiuen Thsiang's (Beal's *Buddhist Records*, II, 273) account of the monasteries and relic mounds, seen everywhere in Sind, marking the spots where the great Arhat Upargupta had rested when he was journeying through the country preaching the law. Hiuen Thsiang, as usual, puts these relic mounds back to the time of Asoka (B. C. 240). The present images, together with the outer casings, if not the entire mounds, are not likely to be older than the sixth century A. D." This is far too late a date as I shall show further on, and in my account of Suḍheran's *stūpa*.

[4] In Plate XXII is seen the headless Buddha, from which this head fell away.

line of wall at a point where there was a sunk panel containing a seated image As the head of the image was only just below the surface, the neck had disintegrated and become separated from the body. As this wall was opened out, other image niches were found, and it was easily seen that we had struck the south wall of the great square basement of the *stūpa*. All four sides were now laid bare to the original ground level.[1] Three sides—the north, east and south—were found to be alike, the upper wall space being divided into five bays by pilasters whose bases rest upon the top member of a great heavy roll-moulding plinth which runs round the four walls, except where interrupted in the middle of the west wall. The three central bays, on each of these three sides, each contained an image niche, occupied by a seated figure of the Buddha, while the end ones at the corners, on each side, contained a similar niche but filled with blind lattice tracery in intricate patterns in imitation of latticed windows, but of these, only two, at the north-east corner, remain.

In order to uncover the four walls, we had to dig through a deep mass of solid burnt brickwork. This had been carefully built against the walls, and extended outward from them some twelve to fifteen feet, and was carried up to the tops of the walls as we found them. The latter, with their mouldings and images, were thus completely, and, apparently purposely, buried at some period not long after their erection, since the great bricks[2] employed for this purpose were of the same size and make as those in the walls. To account for this wholesale burying of the great basement, it first occurred to me that it was probably done upon the first inroads of the Arabs into Sind, in order to hide and protect the images from their iconoclastic tendencies; but, upon clearing the walls completely, down to the original ground level, the reason for this became apparent. From the lines of the mouldings in the basement, which is about 6 feet high, it was seen that the whole *stūpa* had not only subsided about 8 inches into the soil in the middle of the walls, where the weight of the tower above came more directly upon them, but had also bulged outwards to the same extent on all four sides. This bulging downwards and outwards is plainly seen in the photographs, the weight of the tower hardly affecting the corners which were further away from it. This, due to insufficiently strong foundations for the great weight of the tower, must have taken place at, or very soon after, the completion of it; and, as the stability of the whole edifice was threatened, there was nothing left for the builders to do but to buttress it up with this heavy brickwork. Whether the exterior of this additional work was finished off in the same manner as the original walls, with pilasters and images, I had not the time and opportunity to discover by further excavation, but it is to be hoped that at no distant date both this and the exploration of the many other mounds on this site will be undertaken. It is to this buttressing and burying of the walls, that the remarkable preservation of the images is due. The subsidence inwards and downwards of the vault of the central shrine, on the west side, in

[1] Compare with a *stūpa* at Taxila, Archæological Survey of India Annual Report for 1912-13, Plate XII, *a*.

[2] These were so big and so heavy that, damp as they were, one was sufficient for a coolie woman to carry away at a time.

itself shows the danger that was threatening the whole edifice, which had to be immediately provided against. Had the tower been still standing when we cleared this away, we should probably have brought the whole box of bricks upon our heads.

But a silent and destructive force of a different character is ever at work in the soil of Sind. The *kalar*, already referred to, rises with moisture into the porous body of any brickwork accessible to it, and, drying and crystallizing within it, bursts and pulverises the material. So long as the bricks are buried in the moist soil little happens, but, when they are exposed to the air, the alternate drying and wetting that they get soon plays havoc with them. Thus we found bricks which, not so long ago, were stacked by contractors for removal, crumbled to powder on handling them.[1] This *kalar* had already attacked parts of the walls and most of the images of the Buddha, that in the western niche on the north side being found encrusted to a depth of half an inch with an efflorescence of crystals, which had to be carefully chisled away, hot water failing to dissolve it. This salt has been found to be composed of gypsum, sodium sulphate, sodium carbonate, organic matter and sand, of which gypsum forms nearly 89 per cent.

The west side of the basement of the *stūpa* is unlike the other three, and this was probably the front of the building.[2] In the middle of this side, which seems to have had a porch-like projection, were found three little cell shrines, one occupying the centre, and facing west, and one on each side of it, at right angles to it and facing one another (Plate XXIII). In front of these, and common to the three, was a small antechamber (see plan), before which, again, was some further construction, as shown by the foundations, but so ruined as to make it impossible to say what it was—possibly a staircase by which to ascend to the terrace round the base of the tower. The shrines are small, being about four feet square. When the walls around were buttressed up, these appear to have been filled up solid; and, judging from the way the only remaining portion of the roof of the central shrine has been crushed in, the filling up and buttressing was not commenced a day too soon. A portion of the filling-in was removed from these shrines, sufficient to show that in the central one, at least, there had been a bench, or altar, across the back wall, as if for an image. The side shrines probably had the same but they were much ruined. In the central shrine, standing upon the floor, and leaning against the north side wall, was found a large slab of terra-cotta, bearing a male standing figure in relief, which I shall describe further on (Figure 14). It was embedded in the filling-in of brickwork. No other images were found: if images of the Buddha ever rested in these shrines, they must have been removed previously to the buttressing up of the building.

---

[1] Railway contractors, in the past, have been among the worst agents of destruction of ancient buildings in India. At Harapa, in the Panjab, Cunningham says the bricks removed from that site have more than sufficed for the ballast of about 100 miles of railway. We know, too, how the line was ballasted with marble, and a bridge constructed, from beautiful temples which once existed at Chandrāvati in Rājputānā, and these are but examples of scores of other such cases of vandalism.

[2] The Sudheran *stūpa*, near Tāndo Muḥammad Khān, appears to have faced the north.

In the middle and south shrines we have portions of the roofing of each remaining. That of the middle one is wagon-vaulted, the bricks having been corbelled forward upon level beds from the tops of the side walls to the apex, the under sides being dressed to a segmental curve (Plate XXV). The vault thus runs from front to back. In the south shrine, however, we find something calculated to upset a very cherished belief that the Hindūs never built a true arch before the advent of the Muḥammadans, for here we have a fragment of an actual true arch, built with properly formed brick voussoirs, the bricks being placed on edge. There are here portions of some six arch rings, part of an arched vault which formed the roof of this shrine. The top and bottom edges of the bricks are moulded to the curve of the vault, while the other edges radiate towards a centre. The bricks measure 16¼″ from corner to corner along the top, they are 10″ deep and 2⅞″ thick. One or two similar arch rings were found at Brahmanābād.

The horizontal lintels of the doors of these shrines were of wood, some of which still remained, but thoroughly decayed and mostly reduced to powder.

At either end of this west wall,[1] on the face of it, there had been very large panels or niches, the sills only remaining, with the bases of the two flanking pilasters which framed them in. These are seen in the photograph (Plate XXII). Under the sill of that at the south end, in fact, forming part of the sill or bottom of the frame of the niche, is a band of decorated bricks, about 8¼″ high with a little female figure standing and holding a waterpot, in the centre and at each end. It is a great pity that the rest of the niches and their contents have disappeared, for it is quite likely they held some kind of groups in terra-cotta representing such scenes as the birth of the Buddha or his great renunciation, as we have found upon a smaller scale at Ṭhūl Mīr Rukān. Between these large panels and the shrines were two smaller panels, one on each side, of a peculiar shape, that on the north side holding a small image of the seated Buddha, whose hands are broken off, while that on the south side has been mostly destroyed. He wears his robe over both shoulders in the same manner as in the other images in the large niches, and is seated upon a lotus with a background made up of flame-like leaves spreading out from the back of the body all around (Plate XXVI).[2] The eyes are quite shut, the upper and lower lids meeting. The arms have been broken off from the elbows: they were probably placed in the lap, but of this it is impossible to be certain, as there

---

[1] Not the east wall, as was stated, by mistake, in my account in the Archæological Survey Annual for 1909-10.

[2] A Gandhāra image, with a similar background, may be seen illustrated in the *Journal of Indian Art*, Vol. VIII, Plate 18, Figure 1. The figure, in this case, which occupies the centre of a pedestal, upon which are the crossed legs of what was probably an image of the Buddha, appears to stand against a background of foliage rather than flames, of the acanthus leaf style. Of this figure Dr. Burgess wrote: "It seems to have been the base of a figure of the emaciated ascetic [*i.e.*, the figure to which the legs belonged]. The figure rising from the leaves suggests to us the tree Deva called Akubha or Kakubha, who assisted the fainting Bhodisattva at this period." (Beal's Romantic Legends, p. 194). In Prinsep's *Antiquities*, Vol. I, Plate viii, there is an image of the Buddha shown with flames (? leaves) rising from the back of each shoulder, with this remark: "The lambent flame on the shoulders is a peculiarity not observed in any image or drawing of Buddha that I have seen. It seems to denote a Mithraic tinge in the local faith." This image was dug up 2 miles south-east of Kābul, and is clothed in the same manner as those at Mīrpūr-Khās.

appear to be no fractured surfaces upon the upturned feet or legs to show that they had been in contact with them anywhere, except at the toes of the right foot. Being moulded in clay, they may not have been so intimately connected with the rest of the body as they would have been had the image been carved in stone. It is possible the hands may have been raised in front of the breast in the teaching attitude.

The arched arrangement above the Buddhas in the niches, especially that in the centre of the north wall, are very interesting and look like the original from which the façade of the Visvarkarma cave at Elura was derived; the Buddha in the niche, here, corresponding to the Buddha before the *dāgoba* in the cave, as seen through the frame of the doorway below[1] (Plate XX).

In front of the three shrines was a great quantity of loose debris, which seems to have rolled down from above, perhaps from the platform in front of the base of the tower; and irregularly embedded in this were found over a hundred votive tablets in unburnt clay, of different sizes and patterns. Scattered about amongst them were found copper coins, thirty-six of which were recovered, but all as lumps of green verdigris in which it seemed hopeless to expect to find a copper core. These finds were all located in the debris *about six feet above the original ground or floor level in front of the shrines*. But, upon the ground level, to the left in front of the central shrine door, was found a stamp or mould for making such tablets, in burnt clay or terra-cotta.

The well which we sunk down through the middle of the *stūpa* was continued until a depth of 25 feet from the summit of the mound was reached, when, in the centre, we came upon a square area of red burnt brick about 4 feet square. As the upper layer of bricks was removed, a little chamber in the middle, about 15″ square was disclosed, whose sides were set parallel with the sides of the *stūpa*. Within this, reposed two blocks of stone, roughly dressed to a circular shape, about 13″ in diameter and 5″ to 6″ thick, placed one upon the other.[2] When the upper slab was raised it was found that in the middle of both was a cup-shaped hollow, about 3″ in diameter, the lower one being 2½″ and the upper, the lid, as it were, 1¼″ deep. Standing within the cavity, in the lower stone, was a small crystal bottle, while around it, and upon the surface of the stone, were sprinkled, amidst a quantity of white sand, from which they had to be sifted, a number of offerings consisting of 63 coral beads, 7 crystal beads, drilled and undrilled, 2 small crystals cut to simulate diamonds, each about half the size of a pea, 30 very small seed pearls, most of them not much larger than a pin's head, and all drilled; 4 gold beads, two being ribbed and melon-shaped, and about three-eighths of an inch in diameter, 1 small gold wire ring, 10 copper coins, some small lumps of charcoal, a few grains of wheat, and some other small beads and chips (Plates XXIII and XXV).

---

[1] See page 378, *Cave Temples of India*, by Fergusson and Burgess.

[2] Similar to that found in the ruined *stūpa* of Panahiām Jhār at Sahēṭh-Mahēṭh, which Sir John Marshall attributes to about the 3rd or 4th century B. C. (Annual Report, Archæological Survey of India for 1910-11, p. 11). A similar receptacle for the relic caskets was found in the Boria *stūpa* near Junagadh in Kathiawad (*Journ. As. Soc., Bengal*, LX, Part I, No. 2, 1891).

Upon the mouth of the crystal bottle was a small flat silver cap, much corroded, and on the cap rested a copper finger ring, encrusted in verdigris, the corrosion adhering to the cap so tightly as to cause it to break when being taken off. Inside the bottle was a small silver cylindrical case with a slip-on lid, but so corroded that the lid came to pieces in taking it off. The case had been wrapped round with gold leaf, which was as fresh and bright as on the day it was first put on. This case measures 1″ in length by $\frac{5}{16}$″ in diameter. Within this silver case was a very small gold one, of the same shape[1], out of which, when it was opened over a clean sheet of white paper, rolled a very minute substance about the size of a pin's head, together with a speck or two of dust. There was nothing else in the case. But, within the crystal bottle, *underneath the cases, and not in them,* was found about an egg-spoonful of what appears to be brown cremated ash, some lumps of which have the texture and convex surface, as seen through a magnifying glass, of charred bone [2] (Plate XXIII).

In each of the south-east and south-west corners of the brick chamber, and between the bricks and the stone receptacle, was a little earthen pot, with narrow mouth, filled with sand; but, when the latter was removed and carefully sieved nothing else was found. The pots are of an interesting shape, the surface being grooved round in narrow rings (Plate XXIII).[3]

As already stated, a considerable amount of the brick buttressing, and fallen debris around the *stūpa*, remained undisturbed by us: we merely removed suffi-

Fig. 9. Buddhist compared with classic ornament.

cient to lay the walls bare. In the debris were found carved bricks in a great variety of patterns, as shown in the illustrations (Plates XXIV and XXV), and of very superior workmanship, so much so as to merit the term terra-cotta

---

[1] Just such another was found by Sir John Marshall at Taxila, with much the same contents, see *Archæological Memoir*, No. 7, p. 8 and plate X*h*.

[2] All these things were brought away and will be placed in the Prince of Wales Museum at Bombay when that building is ready to receive them. Several of the terra-cotta images will accompany them.

[3] Similar in size and shape to one found at Taxila. See *Arch.* Sur. Memoir No. 7, p. 52 and plate XXVI*b*.

rather than brick being applied to them.[1] Among the designs were found several forms of the key pattern or Greek fret; indeed, Greek influence, in ornamental details, is very apparent in several of the very few fragments retrieved by us, and, in this respect, connects the work closely with that of the Indo-Greek remains of Gandhāra. In the accompanying illustration I have compared a few specimens of Greek ornament, as taken from Nicholson's *Principles of Architecture* with some of the carved bricks from this *stūpa* (Figure 9).

Two medallions were unearthed bearing the image so frequently found and which is supposed to represent Kubera, and several square tiles with grotesque faces (Plate XXV). From the number of tiles, with the face as shown in the right lower corner of the illustration, it would seem that there must have been at least one whole string-course of them. The so-called Kubera image, both here and elsewhere, might very well be the conventional way they had in those days of representing the donor, or person who provided the money for the construction of the work upon which it appears, the money bag which he holds in his right hand indicating this. I do not think that we should necessarily take it as the image of the god of wealth.[2] A few fragments of the capitals of the pilasters, which were placed at intervals around the tower, such as are seen on the Ṭhūl Mīr Rukān, were recovered, and from them, in Plate XIX, I have endeavoured to reconstruct one of these capitals. The little image of the standing Buddha, in the middle of the capital is found in Græco-Buddhist examples, and the capital, itself, is a lineal descendant of the Corinthian order through Gandhāra.[3]

There is little now left to give us any clue to the original shape of the *stūpa*, but, by comparing the little there is with what we know of other *stūpas*, it is not difficult to imagine the outline of the complete building. To begin with, sufficient remains to show that the lowest part of the structure was a great square basement, 53′ 6″ from corner to corner of the plinth, rising, in its ruined state to a height of 14″ 6″. Allowing for missing mouldings above the capitals of the pilasters, the basement was at least 17′ high. Upon this rose a cylindrical tower, with domed top, to about the same height as its diameter, about 37 or 38 feet, thus leaving a flat terrace around the base of the tower, and on the top of the great basement, to serve the purpose of *pradakshiṇā* or circumambulation. This would give a total height of about 55 feet, or about as high as the square of the basement at the ground level.[4] Like Ṭhūl Mīr Rukān, the tower was probably decorated with one or more bands of pilasters, numerous string courses, and mouldings of sculptured or moulded bricks. When complete, the dome was possibly crowned with a wooden umbrella. There were no signs

[1] For similar carved bricks see article on "Set Mahet" (Sahēṭh-Mahēṭh) by W. Hoey in the Journal of the Asiatic Society of Bengal, LXI (1892), Plate XXVI; also, Annual Report, Archæological Survey of India, 1903-4, Plates LXVI and LXVIII.

[2] Somewhat similar medallions were discovered at Sahēṭh-Mahēṭh, (Archæological Surv. Annual for 1910-11, Plate 3 and p. 6.

[3] See Fergusson's *Indian and Eastern Architecture*, Revised Edition, Vol. I, p. 214, and Cunningham's Report, V, Plate XXIV.

[4] Ṭhūl Mīr Rukān and the Giryek *stūpa* give an idea of what the tower of this one was like. See Cunningham's Report, Vol. I, p. 17.

of early railings, but, of course, these could not have been well constructed in brickwork; and, as stone was not easily obtained, any that may have existed would probably have been in wood.

As previously stated, there were three images of the Buddha upon each of the three faces of the basement—the north, east and south. Of these nine, seven were in position when I uncovered the walls. Two were missing, namely, one from the niche on the south side of the central one on the east side, and one just round the corner, east of the centre on the south side. Both of these are accounted for: they were extracted by Mr. Woodburn as already noticed; or, rather, he found a whole image and a head, the body of which was probably broken in removal.[1]

All these images, which are about half life size, are seated cross-legged in the meditative attitude (*dhyāna-mudrā*), with both hands in the lap, one upon the other, with palms upwards (Plates XXVI and XXVII). The Buddha is represented in some seated upon a lotus and in others upon a four-legged stool. The images had all been painted, those of the Buddha having red robes and a golden coloured complexion, with black eyes and hair; and, for this purpose, they appear to have been covered with a thin egg-shell layer of very superior clay before baking. His body is fully clothed with an ample robe which covers both shoulders, and hangs in folds. Under the robe he appears to wear trousers, the legs of which are very clearly shown beneath the bottom of the robe.[2] The end of the robe, in front, hangs down over the seat under him; and both arms, to the wrist, are covered. In all the images, save one, the hair is of the short

FIG. 10.—Head of a Buddha.

[1] These are illustrated in the *Journal of the Bombay Br. R. A. S.*, Vol. XIX, pp. 44 ff.

[2] The robe over both shoulders, and the trousers, show plainly that the Buddhist iconography of Sind, of that date, came from Gandhāra. In the votive tablets, however, which are of a much later date, he seems to have the right shoulder bare, and no trousers, after the fashion of Indian sculptures.

curly kind exception, in the eastern image on the north side it is represented straight, and dressed back from the front Between the eyes, in most of the images, is a small circle to indicate the *ūrṇā*, one of the Buddha's special marks denoting enlightenment (*bōdhi*). As it is a grooved ring and not a protuberance, possibly some metallic button was attached. The knob (*ushṇīsha*) on the top of the head is present, though not very prominent. The ear lobes are long and pendulous, and the eyes in some are fairly open, while, in others they are half closed. Behind the head is a decorated nimbus, alike in all except the straight-haired image, where, instead of a circular band of square and round lotuses, it has a scroll band of conventional leaves[1] (Figure 10).

FIG 11.—Votive tablets

As the *stūpa* is in such a ruinous condition, and so little of it left, I removed six Buddha images from the walls for safer custody, and they will be eventually housed in the Prince of Wales Museum at Bombay. Exposed, as they would now have been to the air and rains, the *kalar*, with which they are more or less impregnated, would soon have caused their disintegration. With a Muhammadan population in close proximity they would also have been, in their isolated position, exposed to wanton damage Three Buddha images were left, namely, two on the east and one on the south face.

[1] These haloes resemble, very closely, those of the large images at the Sanchi *stūpa*.

The clay tablets which we found in the fallen debris, out in front of the west face, some 6 feet above the original ground level, and therefore of later

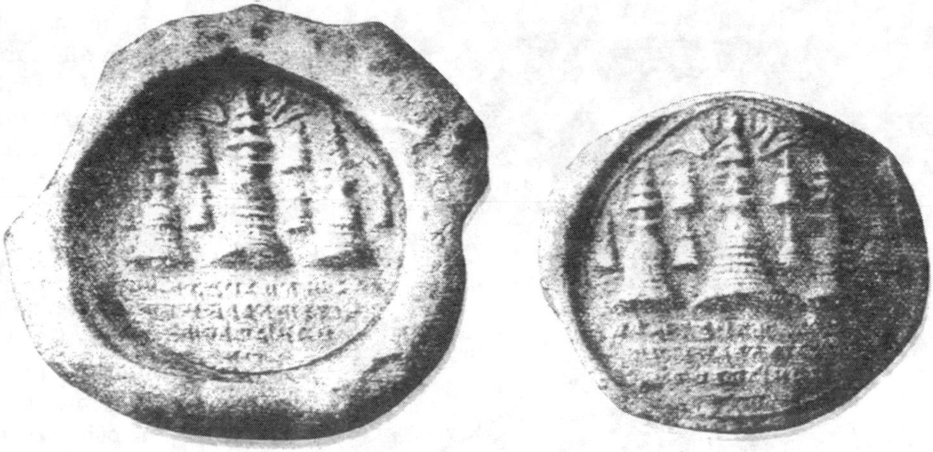

FIG. 12.—Votive tablets.

date than the original building, were all in unburnt clay. They show that the *stūpa* was an object of worship or reverence after it had become ruinous. They are of different sizes varying from 1½" to 6" in their greatest length, for they are mostly oval in shape (Plate XXVII). Some have an impression of Buddha

FIG. 13.—Votive tablet inscription, enlarged.

seated cross-legged with the right hand pointing downwards in the witness attitude (*bhūmisparśa-mudrā*) representing him at the moment of enlightenment (*bōdhī*), the foliage of the Bōdhī tree being shown over his head. Others have him seated in the European fashion, with the legs hanging down, and hands before the breast, in the preaching attitude (*dharmachakra-mudrā*), delivering his address in the Deer Park. The robe is not shown very distinctly, but on some the mark of its edge is shown from the left shoulder to the right waist, and thus, unlike the older images on the walls, it leaves the right shoulder bare, as we find it in such sculptures as those in the Ajanta Caves and elsewhere in the peninsula. Many of the tablets have, instead of an image of Buddha, representations of very attenuated Burmese-looking *dāgobas*—one, three, ten, or more than a hundred being impressed on each tablet. The last are circular tablets, and the *dāgobas* are arranged in rows, which being small, make the tablets look like sample cards of little screws, of different sizes, standing on their heads. Under the Buddhas and *dāgobas* is, in each case, the Buddhist formula, *Yē dharmā,* etc., in letters of different periods ranging from the beginning of the 7th century or earlier, to the end of the 8th century or later.[1]

With these tablets were found about 36 copper coins, which had evidently been placed there as offerings with them. They were but round lumps of verdigris within which was found a much corroded copper core, upon many of which were portions of Arabic inscriptions. Some had the four leaved flower upon one side, from which, as well as from the letters legible, it is easy to identify them as coins of the early Arabs in Sind, such as have been described in the account of Brahamanābād. The position in which these tablets were found, and the Arab coins, would seem to show that offerings were made at the *stūpa* after the advent of the Arabs in Sind, in the early years of the eighth century. The moulds for the tablets were probably fashioned after old patterns; and we must not forget that heavy copper coins would naturally sink through soft debris much more easily than clay tablets, so that the coins may have joined them from a higher level of a later date. The unbaked and soft clay tablets would indicate that there were Buddhist priests, or *sāmānīs*, there to make them in exchange for the pilgrims' money offerings;[2] the copper coins lying there unappropriated would tend to show that, when the few pilgrims who visited the place dropped them there, the *stūpa* was deserted, and there were no priests to gather them up.

To return to the relics. The ten copper coins, found with the other offerings in the relic chamber, were but lumps of verdigris; and, except for their shape being rectangular, could hardly be distinguished from the coins found with the votive tablets. The extent of corrosion being nearly the same in both cases shows clearly that those in the relic chamber, hermetically sealed, as it were, within the mound, to have attained that amount of corrosion, must have been deposited there several centuries before the others were placed on the outside, where they have been but a few feet below the surface, subject to wet and dry seasons for, perhaps, a thousand years.

The crystal reliquary had been broken and the bottom portion lost, after which it had been mended by putting a tightly-fitting case of silver on the bottom reaching halfway up the phial. The lip, around the top, had also been chipped. It is probable that an accident happened at or before the time of enshrining the relics in the present *stūpa*, when the little bottle fell from the

---

[1] Votive tablets from Burmah, like these, are described in the Journ. Bom. Br. R. A. S. for 1898. See also tablets illustrated in the Journ. R. A. S. for 1900, from Sohnāg, p. 431 ff. A very similar tablet is illustrated at page 180, *Buddhist Art in India*, edited by Dr. Burgess, but the image is more of a Burmese type.

[2] The *sāmāni*, whom Chach visited in his temple or monastery, near Brahmanābād, was engaged in this very work of preparing tablets for visitors when the latter called upon him.

careless hands of some persons who was holding it. The fact of a new silver bottom having been provided, and a silver cap to take the place of a crystal stopper or lid, instead of providing a new bottle, would lead one to suppose that this reliquary had already held the relics for so long a time that it was felt it would have been sacrilege to throw away the old phial for a new one, even in its shattered condition. When placing the small stone pot, containing the inner caskets and relics, into the coffer at the Boria *stūpa* at Junagadh, a similar accident seems to have taken place, for we found the fragments of the lower part of an exactly similar pot buried in the mound about four feet from the relic coffer.[1] I have already noticed the discovery of a vase or pot in the upper part of this Mirpūr-Khās *stūpa*, containing "some pieces of crystal and amethyst." Could these have been the missing fragments of the broken reliquary ? It certainly seems that the relics must have existed for some time before the present *stūpa* was built over them. Is, then, the present *stūpa* a reconstruction of an older one—of one of the many built by Aśoka when he redistributed the relics of the Buddha in order that the actual bodily presence of the Great Teacher might pervade the land through all its length and breadth ? If so, this would account for the very small relic, if relic it is, and I have little doubt of it, found in the gold case. And, possibly, the ashes in the phial, beneath the gold and silver cases, may be some of those of the faithful disciple, Upargupta, the friend and erstwhile religious associate of Aśoka, who made the oversight of the Buddhist cult in Sind his especial care.[2] That it is not unusual to find relics of more than one person in the same *stūpa*, we know from the fact of the relics of four *Arhats*, in four reliquaries, all inscribed, in one *stūpa*, No. 2, at Sanchi, as described by Cunningham in his *Bhilsa Topes*.

It is recorded by Hiuen Tsiang (in the 7th century A. D.) that in his day there were several hundred *saṅghārāmas* in Sind, occupied by about 10,000 priests, and that they studied the Little Vehicle. He also adds that "when Tathagata [the Buddha] was in the world, he frequently passed through this country, therefore Aśōka-rāja has founded several tens of *stūpas* in places where the sacred traces of his presence were found. Upargupta, the great Arhat, sojourned frequently in this kingdom, explaining the law and convincing and guiding men. The places where he stopped and the traces he left are all commemorated by the building of *saṅghārāmas* or the erection of *stūpas*. These buildings are seen everywhere."[3]

The silver case, holding the smaller gold one, was wrapped around with gold leaf, which, even now, is as bright and fresh as on the day it was put there —gold leaf, too, as fine as any produced at the present day. If the small particle, found in the otherwise empty and clean gold case, which was again enclosed in the silver one, was accidental and counted for naught, it is difficult to understand why the silver case should have been so carefully enveloped in gold leaf. Those who applied the gold leaf thought they were wrapping up

[1] Journ. Asiatic Society of Bengal, LX, Part I, No. 2, 1891.

[2] We are told that Aśoka opened up seven of the eight *stūpas*, containing the relics of the Buddha, and redistributed them amongst 84,000 *stūpas* which he had caused to be built.

[3] *Si-yu-ki. Buddhist Records of the Western World* (Beal's trans.), Vol. II, p. 272.

something more precious than mere empty cases. If, then, we accept it as the relic, it must, indeed, have been very, very precious to be such a mite, and hence the probability is that it was thought to be of the Buddha himself.

The statue slab found in the central shrine on the west face of the *stūpa* is very interesting and curious. On digging out the core of brick buttressing, with which the cell had been filled, this slab, which measures 30½ inches high by 12½ across, was found standing upon the floor leaning against the north wall. The feet were broken off and were not found. The statue appears to be the portrait of some male person of note, and reminds one very forcibly of the portrait statues of Vanrāj at Anhilvad-Pattan, in almost exactly the same pose,[1] and those of Tejpāl, Vastupāl and others in the Dilwāra temples at Abu. It is not a Bōdhisattava, or it would have had a halo round the head, and would have been in other respects more like those images as we find them elsewhere. The figure is standing full to the front, resting upon the right leg; the right hand, raised almost to the centre of the breast, holds a small lotus flower, while the left rests flat upon what appears to be a wallet slung loosely round his waist and hanging from his left thigh. He is not, as is so often seen in such figures, grasping a knot of his garment. His clothing is simple in the extreme, and is just such as one sees on Jain worshippers as they enter their shrines for worship; it seems to be but a single waist-cloth whose folds hang to the back on the left side. It is possible that there is an under garment, the ends of which are seen across the knees; or they may simply show the inner folds of the one cloth. He wears an elaborate head-dress, arranged in rows of horizontal curls, from underneath which bunches of vertical curls fall upon each shoulder. There can be little doubt, I think, that this is a wig, and similar wigged figures may be seen in one of the Buddhist caves at Aurangābād;[2] they are not uncommon in early statuary. The statue has been painted: the complexion was "golden" or wheat-coloured; the waist-cloth which, though scanty, is rich, was

FIG. 14.—Image found in the *stūpa*.

[1] *Architectural Antiquities of North Gujarāt*, by Dr. Jas. Burgess, p. 44.

[2] Archæological Survey Reports of Western India, Vol. III, Plate XLIX, *see* also Progress Report of Arch. Survey of Western India, for 1903-4, pp. 22 and 26; and the *Indian Antiquary*, V, 240.

red, while the wig, eyebrows, pupils and moustache were black. I am inclined to believe that the statue represents the builder of the *stūpa*, the wallet or money bag under his left hand indicating the source of the funds.[1] If so, this would account for the image being left with the *stūpa*, it not being a sacred image.

Taking everything into consideration, I cannot see how this Mirpūr-Khās *stūpa* can be ascribed to a later date than A. D. 400: it may be earlier. It is probable that it is a reconstruction of a ruined one formerly erected under Aśoka's orders, and, possibly to contain a relic of the Buddha, the other relics —the spoonful of ash—being put into the bottle at the time of its reconstruction. But, of course, this is pure surmise. The fact, however, remains, that the sites of what were once monasteries surround the *stūpa*. The trenches, from which the bricks of the walls of one of these have been removed, gives us a plan very like those of some of the Gandhārā monasteries.

This *stūpa* was not an isolated building of its kind in Sind, for we have of the same period, judging from the remains of sculptured brick which adorned them, the *stūpas* of Ṭhūl Mīr Rukān near Moro, Depār Ghāngro near Brahmanābād, Suḍheran-jo-dhaḍo near Tāndo Muḥammad Khān, and the one near Jarak.

In most cases, if not all, the brick ornament was carved upon the moist clay with a sharp tool and was not shaped in a mould. It is of the same character as that found at Jamāl-Gaṛhī in the Yūsufzai country, almost on the borders of Kaśmīr, near Peshāwar, which General Cunningham, in the fifth volume of his Reports, called the Indo-Corinthian style, and which he thought was practised in that region at the beginning of the Christian era. As I have already noticed in my account of Depār Ghāngro, General Haig tells us that the Buddhist settlement of Sāwandī is mentioned in the legends of the *Mujmal-al-Tawārīkh*, "as having been built by the King of Kashmīr during an expedition to Sind. The legend is full of absurdities, but we may perhaps safely infer from it the antiquity of Sawanḍi" [? Depār Ghāngro].[2]

About the middle of the 7th century, we have learnt that Chach, the Hindū king of Alor, paid a visit to a Buddhist devotee in the vicinity of Brahmanābād, when the latter complained that the "temple" (? *stūpa*) and monastery had fallen into a state of disrepair due to the wear of time. If we take it that the place had been in Buddhist hands continually from its establishment to that time, and had not fallen into disrepair from absolute neglect—and the wear must have been very slow and gradual in a country where there was little rain— we are forced to put back the *stūpa* of Depār Ghāngro (Sāwandī) to the early centuries of the Christian era, but the want of sufficient data prevents any very

[1] For references to some other portrait statues see *Aśoka* (Rulers of India Series), 20, of Aśoka ; Prog. Report of the Arch. Surv. of Western India, 1903-4, 30, 31, 33, 40 ; 1904-5, 53, 56 ; 1905-6, 57 ; 1906-7, 29, 32 ; Annual Report of the Arch. Surv. of India, 1903-4, Pl. LXVIII ; Journ. Bom. Br. R. A. S. XII, 404 ; and Cunningham's Reports, I, 240, and V, 27, 40, 41, 49. Curiously, Cunningham found portrait statues with the feet broken off like the Mīrpūr-Khās one. This may be due to their having been thrown down, when fixed to the seat by a tenon under the feet, which would not give way. For similar statues at Jamāl Gaṛhī, see *Indian Antiquary*, III, 142.

[2] *Journ. R. A. S.* (n. s.), XVI, 292. See also the *Indian Antiquary*, III, p. 142.

approximate estimate of its age being made as yet. And this conclusion applies equally to the *stūpa* of Mīrpur-Khās, for all the *stūpa* remains in Sind are of one class and manifestly of the same age, and we have found nothing else of a greater age. The very same moulded or carved bricks as are found in Sind were also found by General Cunningham further north at Shorkot, in the Panjāb, and these he likens to the work on Yūsufzai remains. He found letters and writing on the bricks, being, he thinks, instructions to the builders as to the positions they were to occupy. I found two fragments at Ṭhūl Mīr Rukān with parts of letters upon them. The patterns, as figured by him in his Report are identical with those in Sind. The Shorkot bricks, judging from the style of letters upon them, he places from A. D. 79 to 319.

A great deal of excavation work which, until lately, was more or less impossible owing to lack of funds, remains to be done in Sind, which may throw a great deal of light upon the Buddhist period in that province. Ṭhūl Mīr Rukān might be further explored, and the hopeless looking ruin of Depār Ghāngro would probably repay further research. There are many other promising sites in the north of Sind and the delta.

Since the above was written, my successor, Mr. D. R. Bhandarkar, made further excavations on this site. In his Progress Report he tells us that his excavations of an adjoining mound "yielded quite a wealth of minor Buddhist antiquities. A regular forest of smaller *stūpas* was here extricated. Those that were opened were found to enshrine relic pots containing bones. Votive objects, such as diminutive clay *stūpas* and tablets of various sizes and description, were found in numbers. The remains of two monasteries were also exhumed. ....Particularly interesting was the colossal standing stucco figure of Buddha or Bodhisattva covered with gold leaf, not unlike those found in Khotān by Sir Aurel Stein."[1] Further excavation here will well repay the expense and trouble.

[1] See the Progress Report of the Archæological Survey, Western Circle, for the year ending 31st March, 1917, pp. 4 and 47.

ṬHŪL MĪR RUKĀN.

LIKE the *stūpa* at Mīrpūr-Khās, that known as Ṭhūl Mīr Rukān, 14 miles to the south-west of Bāndhi railway station, and 8 miles south-east of Dāulatpūr, has no history and little legendary lore connected with it; nor is there any explanation of the name, Mīr Rukān, that it goes by. It sounds like a Muḥammadan name, and may be that of a former possessor of the land in which it stands. There is now no sign of village or other habitation near it. It is the only *stūpa* in Sind, so far as we are at present aware, with so complete a tower. That it had a great square basement, as at the Mīrpūr-Khās one, which was 66 feet square, we learn from Mr. Gibbs' note which is quoted below; but as the ruined structure is so temptingly close to the line of railway, in a country where ballast is not easily obtainable, it is more than likely that, like that of the other *stūpa*, its material was found very useful by the contractors.

It is a solid cylindrical structure, slightly tapering towards the top, about 60 feet high, which is constructed, so far as its outward casing is concerned, of excellent burnt brick. What is now left shows three bands of decorative pilasters in tiers one above the other; below these the surface has all been broken away. Some part of the basement may still be found beneath the present ground level around the base of the tower (Plate XXVIII). The capitals of the pilasters of the upper band, as well as some projecting string courses, are decorated with beautifully carved brickwork in floral scrolls and other designs (Plate XXIX). In the capitals the clay was carved while wet, and does not appear to have been moulded, and the edges are sharp and crisp still; but, in some of the more elaborate scroll-work of the string courses, above, the bricks were, no doubt, moulded. The debris around the base, when it was examined by us, was piled up against it in some places ten feet above the surrounding ground. A villager, who professed to know all about the *stūpa*, imparted the information that some years ago a number of Muḥammadans, who were celebrating some *id* close by, rushed into it, through a door in its side, to escape a sudden storm of rain, when the interior collapsed and buried them all. He also said that a former Collector found, on excavation of some of the surrounding heaps, an earthen pot about ten or twelve inches in diameter, containing a pair of bronze anklets. Other villagers volunteered the information that an Irrigation Engineer, who excavated the fallen debris, which encumbered the base of the tower, dug out several images and took them away. After my visit, the local Executive Engineer, in carrying out some conservation measures, found a number of terra-cotta images of the Buddha and two other representations showing the birth of the Buddha from his mother's side under the *sāl* tree, and the Buddha taking farewell of his sleeping wife. These terra-cottas, which are, roughly, about six or seven inches square, must have formed portion of a frieze, probably

FIG. 15.—Terra-cottas from the *thūl.*

above the upper band of pilasters where the little square holes are seen in the photograph (Figure 15).

Mr. J. Gibbs (afterwards Member of Council), in company with Sir Bartle Frere and Mr. Shaw Stewart, proceeded to explore this *stūpa,* which he calls Rukān-jo-Thūl. He says: "We had previously sent men out to clear the base and sink a shaft down through it, in order, if possible, to find the relics, if any. In the evening I ascended the Thūl by means of a rough jungle ladder, and found the men had sunk the shaft about 8 feet. Three days after, on the 27th idem [27th February, 1858], we encamped at the Thūl, and the workmen completed the shaft down to the base without finding anything. The Thūl was of ordinary masonry; but the stones,[1] of which it was composed, must have been brought from a great distance. The square base, when cleared, measured about 66 feet on each side." The Sind Gazetteer (p. 638) tells us that "an excavation was made under this tower by the late General John Jacob, when acting Commissioner in Sind, but nothing of interest was discovered." It does not appear that any tunnel was ever made horizontally into the tower from the outside.

Of current traditions regarding the *thūl*[2] the following are specimens:

A wealthy fisherwoman, named "Rukān," had this tower erected with the object of landing her wares from the summit, to which, however, there is no visible means of easy access.

A King, who had no son, wishing to perpetuate his name, was induced by his councillors to erect this tower.

A third explanation is that Mīr Rukān, a Hindu rājā, who ruled here in A. H. 600 (A. D. 1203) had two brothers named Bhim and Bahman. The kingdom was divided between the three, and Mīr Rukān built this tower within his division. So much for tradition!

[1] Mr. Gibbs' memory has failed him here. The entire *thūl* is built of bricks and mud, made locally. He wrote his note in the end of 1877 (Memorandum No. 8, Archæol. Surv. of Western India, p. 33). The Deputy Collector of Naushahro, describing the *thūl* in 1876, says it is "a solid circular block of burnt brick and mud."

[2] *Thūl* is a Sindhi word meaning a tower or bastion. See my note upon this word under my description of Brahmanabād.

SUDHERAN-JO-DHADO (STŪPA).

THIS is another of the many *stūpas* which were spread over Sind in the days when Buddhism held its own in the land—a mound of earth, out of the centre of which rises a rough tower of the same material. It has been long enough in its ruined and unrecognisable state to have gathered about it a decent collection of the cobwebs of superstition and legendary tales. Like the Boria *stūpa* near Junagadh in Kāthiawād,[1] which was opened up some thirty-three years ago, it has been credited with the presence of a guardian serpent, ever on watch over treasure supposed to lie buried beneath; and this belief was so strong in the minds of the people living in the neighbourhood that Mr. Bhandarkar, who lately opened up the mound,[2] had no little difficulty in inducing them to take any hand in its excavation. The prospect of ample and prompt payment, however, generally decides the wavering coolie, and when he finds the snake puts in no appearance, he soon settles down to regular work. The name Suḍheran is connected by tradition with a mythical Hindū King Nerū who reigned at Haidarābād—hence its old name, perhaps, of Nerūn (or Nīrūn) Koṭ. The ever recurring story of surreptitious love-making—in this case between the King's nephew, Suḍheran, and the queen—led to its exposure, and his escape from the palace and disappearance into the earth at this place. The mound raised over him became known as Suḍheran-jo-dhaḍo, and in time became an object for local pilgrimages. The eṛring queen is said to have been buried in a smaller mound close by, which, like Absolom's Pillar at Jerusalem, is regularly pelted with brickbats and mud by indignant devotees. The proof of the truth of the story is, as usual, the existence of the object which gave rise to it!

In a note on the remains of Buddhist ornamental architecture in Sind in the Journal of the Bombay Branch of the Royal Asiatic Society for 1857,[3] is a notice of certain terra-cottas that had been sent to the Society from Sind, which says: "Among the fragments of *terra-cotta* ornaments mentioned in the presents to the Museum[4] are a figure of Buddh in a sitting posture with the

---

[1] Journ. As. Soc. Bengal, LX, Part I, No. 2, 1891.

[2] For his own account of the excavation of the *stūpa* see the Archæological Survey of India Annual Report for the year 1914-15.

[3] Vol. V, page 688.

[4] Fifteen fragments in terra-cotta, of ornamental parts of a Buddhist temple, found at the southern extremity of the Haidarābād range of hills in Sindh. These remains are precisely of the same kind as those forwarded from the ruined temple near Jerruck, page 665.

legs drawn up; a head with a curled wig similar to those seen in the caves of Elephanta; an elephant's head; and figures of the lotus, together with fragments of cornices. Of these ornamental remains Mr. Frere states as follows:—'We found them in several spots from Syudpoor, about half way between Moolakattyar and Mahomed Khan's Tanda, to Sidh Soodemu, where the ruins of a tower are situated [Suḍheran's], built of unburnt brick faced with large burnt bricks, at the junction of the Goonee and Fullailee, about six miles north of Mahomed Khan's Tanda. This we were told was the ruins of a lighthouse, which existed here when the sea came up to the Goonee and ships used to come hither, and was built by the Beni Israel, in the time of the prophets, before the days of the Kafir Kings.'"

Writing of this locality Raverty says: "In the plain, close to where the Fulaili branch of the Indus used a few years back to unite with the Gūnī, the country for miles around is covered with broken bricks and the ruined foundations of large buildings. Tradition says that a large and flourishing city once covered the plain and extended as far as the range of limestone hills on the extreme northern part of which, some eighteen miles further north, Haidarābād stands."[1]

The mound, before excavation, rose to a height of about 20 feet, with a base diameter of about 137. Out of this rose a weather-worn and deeply scored mud cone or tower—all that was left of the original brick tower of the *stūpa*—which, like others of its kind was built of sun-dried bricks, regularly laid, with an outer shell or casing of ornamental burnt brick (Plates XXX and XXXI). But the latter has disappeared, much of it, possibly, having been used up in the canal construction close by. The original tower must have been about three times the diameter of the present mud cone.

It was not an isolated building, for the ground to the south-west, for a mile or so, is still covered with small mounds of brick debris and pottery sherds, the remains, perhaps, of monks' establishments; and, as Raverty shows, it must have been in the neighbourhood of a large town or city. The small mound close by, which is said to cover the remains of Nerū's Queen, is evidently a spot upon which cremations took place, as it was found to be composed of layer upon layer of ashes interspersed with potsherds.

The lower courses of the basement walls of the *stūpa* were found in the mound, and these showed that, at the ground level, the lower part of the structure was oblong in plan, measuring 98 feet 6 inches from north to south, and 76 feet 9 inches from east to west[2]. But the excess length, in the one direction, was, no doubt, due, as Mr. Bhandarkar suggests, to the excrescence necessary for the stairways up to the terrace, and, possibly, to one or two small image shrines as at Mīrpūr-Khās. The front of the *stūpa* was thus on the north side, whereas at Mīrpūr-Khās it was on the west. The centre of the tower coincided with the centre of the square formed with the south wall as one side. The

---

[1] *The Mihrān of Sind*, 228n.

[2] I take my account from Mr. Bhandarkar's description as published in the Archæol. Surv. of India Annual Report.

south, east and west walls were found to be alike. The walls may have been plainer than those of Mīrpūr-Khās, but of this it is difficult to judge as there is so little left But upon the lower four feet of the walling, from the level of the pilaster bases upwards—the most that is left at any part—there were no image niches to be seen, so that, if such did exist, as at Mīrpūr-Khās, they must have been higher up the wall, and consequently smaller. The walls could not have been wholly devoid of decorative detail, apart from the plainer mouldings, since a smaller *stūpa* upon the hill, about two miles to the north-west, was fully decorated in the usual way, as may be gathered from the quantity of beautifully moulded brick which I found there (Plate XXXI) Some similar fragments were also found built into the repairs which had been subsequently made to this *stūpa*. The bases of the pillars, which still exist, are of the same style as those at Mīrpūr-Khās and those at Thūl Mīr Rukān, and it may fairly be inferred that the capitals were the same, which in the Thūl Mīr Rukān are very rich (Plate XXIX). Within the four walls, the mass of the substructure, like the tower, was of sun-dried brick laid in mud.

As mentioned, Mr. Bhandarkar found the centre of the *stūpa* to be that of the square having the south wall for one side, and he considered that it was here that relics, if any had been buried, had probably been placed, but subsequently removed. He first sunk a well over the centre of the oblong base of the mound, as found by the intersection of its diagonals, which fell just within the north face of the base of the tower. But here, at the ground level, as was to be expected, no signs of relics were found He then tunnelled south, on the ground level to the centre of the square, that is, immediately under the centre of the tower. Here he found the sun-dried brickwork, which was perfectly solid and well laid in the parts he had cut through, had apparently been disturbed, opened out and subsequently filled up again with big lumps of dried mud. He says: "Evidently a fairly large hole had been cut here with the express object of removing the relics, and it was afterwards filled with wet earth. The formation of the hole clearly showed that it was bored from the south. The motive in carrying away these relics cannot be plunder, for the plunderer certainly would not have cared to close the hole with wet earth But as this gap is purposely filled with big lumps of clay, it is not unreasonable to infer that they may have been anxious for the safety of the relics and removed them to a more secure resting place." Now Burton, in his *Sind Revisited*, says: "Easily climbing to the top by one of the wide clefts which rain had dug in the side of the tumulus, I found a shaft sunk to the foundation. Below the base was a tunnel, into which I penetrated, despite the fiends and dragons, the cobras and scorpions, with which my native friends peopled it: it was about seven or eight feet in length, and it led nowhere. These diggings, I afterwards heard, were the work of Ghulām 'Alī Talpur, one of the late Princes, who, suspecting, as an Oriental always does, that treasure was to be found in, under, or somewhere about the mysterious erection, took the most energetic and useless steps to discover it." The hole Burton looked into from the top—he does not say that his agility in climbing the tower was equal to descending into it, whence it might have been more troublesome to get out—was, probably, the hole made when the relics were fished out of the *dāgoba* which was found in the base of the tower, which had become partly filled in again with earth from the sides. This gradual filling in would have gone on very slowly since the sides were of solid sun-dried brick, and the rains in that region are so light as to be practically negligible. He does not say that this is where Ghulām 'Alī excavated, for, if he had, he did not go far enough to disturb the *dāgoba* which had not been destroyed. If the Tālpūr did excavate in the mound, it is likely he did it from the side by tunnelling, and this may account for the disturbance in the centre of the *stūpa* below the *dāgoba*. It was probably into this tunnel that Burton ventured, and eight feet was not very far.[1] As the tower was an object of veneration throughout the countryside, Ghulām 'Alī may have had the decency to fill it up again, if, indeed, his object was not to prevent others from benefiting by his excavation in prosecuting a more successful search. Or, if this were not so, it is possible a hole was left when building the *stūpa* through which to place the relics on the ground level, as at Mīrpūr-Khās, but that a change in their plans decided them to place them on the terrace level. The hole would then have been filled up, but I must say, that, in such a case one would suppose the builders would have built in the hole properly, so as to make a firmer base for the *dāgoba* above it.[2]

FIG. 16.—*Dāgoba* inside the *ṭhūl*.

And now we come to the interesting find of the *dāgoba*. Mr. Bhandarkar, whose curiosity was aroused by a layer of sand in the masonry of the mud tower, drove in a tunnel from the north side into the middle of it on the level of the top of the terrace which originally surrounded the base of the tower. Here occupying the centre, he came across a *dāgoba*, such as we find in the cave temples, standing 6 feet 9 inches high, composed of sun-dried bricks covered with plaster, the surface of which had been painted (Figure 16). It was completely built in and embedded in

[1] Burton speaks of "diggings" in the plural, which would mean the hole from the top, and the horizontal tunnel into which he went, below.

[2] Burton, looking down the hole from the top, evidently misjudged the depth of it, for it was certainly not deeper than the top of the undisturbed *dāgoba*, unless he considered the tower to be the whole structure, and the top of the mound its base.

the tower. "Through the centre of the domed top ran a round shaft reaching down to the base of the *dāgoba* and containing traces of wood powder indicating that it held a wooden staff probably surmounted by a tee and umbrella. The shaft could be easily traced nearly 2 feet above the dome, and I suspect that it went at least one more foot upwards." He opened the *dāgoba* but found nothing in it, and goes on to say: "No doubt, this *stūpa* [*dāgoba*] once stood alone on the platform and, as its sanctity and fame increased, it was encased in a larger structure . . . The walls of the tower were from the top to the bottom constructed of sundried bricks well-laid and arranged in regular courses and with due regard to the rules of bonding except for about four feet immediately above the small *stūpa* [*dāgoba*] which were loosely built. This is explained by the fact that immediately above the small *stūpa* [*dāgoba*] came the wooden tee and umbrella and that in erecting the new superstructure they had to build more or less loosely immediately round them to prevent their being damaged."

I can hardly think that a small *dāgoba*, of sun-dried brick covered with plaster, was ever intended to stand alone upon the platform, in the open and exposed to view. This would mean that half a *stūpa*, that is a basement and terrace, without a tower, was to be the finished design. Again, the basement, with its richly moulded and decorated base in burnt brick or terra-cotta, would have shamed the clumsy and shoddy-looking mud and plaster *dāgoba* holding the precious relics! Such an arrangement would have outraged the finer feelings of the builders, and would have been altogether incongruous.

My own opinion is that this *dāgoba* was, in reality, the relic chamber instead of a rough brick one as at Mīrpūr-K͟hās, and that the relics were lowered into it down the shaft which Mr. Bhandarkar discovered, the top opening being closed by the "tee," there being no umbrella. By digging down the centre of the tower the relics were easily removed in the same way; and it was, perhaps, as short a way to them as it would have been by tunnelling twenty-six or twenty-seven feet in from the side. Moreover, if they thought of returning to the spot, when peaceful times came round again, the *sāmānīs*, in charge, would refrain from mutilating the outside of the *stūpa* as far as possible. A somewhat similar shaft to that down the centre of the *dāgoba* was found leading down to the relic chamber of the Sue Vihār *stūpa* near Bahāwalpūr, not far north-east of the Sind border, in which was found an inscribed copper plate of the time of the Emperor Kanishka, with coins, pieces of iron, a few beads and fragments of ornaments, mixed with ashes. The floor of this chamber was thirty-five feet above ground, and, presumably, like our *dāgoba*, on the level of the top of the terrace on which the tower stood.[1] The relics, with their coffer and caskets, which were found in the great Boria *stūpa* near Junagadh, in Kāthiawād, occupied the same position in the *stūpa* as the *dāgoba* does in this.[2] Mr. Bhandarkar says the shaft down the centre could be traced nearly two feet above the dome. I do not quite see how this could be, for any hollow

[1] *Journ. As. Soc. Bengal.* XXXIX, 1870, 65.
[2] *Journ. As. Soc. Bengal*, LX, Part I, No. 2, 1891.

matrix above the dome should be that of the "Tee" rather than that of the smaller shaft of the umbrella, and it is not at all likely that the *dāgoba* would have an umbrella without the "Tee," but, like many votive *dāgobas*, it might have the "Tee" without an umbrella. I certainly do not think there was any umbrella, and the "wood powder" was perhaps, remains of some sacred powder such as we found in the caskets of the Boria *stūpa*. That *dāgobas* contained relics is, I think, clear from the fact that I found in the top of the "Tee" of the rock-cut *dāgoba*, in the great *chaitya* cave at Kārli, a square hole, about ten inches square, filled with ancient sawdust, which had been closed with a closely fitting slab, flush with the top of the "Tee," evidently intended to hold relics. Had the relics in the Sudheran *stūpa* been placed at the ground level, it is very improbable that all signs of the relic chamber and its bricks would have been removed together with the relics; and it is less probable that the relics would have been deposited there without a protecting chamber of some kind.

Mr. Bhandarkar thinks the original *stūpa* cannot be later than the time of Kanishka (Cir. A. D. 100), "and that we shall not be far wrong if we assign it to the beginning of the Christian era." If we accept this for this *stūpa*, we must also accept it for Mīrpūr-Khās, Thūl Mīr Rukān and others of similar construction and decoration in Sind. As already referred to in my account of Brahmanābād, General Haig tells us that Sāwandī, which was near that place, is mentioned in the legends of the *Mujmalu-t-tawārīkh* as having been built by the king of Kaśmīr during an expedition to Sind. Sāwandī was a great Buddhist establishment, and I have identified it with Depār Ghāngro, where I found that the large mound was the ruin of a *stūpa*. This, then, was probably what the Kaśmīr King is credited with having built. The King referred to, I gather, was Kanishka "who alone among the Kushān Kings has left a name cherished by tradition, and famous far beyond the limits of India."[1] His dominions included Sind. He is said to have erected numerous monuments in Kaśmīr, and what more natural than that he should extend one of his southern expeditions to the mouths of the Indus to gratify his curiosity to gaze upon the great ocean as did Khān-i-Khānān Mīrzā 'Abdu-r-Raḥīm long centuries afterwards; and to commemorate his visit to the province, he may have caused to be built many of the *stūpas* of which we find the ruins following the line of the great river all down through the Punjāb, Bahāwalpūr and Sind. We are told that the kings Huvishka, "Jushka" and Kanishka were given to acts of piety and built at various places *maṭhas*, *chaityas* and similar structures,[2] and these *stūpas* must have been very small affairs compared with the great *stūpa* built by him at Peshāwar, which was at least five or six times the height of any in Sind.

I would not lay much stress upon the shape of the *dāgoba* for giving any very definite indication of date. There may be a general rule, but there are many exceptions. For instance, the base of the drum of the *dāgoba* in the *chaitya*-cave at Bedsa is more than twice the height of the dome, the base being

[1] *Early History of India*, V. A. Smith, 3rd Edition, 255.

[2] *Rājataranginī*, translated by Stein, Bk. I. vv 168-171.

in two tiers, the lower tier being, alone, nearly twice the height. In the *dāgoba* at Kārli it is one and a third times the height.

As to the point about the Hīnayāna school of Buddhism being paramount in Sind in the 7th century, as Hiuen Tsiang tells us, and the amount of image sculpture upon these *stūpas* proclaiming them as of the Mahāyāna school, we must remember that a good few centuries intervened between the time of their building and Hiuen Tsiang's time, during which many changes may have occurred. Kanishka favoured the school then most in vogue—the Mahāyāna. There is little doubt but that the Suḍheran *stūpa* also had its images, for, as we have seen, among the fragments of terra-cotta ornament sent to the Bombay museum, about 1857, was an image of a Buddha in a sitting posture, and a head with a curled wig (? "Kubera"), and these were found in the immediate neighbourhood, if not at the *stūpa* itself. So little in the way of moulded brick was found then, sixty years ago, and so complete is the ruin of the structure, that it is not to be wondered at that so very little remained for Mr. Bhandarkar to find.

The date of the votive tablets prove nothing as to the date of the structure, they only shew that at the time indicated by the style of the letters upon them the *stūpa* was still an object of worship. The same may be said of the coins, except that in the case of the one of Kanishka, which would hardly have been placed there as an offering unless it was to some extent still a current coin, and, therefore, at some time during that King's reign or not very long after it.

About two miles to the north-west of Suḍheran's *stūpa*, upon the hill, are the remains of another small one, which consists of a few heaps of debris from which I recovered a few moulded bricks, some of which are shown in plate XXXI. This is, perhaps, the one that Burton describes: "On the Ganjah hills, about three miles from Suḍheran's Thūl, there is another tower, similar in all things to this, except that it is now in a ruinous state. The people have named it Kuttehar, after a dog whose superior sagacity discovered the spot in which thieves had buried his owner's property.[1] Like Suḍheran's fate, the poor animal's runs in the established groove; it lost its life by the master's hasty choler, and, in due time, that is to say when too late, the master discovered his mistake, repented his conduct, and erected this monument to the memory of his Kutto."

[1] The *stūpa* at Supāra, near Bombay, which was opened up by Sir J. Campbell and Dr. Bagwanlāl Indraji, was discovered by the police, who ran certain thieves to earth, hiding in a depression in the top of it. H. C.

BUDDHIST REMAINS NEAR JARAK.

THE town of Jarak is picturesquely placed amongst the rocks, upon the right bank of the Indus, some twenty-four miles below Haidarābād. Two and at half to three miles south of this again, and between the Jarak-Ṭhaṭhah road and the river, is a low flat-topped hill upon which are the remains of a Buddhist *stūpa* (Figure 17). At present there is nothing but a shapeless low heap of brick debris, in which there are hardly half a dozen carved bricks to be found, and not even a fragment of the walls remains. In the centre a hole had been dug to the ground level; and, though I made further excavation when I examined the mound, nothing of any importance was found. There are signs of basements of other rough rubble buildings upon the hill-top, showing that there must have been a small community up there at one time. Most of the bricks found measure 18″×10½″×2½″, from which it may be gathered that the *stūpa* was as old as that at Mīrpūr-Khās. Fortunately, however, we know a little more about these remains since they were examined about 1852 by Mr. W. Cole, Deputy Collector of Karachi. In a letter addressed by the Commissioner in Sind to the Secretary of the Bombay Branch of the Royal Asiatic Society, dated in 1853, the place is thus described :—" All the ornamental parts strike me as very similar in character to those found in the later Buddhist cave-temples; and fragments are found bearing the figure of Buddha, sitting in the attitude of contemplation. The head is invariably cut or broken off, probably by the Mahommedan iconoclasts who destroyed the temple; but the large pendulous ears and other characteristics of Buddha are still clearly traceable.

" Some of the ornaments are stamped [? moulded] others appear to have been cut while the clay was soft; and the patterns are of great variety.

" The spot where the remains were discovered is a low hill overlooking the Indus, about 3 miles below Jerruck, and close to the hamlet of Shaik Taroo.

" It was pointed out to Mr. Cole as a ' Kaffir Kote '; the only local tradition was that it was the residence of ' Munjeera,' an infidel King, who reigned before the Mahommedan invasion of Scinde.

" The flat top of the hill, which is of small area, appears to have been formerly surrounded by a wall of large stones, the remains of which are in places still traceable. A projecting portion at the east side appears to have been separated by a wall still traceable by a raised ridge of loose stones and rubbish ; and there are traces of stone enclosures inside, the character of which may, perhaps, hereafter be discovered, when the rubbish which covers them has been removed.

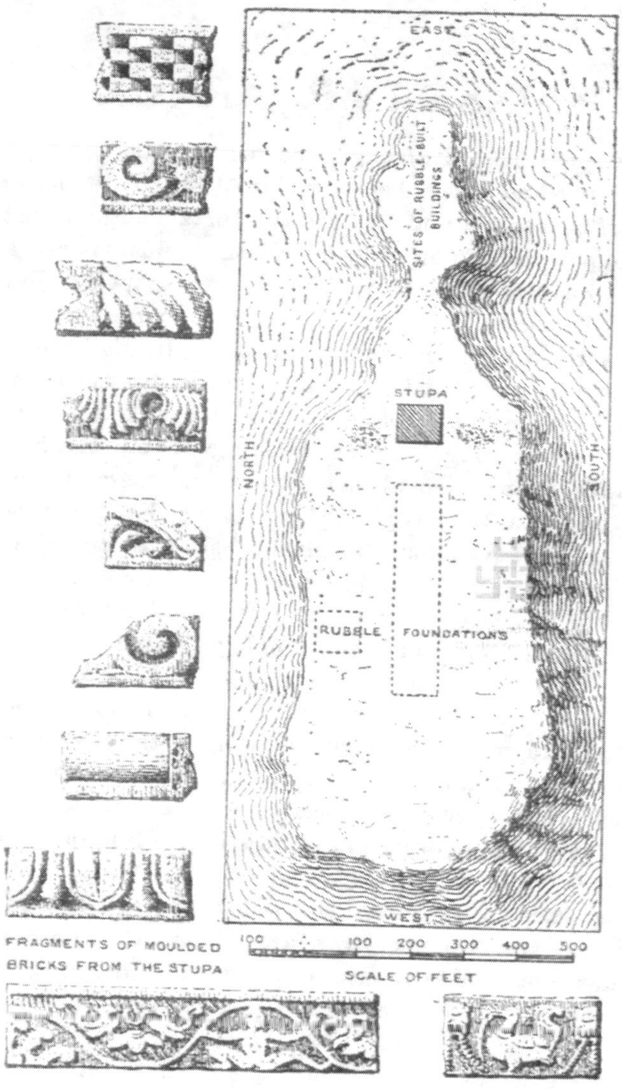

FIG. 17.—Plan of *stūpa* hill, and terra-cottas.

"Mr. Cole's attention was attracted to the mound by finding a fragment of a very large and fine-grained brick, one side of which had been bevelled off. It struck him as unlike any brick he had seen before in Scinde, and he employed men to trench across the mound. They soon came to the top of a wall, and, by clearing it down to the level of the surface of the hill, and following the wall, he exposed the remains of a building $85\frac{1}{2}$ feet square, constructed of large and heavy well made bricks $15\frac{1}{2}'' \times 9\frac{1}{2}'' \times 2\frac{3}{4}''$, laid with very little cement, and that apparently the fine mud of the Indus,[1] mixed occasionally, Mr. Cole thinks, with some fibrous substance.

"The base of the building was ornamented by a bold moulding, the character of which will be seen by the section. At intervals of 6 feet there were square projections, as if for pilasters.[2]

"With the exception of the moulding, none of the ornaments were found *in situ*. They were dug out of the rubbish which buried the remains of the walls, as though they had belonged to the structure above, and all bearing human figures had been defaced with some care.

---

[1] This fine mud cement has been found elsewhere in very early brickwork. It was found, for example, in the old brick temples at Sirpūr in the Central Provinces. See the Progress Report of the Archæological Survey of Western India for the year ending 30th June, 1904, p. 20. H. C.

[2] This is the same arrangement as found in the Mirpūr-Khās *stūpa*, but much closer together in proportion. This was a larger *stūpa*, having a base 80 feet square against 53 feet 6 inches of the Mirpūr-Khās one. H. C

"Since writing the above, Mr. Cole has discovered an inscribed stone at a spot a few miles from the remains of the temple.[1] It was lying about a quarter of a mile from one of the large square enclosures, built of unhewn and uncemented stones, of great size, which are commonly known to the hill shepherd as 'Kaffir Kote.'"[2]

Across the river, at Budhke Tahar, opposite Jarak, Mr. Carter has discovered two tumuli "which, judging from the shape and the size of the bricks, poking out from the surface, the colour of the coloured pottery and the name, must cover two small Buddhist shrines of the same age as the *stūpa* at Mīr-pūr-Khās." On the tumuli he found a quantity of "flints."

---

[1] Cunningham said he read on it the words *putrasa* and *Bhagavatasa*, only, with a few letters in different parts which show it to have been a Buddhist inscription (*Ant. Geo.*, 288). H. C.

[2] The description of the carved bricks, sent with the above letter to the Society, is as follows :—"Bricks, mouldings and cornices from the remains of a Buddhist building, discovered by Mr. Cole in a mound three miles below Jerruck, on the Indus, Lower Scinde, bearing designs slightly allied to Grecian*(?) style, *viz.*, human figures, a running pattern of pelicans and the lotus with its shoots and leaves in the form of scrolls, lions' heads, the lotus by itself, &c., &c. On the surface of one brick is a figure of Buddha seated cross-legged on the lotus, with the hands in front of the lower part of the chest, and the little finger of the left between the thumb and forefinger of the right hand ; a vest over all the body except the neck. Two rams erect, one on each side, their backs turned towards the figure ; and two lions couchant under the lotus. Other figures appear to have existed on each side of the head, (crocodiles' mouths ?) but they, with the head of Buddha himself, have been broken off." *Journ. Bom. Br. R. A. S.*, Vol. V, pp. 355, 367, and 371. 113 specimens were placed in the Karachi Museum, then in the Frere Hall, one of which was an alto-relief image of Buddha, seated, but these appear, by the descriptions given of them, to be the same as the above. H. C.

DEWAL-ṬHAṬHAH.

THE town of Ṭhaṭhah, or Tatta as it is now commonly spelt, but which is known to the natives of the place as Nagar-Thaṭo, is situated some 55 miles east of Karāchi, and about 50 miles south by west of Haidarābād, at the apex of the delta of the Indus, and within three miles of its right or western bank. It is now reached from Jangs͟hāhī, a station on the North-Western Railway, from which it is thirteen miles distant.[1]

The present town was probably founded about the middle of the fifteenth century.[2] The site of Sāmuī, Sammanagar or Sāminagar, the older capital of the Sammah dynasty, lies about three miles to the north-west of Ṭhaṭhah, under the Maklī hill, where ruins are to be still traced. The *Tārīk͟h-i-Tāhirī* tells us that, when the Sammahs came into power, they founded a town and fort below the Maklī hill. The former they called Sāī [Samūī] and the latter Taghurābād [Kalyān Kōt], of which Jām Taghur or Tughlaq had laid the foundation, but had left unfinished. It also informs us that, after Jām Nanda *bin* Bābiniya had dwelt some time in the city of Sāī, "the thought entered his mind to build, at some auspicious moment, a new town, where happiness might remain for ever. Brahmans and astrologers having settled a lucky day and having sought a spot in the neighbourhood of Samūī, they selected an eligible place, where now stands the city of Tatta, and there with the assent of the Jām, the foundation was laid."[3] According to the *Tuhfatu-l-Kirām* the city was founded by Jām Pāniya.[4] McMurdo refers the foundation of Sāmuī to the time of Alāu-d-dīn of Delhi (A. D. 1295-1315), and that of Ṭhaṭhah to the reign of Jām Niẕāmu-d-dīn (Jām Nindo) in the year A. D. 1475.[5] Raverty says that Ṭhaṭhah was founded by Jām Tamāchī, who became known as Jām, the Bani-i-Ṭhaṭhah—the Founder of Ṭhaṭhah—and he thinks that the *Tārīk͟h-i-Tāhirī* has confounded Jūnān with Nandah.[6]

---

[1] The name is variously spelt. Raverty says it is written in all Persian histories as ٹهٹه Ṭhaṭhah, (*Mihrān of Sind*, 329n.). The Sind Gazetteer says it is Thattah. Captain Wood spells it T'hat'hah, and so on. Cunningham gives the origin of the name as *ṭhaṭṭha*, shore or bank, but Raverty thinks it is from ٹهٹ, *ṭhaṭh*, a crowd, throng or assemblage. Captain Hamilton, in 1699, says it was about two miles from the Indus (*New Account of the East Indies*, I, 123).

[2] It was probably not fortified until after it was sacked by the Portuguese in 1556 Raverty tells us that the name "Ṭhaṭhah," as a city or fortified town, will not be found in any history written previous to the historian Ziyau-d-din, Barani, of Sultān Firùz Sháh's reign. (*Mihrān of Sind*, 272n.)

[3] Ellipt's *History of India*, I, 272 and 273

[4] Elliot's *History of India*, I, 402.

[5] Cunningham's *Ancient Geogra·hy*. 288.

[6] *Mihrān of Sind*, 329.

The Maklī hill table-land, which runs from north to south for four or five miles, is one vast cemetery—the Valhalla of Sind—which has been in constant use for hundreds of years, and is still the principal burying ground for the Musalmān population of Ṭhaṭhah. Kennedy, who wrote of these ruins, calls it a vast cemetery of six square miles, which contained, at a rude guess, not less than a million tombs. Standing within this great necropolis are the more pretentious mausolea of many of the former rulers of Ṭhaṭhah. Captain Wood has remarked that, "Here, neither labour nor expense has been spared, but only for the absurd purpose of giving the dead better accommodation than the living."[1] From the northern towards the southern end, these dilapidated fabrics run, approximately, in order of their dates, and embrace the last resting places of princes of the Sammah, Arghūn and Tarkhān families. The ground is thickly crowded with graves and tombs, in all stages of decay, from the more costly structures to the simple and inexpensive whitewashed cairns of the present day, the larger ruins rising out of a forest of cactus bush, which disputes with them the possession of the ground. The hill is said to have taken its name from that of the occupant of one of the earlier tombs —a woman called Maklī—and it is also said to be derived from "Makkali" or Makka-like, a name given to a mosque built here by Jām Tamāchī, one of the Sammah Princes. Burton says he built this mosque by order of the holy Shaikh Hammad, [? Shaikh Himād Jamāli.], who directed that people should be buried around it instead of being carried for sepulchre to Pīr Paṭho.[2] He also quotes the *Tuhfatu-l-Tāhirī* as saying, "Mohammed Aazam enumerated between seventy and eighty saints of the first magnitude, whose sepulchres grace the Maklī hills, near Tattah," and gives a list of some of them.[3] Close to the spot, where the road begins to debouch into the plain, stands the Travellers' Bungalow, which consists of two small plain cenotaphs connected together.

The larger buildings are of two distinct styles of work. In the one they are constructed of cut-stone covered with carved surface tracery, similar to that on the buildings at Fatḥpūr-Sīkrī, while, in the other, they are built of brickwork, all except the plinth on which they stand, and depend for their decoration upon a lavish use of enamelled tiles. The stone foundations and plinths are rendered necessary by the salty character of the soil of Sind, the *kalar*, or *kalarathi*, as this salt is called, being very destructive to brickwork, through which it rises when damp, and, crystallizing, disintegrates it.[4] The brickwork of the latter class is very superior, the bricks, or, at least, those on the surface, being made of the best pottery clay, perfectly formed and dense, having cleanly-cut sharp edges, and of a rich dark red. The enamelled bricks are glazed, upon their outer surfaces, in light and dark blue and white.

---

[1] *Journey to the Source of the Oxus* (1872), p. 8.

[2] *Sind Revisited.*

[3] *Sind and the Races, etc.* 222.

[4] An analysis of this salt is given in my article on the Mīrpūr-Khās *stūpa* in the Annual Report of the Archæological Survey of India for 1909-10.

The joints between the bricks are exceedingly fine, and are almost invisible; but imitation mortar joints, which, however, are too white and clean and sharply defined to be mistaken for the real thing, about ⅜ of an inch wide, are moulded upon the edges of the bricks themselves, as sunk bands of white enamel. When used in the inner lining of domes these enamelled bricks have been worked into zigzag patterns, in radiating divisions, from the apex to the springing line, and look remarkably well though quaint. This class of work is best seen in the decorated doorway of the tomb of Mīrzā Jānī Beg (Plate LIII). The tiles are fixed with a thin coat of strong cement, in which powdered brick is used, overlaying a rough brick backing, and the elaborate patterns are worked in colour, being further helped out with variously-shaped tiles. The coloured dadoes are an especially fine feature. Some of the colours have run slightly in the firing, the light blue particularly so, which, blurring the hard edges of the patterns, softly blends the tints and gives the whole a waxy translucent appearance which is one of its great charms. A single design, without duplication, will sometimes cover several square yards of surface, such as on the spandrils of arches and in some of the dadoes, each tile being different from its neighbour. Then, again, some tiles are as small as half an inch square, and over a hundred are used in a square foot, of mixed sizes, forming a perfect mosaic. Such tiles are found upon the Jāmiʿ Masjid in the town. They required the greatest skill and care in piecing the designs together within their exact limits (Plates XXXII and LIX).

The colours chiefly used in the older work are two blues—a rich dark purplish blue and a light greenish or turquoise blue—and white. These are very transparent colours, and, in their treatment, acquire an effect of great depth and richness. Now and again a yellow is found, but very rarely, if at all, in the older work, its place being taken by a self-coloured buff unglazed tile which, being of a soft and subdued tint, harmonises better with the blues and, acting as a foil, emphasises their brilliance. In later work at Haidarābād and elsewhere in Sind, are found a bright yellow, a yellowish brown and a green glaze in two tints. In one panel, only, at Ṭhaṭhah, in the Jāmiʿ Masjid, was found a design upon a purplish red ground, but it would seem that this colour was a failure and did not burn well, and was consequently not repeated.[1]

The great Jāmiʿ Masjid has the greatest quantity and variety of designs of any building in Sind. It is not, in itself, remarkable for its general design or the finish of its masonry; the architect depended entirely upon the tile mosaic for his decoration and effect, and rich, indeed, it is, though, perhaps, somewhat overdone. He forgot the principle of leaving sufficient plain surfaces as a foil for his decoration (Plates LVII—LXII).

In many of the tombs in Sind, plain light blue tiles are used for paving the interiors. The glaze, at its best, is not very tough, so, were it not that persons entering these buildings went in barefoot, it would not have stood so

---

[1] This tile work is fully illustrated in my Portfolio on Sind Tiles, published for the Government of India, in 1906. Very similar terra-cotta tiles, of the 13th and 14th centuries, coarsely enamelled in yellow and brown patterns, have been dug up on the site of St. Augustine's monastery at Canterbury.

well as it has for this purpose. It would not stand, in ordinary buildings, where boots are used. This light blue tile has also been largely used to cover the exterior domes, and, in this position, in the bright sunlight, it has a very fine and brilliant effect.

In Sind these enamelled tiles are always laid in flat surfaces upon one level, but in Multān, as may be seen on the tomb of Ruknu-d-dīn, they are sometimes sunk and raised alternately, thus giving a play of light and shade apart from the general colour scheme. Another noticeable thing in that building is the ornamental carved plain brickwork in raised patterns.

Sind tiles seem to have travelled further afield than Sind itself. They have been found forming a dado in the gallery and near the altar, on either side, in the old ruined church of the Jesuits at Bassein, near Bombay.[1] They have been sparingly used, together with Panjāb tiles, in some of the old buildings at Bijāpūr; and the whole front of the old *madressa* at Bīdar, now in ruins, in the Nizam's territory, has been covered with them. A great deal of enamelled tile work is found in the Panjāb, especially in Lahore, but it is of a different material, and of different treatment both in colours and patterns.[2]

Hālā, thirty-five miles north of Haidarābād, is at present the home of this art, where it is still being carried on by a few families, but of inferior quality (Figure 29 and Plates C and CI). There are one or two other places in Sind where it is also practised to a small extent, one of which is Nasrpūr, some seventeen miles to the north-east of Haidarābād, but the Hālā work is best known. It is also made at Multān, in the same manner as in Sind, but the work there compares unfavourably with that of Sind. Besides tiles, ornamental pottery is also turned out.[3] It was started at the Bombay School of Art, potters from Sind and Multān having been brought there for a time to superintend.[4]

Reverting to the buildings upon the hill, it will be best to notice them in the order in which they occur, commencing with the earlier ones at the north end. The furthermost in that direction is the mausoleum of Sayyid 'Alī Shāh Shīrāzī who died in A. D. 1572, but of whom we know very little. His son, Sayyid Jalāl, was one of the victims of Mīrzā Bāqī, when that ruler turned "Berserk" and madly imbued his hands in the blood of many of his nobles and prominent religious leaders. The building is oblong in plan, measuring 48½ feet by 33, and is roofed in by a large and two small fluted domes. It is said to have been built by the Jokiahs, who came to notice in the reign of Muhammad Atur Khān, when some of the tribe fell upon

[1] See the Progress Report of the Archæological Survey of Western India for the year ending 30th June, 1898. This church was built in 1548, only eight years before the Portuguese sacked Ṭhaṭhah, when, pleased with the effect of these tiles upon the mosques and tombs at that place, they probably brought away some of them to decorate their new church. The patterns upon some specimens of those, which have been recovered, are identical with those found in Sind in both design and colours.

[2] See the Progress Report of the Archæological Survey, Panjab, for 1901-2. Also the *Journal of Indian Art*, Vol. II, p. 17.

[3] For an account of the method of manufacture, see Dr. Stocks' description in the Sind Gazetteer, 2nd Edition, p. 218, and under "Hala."

[4] Illustrations of this quasi-Sindhi pottery may be seen in *The Journal of Indian Art*, Vol. II, 2.

Ṭhaṭhah, in open daylight, and plundered the quarter of Mūlah Talahtī. There are inscriptions upon some of the small tombs within the enclosure, but none upon the Sayyid's.

At a short distance south of the last is a group of old dilapidated structures, amongst which is a small domed brick building with some good coloured tile work within. It stands a little way from the north-west corner of Jām Niẓāmu-d-dīn's tomb. Within it are two graves, one being that of a woman, Maklī, after whom the hill is said to have been called. The tomb is supposed to have been built about A. D. 1410. Close by are other very early and very plain brick tombs, now in ruins.

The tomb of Jām Niẓāmu-d-dīn, of the Sammah dynasty, commonly known as Jām Nindo, who died about A. D. 1508,[1] is situated at a distance of about a mile and a half from the Travellers' Bungalow (Plates XXXIII and XXXIV). It is a great square unfinished building enclosing a square sepulchral chamber, which has never been roofed in, the work having been apparently stopped when the four walls had almost reached the springing line of the dome. It was intended to have been a building of considerable pretensions, and it is rather remarkable in its way, for it is built almost entirely of Hindū elements, that is, such as generally found in Hindū temples. Indeed, there seems to be sufficient proof that much of its sculptured material had been removed from one or more such temples of a later date than the eleventh century A. D. This is particularly noticeable in the pillars, with parapet walling below them, as seen in the upper balcony of the exterior on plate XXXIII. The whole of this projecting mass of sculpture forms the outside buttress of the *mihrāb* niche within, such as we find in the decorated mosques of Gujarāt. In this case the building is a tomb and mosque combined. It was always the custom, with mausolea of any pretensions architecturally, to include a mosque in the general design, in which the relatives could pray for the welfare of the deceased's soul. But in these Ṭhaṭhah tombs, instead of having the mosque as a separate building, a prayar niche or *mihrāb*, worked into the west wall within, served its purpose.

Again, on the same plate, notice the miniature *śikhara*, or temple spire, at the corner, about half way down. This miniature, in constantly recurring repetitions, was a very favourite ornament upon Hindū temples, but altogether foreign to Muḥammadan work, where domes were employed, and not spires, to surmount their buildings. It will be seen that the corresponding features, on either side of the vertical centre line of the buttress, are odd, and the centre part is manifestly too much of a patchwork to be an original design worked out in freshly dressed material. The little corbles, or consoles, above the narrow pillarettes, would, in Hindū work, support the ends of flying arches, or *torāṇas*, or small bracket images leaning forward from the capitals of the pillars, but here they are meaningless, since they carry nothing. The basement is thoroughly Hindū, not of the very ornate style of the tenth and eleventh

[1] The length of his reign is variously given by different writers as 73, 63, and 43 years. The *Tuḥfatu-l-Kirām* gives the date of his death as A. H. 914 (A. D. 1508) which by some, is considered to be correct.

century, but of a considerably later period. Had this tomb been built of virgin material, the same basement would have run all round it; but as there, apparently, was not enough of it, what there was was reserved for the decorated *mihrāb*, with a little bit more which just turned the corner. We find that, all over India, the earliest mosques and tombs, built by the conquering iconoclasts, were, in most cases, constructed of pilfered material from Hindū or Jaina temples. We are told that a governor of Ṭhaṭhah, Nawāb Āmīr Khān, *alias* Mīr Abūl-Bāqā, built a mosque on the site of a Hindū temple in the street of Bhāī Khān, and we also learn that Jalālu-d-dīn founded a Jāmi' Masjid at Dewal on the ruins of an idol temple.

The doorway, at the side, has the Hindū projecting block on the threshold as well as the lintel, the latter being the dedicatory block in a Hindū temple, but in a Muḥammadan building it is without meaning. The lintel, however, appears to have been cut anew for the doorway, in which case, the explanation would probably be that it was prepared by a Hindū workman who was accustomed to temple building. Some of the bands on the face of the walls are made up of odd patterns, on one of them being seen the sacred geese, which would hardly have been deliberately included in a design for a Musalmān building. The absence of traces of human figure sculpture on these remnants is not surprising when it is remembered that the Hindūs had been living so long under the heel of the uncompromising Muslim iconoclast that they had learnt not to give offence to Islām by displaying images upon the exteriors of what temples they were permitted to erect. On the little pillars already noticed, in the upper balcony, will be seen tiny rosettes where images may have been. In similar panels on temple pillars, which have been re-erected in Gujarāt by the Muḥammadans, the images have been chipped away leaving, in many instances, their distinct outlines behind. Two small pavilions, on the other side of a basin-like depression in the plateau, close by the tomb of Sayyid 'Alī Shāh, as well as one beside this tomb, are built, almost entirely, of Hindū material, and the domes are surmounted by Hindū *kalasas* or finials; while, on the pillars, the places upon the square shafts, and panels where images have been cut away are distinctly traceable (Plate XXXV). Much of the ornament upon the tomb, such as the half-lotus bands and the single medallion lotuses, is identical with what the Hindū masons wrought for the Muḥammadan buildings in Gujarāt, especially those in and around Ahmadābād; and some of the *mihrāb* basement mouldings are also the same as found on the bases of pillars and plinths in those buildings.

Plate XXXIV shows how it was intended to roof in the tomb. The corners of the square chamber are cut off by squinches which span the corners to carry the octagon above, which, again, is reduced in the same manner to a sixteen-sided figure which would carry the circular springing courses of the dome. It is a very simple arrangement. The squinches are splayed arches radiating from points in the corner of the square. By corbelling forward the masonry of the octagon and the sixteen-sided figure above, the diameter of the dome is considerably reduced.

Remains of Hindū temples are very rare in Sind, and this is easily accounted for when it is remembered that the province bore the brunt of successive invasions of Islām in its early days, when its followers were burning with religious zeal for a newly established faith, which held all kinds of idolatry in the greatest abhorrence. Again, it is likely that, in a brick country, the early temples were constructed in that material, which, when desecrated and deserted, became a most desirable supply of building material for the villager.

The masonry of the tomb of Jām Niẕāmu-d-dīn looks very solid and strong, but this is a delusion, for its seemingly great blocks of ashlar are a sham, being nothing more than thin slabs set up on edge, with the interior of the walls filled up with rough rubble. In Mīrzā 'Īsā Khān's tomb, described further on, it will be seen how easily this kind of work may come to grief through its instability and want of thorough bonding of the two shells of the walls which, in places, have fallen away exposing its rubble core.

Some little distance south of Jām Niẕāmu-d-dīn's tomb, and near the edge of the plateau, is the ruined tomb, with a brick dome, known as Juman Jati, while still further southward, and just below the edge of the table-land, is the small insignificant whitewashed tomb of Sayyid Muḥammad Baghdādī.

Next comes a square building, with a curious arrangement of four half-domes, one above each corner of the building which is said to be the tomb of Shaikh Jīa, the religious instructor of Bahāu-d-din Multānī Qureshi, and is supposed to have been built about A. D. 1494.[1] It has an inscription which contains the Throne verse, only, from the Qurān, but no date. Still further along, below the crest of the hill, is a group of stone-built enclosures, that on the north containing the grave of Sayyid Maḥmud Mirākī, Shaikhu-l-Islām, from Kandhār. Date, A. D. 1520.

The next enclosure, which is separated from the last by an old *masjid*, contains the grave of Barā (the elder) Mīrzā 'Īsā Khān, the first Tarkhān ruler of southern Sind. It stands in a large court, within which, are two smaller courtyards, and is entirely of carved stone, with perforated slabs introduced in a few places. The *Tuhfatu-l-Kirām* gives the date of his death as A. H. 980 (A. D. 1572) which is generally accepted as correct, but the *Tārīkh Ma'ṣūmī* places it in A. H. 974 (A. D. 1566). Slightly further to the south is the tomb of Pir Asad, much ruined, with an inscription over the entrance doorway containing only the declaration of faith, and another on a grave, in the enclosure, gives the date A. H. 1079 (A. D. 1668). An inscription on a grave in the outer verandah records the death of the lady Dunbā'ī in the same year. The tomb of Sayyid Abdullāh Jalāna, from Gujarāt is a white-washed building of no particular account.

The tomb of Nawāb Āmīr Khalīl Khān is a solid octagonal brick building with a rather pointed dome, of the same material, set upon a very high drum. The eight sides of the building have deep arched recesses, those on the north and south being larger than the others and pierced with doorways into the

[1] Shaikh Bahāu-d-dīn Zakariyā Multānī was the celebrated saint of Multān, whose tomb, at that place, is visited by thousands of people to this day. He was a discipl[illegible] Shaikh Shahābu-d-dīn Sohrwardī.

sepulchral chamber. It is on precisely the same plan as that of Dīwān Shuria Khān (Plate XXXVI). The whole building has been covered with enamelled tiles, but these have now almost entirely disappeared The portion of the walls, above the arches and around the base of the dome, has been so completely ruined that it is impossible to say how it was originally finished off—possibly with a little kiosk over each angle of the octagon. The tomb stands in the middle of a courtyard 156 feet square, and upon a stone foundation and plinth. Though the building is octagonal without, the sepulchral chamber within is square, being 21 feet each way, and it contains four graves. It is said to have been built during the reign of Mīrzā Muhammad Bāqī Khān (A. D. 1572-1584). We are told that the Nawāb left directions that his body was not to be buried inside the mausoleum, but near it, so seven *hafizes*, or religious devotees, were buried within.

Not far to the south of the last is a ruined enclosure which contains the grave of Nawāb Āmīr Mīr Abu-l-Bakr. The dome of the *mihrāb* is partly demolished, and the walls are in a very ruinous state, but it still retains some of its fine enamelled tile work. Its erection is placed in the year A. D. 1627. This is probably Mīr Abu-l-Bāqa, mentioned in the *Tuhfatu-l-Kirām*, whose title was Nawāb Āmīr Khān, and who was the sixth governor of Ṭhathah under the Emperor of Delhi, after the death of Mīrzā Ghāzī Khān, and who, it is said, built the town of Āmīrpūr. He was a very learned and witty person, whom we have already noticed as having built a mosque upon the site of a Hindū temple. It is said of him that he lisped or stammered in pronouncing certain letters of the alphabet, but he was so clever that, while speaking fluently, he managed to avoid words containing those letters, substituting other words of the same meaning in their place. The *Tuhfatu-l-Kirām* tells us that his body was buried in a *rānk* or mausoleum upon the Maklī hill.

The mausoleum of Dīwān Shurfa[1] Khān, next in order, is the best preserved of the brick buildings on the hill (Plates XXXVIII—XL). It is a massive square structure, standing on a platform 38 feet square, with heavy round towers at the corners, and is constructed of fine brickwork "pointed," in the joints, with strips of dark blue tiling The dome is much like that of the tomb of Nawāb Āmīr Khalīl Khān, only that the drum is not so high, and has been covered with light blue tiles, only a portion of which remains. There is sufficient of it, however, together with the noticeable red brick of the building, to make this the most conspicuous note of colour on the hill. The central gravestone, within, is very elaborately carved with surface tracery in geometric patterns and interlaced Arabic writing. The *mihrāb* which, like others on the hill, is constructed in the west wall of the enclosure, has been decorated with blue and white tiles. The gravestone, just mentioned, is a particularly fine piece of work. Its general design and its surface decoration are in very good taste. The upright headstone is divided into compartments which are filled with Arabic writing, forming beautiful traceries of interlaced characters. The sides, top, and end of the upper

---

[1] Also written Shrufa and Sharifa.

bed-stone are also divided up, in the same way, into panels of writing. The chain bands separating the smaller panels on the headstone are very effective.

The tomb was built in A.D 1638, during the lifetime of Shurfa Khān, who was the grandson of Mīr Alīkah Arghūn and minister to Nawāb Āmīr Khān until A.D. 1644. The date 1048 (A.D. 1638) is given in the inscription on the end of the tombstone.

The largest, and most important-looking building on the hill, is the resting place of Mīrzā 'Īsā Tarkhān, the second of that name, and governor of Ṭhaṭhah under Delhi, situated not far from the Travellers' Bungalow (Plates XLI—XLVI, L and LI). Inclusive of the courtyard it covers 4,900 square feet. The great central chamber, containing the graves, rises through the whole height of the building to the dome, and is surrounded, upon all four sides, by pillared verandahs in two storeys. It is constructed throughout of a buff-coloured sandstone brought from Kathiawād, and is covered with surface tracery similar in treatment to Akbar's famous work at Fatḥpūr-Sīkrī near Agra. As it was the custom for rulers to erect their own mausolea during their lifetime, this building was probably raised not long after that, for the Mīrzā died in A.D. 1644, and we are told he began it in his youth. The *Tuhfatu-l-Kirām* says its cost was met by the revenue of the village of Nōrāī, "which was set apart for the repairs of the tombs of his elders. Some say the Mīrzā died while the building was being built and was yet incomplete." He is said to have died at the age of ninety-two years, so he was given plenty of time in which to complete his palace of death. He was cousin of Mīrzā Ghāzī Beg and grandson of Barā 'Īsā Khān, and was governor of Ṭhaṭhah between A.D. 1627 and 1644.

The Hindū custom, observed here, of always having a pillar shaft *in one piece*, between the base and the capital, has, perhaps, helped materially in saving the main building from destruction, for the walls of the enclosure are in ruins. The honeycombed capitals of the lower pillars are worth noticing; those of the upper pillars are of a purely Hindū type. Without a proper proportion of through or bonding stones, this slab-on-edge method of construction is not a very desirable one; it is, indeed, a sham, serving principally for show. The photographs show the disastrous results of such work. There are two styles of surface carving used upon the building. In one, as upon the pillars and walls, it is a fine filigri work in which the design is slightly raised, the ground being sunk, whereas, in the other, the design is sunk, the ground being raised, that is, the dressed surface of the stone forms the ground of the design; in other words, the design is incised or channelled into the surface. Thus, in the first, it is in light, the ground being in shadow, while, in the second, the effect is reversed. The one is quite as pleasing and effective as the other.

In front, or to the east, of the Mīrzā's tomb is the rather dilapidated enclosure of the tombs of the ladies of his *zanānah* (Plates XXXVI and XLVII—XLIX). The surface, here, is particularly rich and delicate, especially upon the great *mihrāb* in the west wall, which is covered with tracery both within and without, making it look, at a distance, as if it were covered with some rich brown lace. The gravestones are also very elaborately covered with this fretted veneer, in beautifully designed panels, filled with interlaced Persian or Arabic writing—extracts from the Qurān. There are few characters which lend themselves better to such ornamental conceits as these; and the artists, employed by the Muḥammadan rulers, have availed themselves of this to the full. They are so interwoven and arranged, with a view to effect rather than intelligibility, that, at first sight, one might easily take the design for intricate geometric ornament. It is sometimes very difficult to read, even by the ordinary Arabic or Persian *mūnshi*, who finds it no easy matter to unravel without considerable practice. A pillared porch has been added before the entrance as an afterthought, where it abuts upon, and covers up, some of the best work on the walls.

One of the graves has the date A. H. 964 (A.D. 1557) upon it. It is probably of one of the family who was buried here long before 'Īsā Khān took in hand the enclosing and beautifying of the old graveyard of the ladies of his family.

On the south side of Mīrzā 'Īsā Khān's tomb is a ruined brick enclosure containing the grave of Mīrzā Bāqī Khān upon a platform in the centre. He died in the year A.H. 993 (A.D. 1584). Mīrzā Muḥammad Bāqī Khān followed Barā Mīrzā 'Īsā Khān, as governor of lower Sind, in A.D. 1572. The tomb is said to have been built in A.D. 1586. It stands upon a stone foundation and has been adorned with coloured tiles.

Next comes a small stone 12-pillared canopy, about 16 feet square, over the grave of Mīrzā Tugral Beg (Plate LV). Small boys have been in the habit of throwing stones at this tomb by way of showing their displeasure at the occupant, and a great heap of stones was recently removed from it. A similar practice takes place, I understand, at the tomb of Absalom at Jerusalem. The pillars which support the dome are richly carved with surface tracery, and we have here, again, the honeycombed capitals which we noticed in 'Isa Khān's tomb close by. The pavilion stands upon a raised platform, upon the western side of which is the sculptured *mihrāb*—a great central arch flanked by two smaller ones. At either end of this, rising above the battlementing, which runs all along the top, is a little pillar-like *mīnār* which makes the whole erection look very like the ordinary *'īdgāh* one sees so often on the outskirts of villages and towns occupied more or less by Muḥammadans. There is a similar domed pavilion not far from this, also supported upon twelve pillars, and decorated in the same way, with the same honeycombed capitals, called the Baradari, which is said to have been built in A.D. 1686, the year in which Tugral Beg died.

Beyond the last is the *rāṅk* or mausoleum of Mīrzā Jānī Beg *bin* Pāindah Beg, and of Ghāzī Beg *bin* Jānī Beg Tarkhān (Plates LII—LIV). Like that of Diwān Shurfa Khān, it is faced with a very superior kind of brickwork, with imitation joints, or "pointing," of sunk strips of white enamel along the edges of each brick. The real joints are so fine, and the courses are so closely cemented together, that a knife blade can hardly be inserted between the bricks. They are laid in alternate courses of red unglazed, and dark blue glazed bricks. Around the basement was a deep dado of enamelled tiles, but these have disappeared, having, most probably, been removed by mischievous hands. Above the entrance doorway, on the south side of the building, is a beautiful panel, still intact, being out of reach, containing a Persian inscription in coloured tiles, the letters being white upon a dark blue ground. The door-frame, and the arched light above the doorway, are delicately worked in stone in a tracery of geometric patterns, the latter being perforated. The little oblong block in the centre of the bottom moulding of the lintel is a reminiscence of the square dedicatory block above Hindū temple doorways, and is here introduced, through force of habit, by the Hindū craftsman.

Within the building, is a fine dado of coloured tiles, corresponding with that which ran round the outside, which is one of the finest pieces of tile work on the hill, but it is badly damaged. Some fine panels of the same work adorn the rest of the walls and the dome. There are three graves, two of marble and one of ordinary stone.

The mausoleum, which is octagonal in plan, with twenty-five feet faces, has been surrounded with a wall which is now ruined, in which, upon the western side, is the usual carved stone *mihrāb*, with an inscription above it, but it is very much damaged. The outer gateway has also been richly carved with surface tracery.

Mīrzā Jānī Beg was one of the more important rulers of lower Sind, and died in A.H. 1008 (A.D. 1599). The *Tārīkh Ma'ṣūmī* puts his death as early as A.H. 1000. His son, Mīrzā Ghāzī Beg, who succeeded him, was assassinated in A.D. 1610, and his body was brought from Kandhār, where his death took place, and was "buried in a Mausoleum, in the neighbourhood of his father."[1]

Near the last, is a twelve-pillared pavilion covering a grave with a ruined brick *mihrāb* beside it (Plate LVI). The dome, which seems to have been left unfinished, has a peculiar zigzag pattern within it, a reproduction in stone of what is carried out in coloured tiles in the tomb of Jānī Beg; and the pillars have the honeycombed capitals. The photograph shows the regular Hindū method of cutting off the corners of the square to form an octagon; thus the dome is really supported by the two central pillars in each of the four sides of the pavilion; and corbels in the angles, above the capitals, support the alternate sides of the 16-sided figure above the octagon. Cross-arching, from these sides, reduce, still further, the aperture to be closed in by the dome.

Among the many others buried upon the Maklī hill are Qāzī Abdullah, behind the tomb of Shaikh Himād Jamālī, and Sulṭān Samtiah who was agent or administrator of Ṭhaṭhah on behalf of Miān Nūr Muḥammad.

Leaving the Maklī hill we come to the largest and most important building at Ṭhaṭhah—the great Jāmi' Masjid in the town. There is little in the general design of the building that is in any way remarkable. It is a heavy brick structure of simple construction, built upon a stone plinth, with heavy square piers and walls (Plates LVII—LXII). It is in the form of a great quadrangle, the prayer chamber, or mosque proper, occupying the western side. A corresponding block of building, on the eastern side, forms the entrance, while long corridors, on the north and south sides, connecting these, close in the great courtyard which

[1] Fredunbeg, II. 124.

measures 164 feet by 97, the whole building covering 305 feet by 170. Excepting the façade, the whole exterior is plainly whitewashed, save where the modern town painter and decorator has entered into rivalry with the tilemakers of old by gaudily painting the drum of the dome The façade, in spite of its tile work, is rather bald looking, and not very elegant in outline. But the great feature of the mosque is its coloured tile work within, the whole of the interior being covered with it. Plates LIX—LXII will give some idea of the extent of the work, which is in a fairly good state of preservation, and the plates in my portfolio of Sind tiles, already published, show the colours and the infinite variety and combinations of designs.[1] Plate LXII shows the lining of the main dome, as seen from below, which, owing to the colours used and the mosaic of the design, has the appearance of a starry vault. The cross-arching, leading up to the 16-sided stage and thence to the dome, is well seen in this plate, and plate LXI shows how the corners of the square chamber, below, are cut off to form the octagonal stage above. In plate LX is seen the peculiar honeycomb vaulting in the *miḥrāb*, which rather gives it the appearance of a section through a jelly mould.[2] It is not a very happy device for this position, and, altogether, the design of the *miḥrāb* is poor and weak. The *mimbar*, or pulpit, of four roughly-built steps, to the side of it, is very ugly when compared with the beautiful ones erected in Gujarāt and elsewhere. The roof of the mosque is composed of no less than ninety-three domes, three of which are principal ones, much larger than the rest.

The Jāmi' Masjid was commenced in A.D. 1644 and completed in A.D. 1647, but the floor was not laid until A.D. 1657. The mosque proper, together with the north and south wings, was built by Shāh Jahān as a memorial of his visit to Ṭhathah, when, having quarrelled with his father Jahāngīr, he was, for the time being, an exile from the court The eastern end, including the great gateway, was added in the year A.D. 1658-59. The total cost is said to have amounted to six lakhs of rupees, the whole of which was forwarded from the royal treasury at Delhi.

Upon the outskirts of the town, to the south, is the old brick mosque known as the Dabgir Masjid, which has been very badly ruined (Plates LXIII—LXV). It is, perhaps, the oldest mosque in the place, and may have been the older Jāmi' Masjid in which Shāh Jahān worshipped when he was at Ṭhaṭhah, as it dates back to A.D. 1588. It is also known as Āmīr Khusrō Khān's Masjid. Khusro Khān Charkas, a descendant of Changez Khān, is said to have fallen into the hands of Mīrzā 'Īsā in his infancy, and to have risen to important positions in Sind. When Mīrzā Jānī Beg placed his minor son, Mīrzā Ghāzī Beg, as ruler at Ṭhathah, Charkas Khān was appointed one of the governing council. Subsequently, when left in charge of Ṭhathah, he was accused of embezzlement of public funds and was disgraced; but Mīrzā Ghāzī Beg, who, at that time, was

[1] Very similar work is seen in the great mosque at Fathpūr-Sīkrī (*The Moghul Architecture of Fathpur-Sikri*, by Ed. W. Smith, Part IV).

[2] The very same kind of work is found upon the minaret of the mosque of Sulṭān Kalāun at Cairo which is remarkable for its lace-like fretwork, and which is in the style of the Alhambra, but uncommon in Cairo.

ruling Sind, dying suddenly, he escaped punishment and, later on, retired. During the time he was in office he is credited with having built 360 public buildings, including mosques, tombs, wells and bridges, at immense cost. He did this charitable work by way of penance for having once accidentally seen a neighbour's wife while she was bathing. They say he was about to root out his eyeballs, but learned men suggested that he might do this penance.

The mosque measures 98 by 48 feet, and has three bays surmounted by one large and two small domes. It still contains some very fine coloured tile work; and the *miḥrāb*, which is of stone, covered with the most delicate tracery, is a superb piece of work. Like many of the older buildings in Sind, this one has suffered very much from the *kalar* or salt in the soil, which, when damp, rises through the porous brickwork and crystallizing, disintegrates the brickwork as far up as it reaches. This damage has of late been repaired with stone work which, with the plaster repairs over the top, is not very beautiful. Plate LXIII shows the building before repairs.

Four miles south by west of Ṭhaṭhah is the old deserted Kalān Koṭ, or Kalyāṇ Koṭ, also known as Taghlaqābād. The *Tārīkh Ma'ṣūmi* tells us that this fortified position was constructed by Jānī Beg, when he was fighting with the emperor's troops under Khān Khānān, as a place of refuge should he be compelled to fly before the enemy. He wrote to his father, Pāindah Beg and his son Abu-l-Fatḥ, who were at Ṭhaṭhah, to destroy that city and to betake themselves, with the people, to Kalān Koṭ. This was done and the city of Ṭhaṭhah, we are told, was laid waste.[1] The fort, which is situated upon a limestone hill, and is about a mile and a quarter in circumference, is supposed to stand upon the site of a still more ancient stronghold. It is partly surrounded by an extensive natural moat filled with water, and is now in ruins, the only building left standing within it being an old masjid with a dry tank before it. It was constructed of brickwork, and its fallen walls may be traced all around, heaps of brick debris strewing the area within.

Elliot writes: "Subsequently, the fort of Tughlikābād was built by Jam Taghūr or Tughlik, on the site of the older Kalā-Kot, about 2 miles south of Thatta, but that, as well as its predecessor, was left unfinished by its founder. By a strange vicissitude, the name of Tughlikābād is now comparatively forgotten, and that of Kalā-Kot, erroneously called Kalān-Kot (the great fort), though for a time superseded, has restored the just claims of Rājā Kalā, and still attracts the attention of the traveller. Lieutenant Burton calls it Kalliān-Kot. I fear to differ from so good a local authority, but believe Kalā-Kot to be more strictly correct."[2] Raverty says that Dr. J. Burnes and Sir A. Burnes, following Mr. Crow's statement, considered "Kullan Kot" to be Brahmanābād. "The correct name is Kalyāṇ Koṭ (*kalyāṇ*, Sanskrit, meaning Prosperous, happy, etc.).[3] During the time the Sammahs had been subject to the Sumṛahs, they had founded a town and a fort on the skirts of the Makkahlī hills, the first

[1] Fredunbeg's *History of Sind*, II, 113.
[2] *History of India*, I, 402.
[3] *Mihrān of Sind*, 203n.

being named Sāmū'ī, also called Sā'ī by some few writers, and the other Ṭhākūr-ābād—the chief's abode or place of residence, the foundations of which had been laid by their then Ṭhākūr..............but it had been left unfinished, probably because the Sumrahs would not permit them to finish it. This they now completed [that is, when they came into power] and also founded a number of other towns and villages. This fort was subsequently called, or the name changed into Tughluk-ābād, a Turkish, not a Sindi name; and the author of the *Tuḥfatul-Kirām* states that some of the present defences and erections in the fort of Tughluk-ābād, better known as 'Kalyāṇ-Koṭ,' were the work of the Nawāb, Murūd Khān (a Turk or Mughal) who was the feudatory of the Ṭhaṭhah province in 1099 H. (1688 A.D.)."[1]

Hidden in the cactus bush, at a short distance from the Travellers' Bungalow, is the grave of an Englishman, Edward Cooke, who died at Ṭhaṭhah in 1743. It is not known who he was, but it is supposed a private merchant. In 1758, during the reign of Ghulām Shāh Kalhōrah, an English factory was established at Ṭhaṭhah, but it was withdrawn in 1775. Again in 1799 another commercial mission was attempted under the same auspices, but this, like the former, terminated unsatisfactorily. The house belonging to the factory at Ṭhaṭhah was, up to 1839, in good repair, and in that year it was occupied by a portion of the British garrison. It is thus evident that Edward Cooke was one of the first Englishmen to visit Ṭhaṭhah. The tombstone lies north and south, like those of the Muhammadans, and on the top is a long inscription in highly-raised letters, closely packed, which runs as follows :—

> Here lyes the manes of Edward Cooke, who was taken out of the world in the Flower of his Age, a person of great merit and in great esteem and much lamented by his friends, learned in many languages, of great humanity, a sound judgment and generous disposition, who departed this life on the 8th of May 1743. Ætatis suæ 21.
>
> As blooming lilies grace the field,
> So for a day they shine,
> Like him to God, so they yield
> Their selves, but not their name resign.
>
> To whose memory his servants erected this tomb.

Beside it are the graves of some Muḥammadans, possibly his servants referred to.

There has been much controversy as to whether Ṭhaṭhah occupies the site of the more ancient town of Dewal or Debal, one of the first cities of Sind, as we have seen, to be attacked by the Arab invaders of the eighth century. I am inclined to believe it does, allowing for the slight shifting of the site from time to time on account of the movements of the river.[2] General Haig, who gave the subject very considerable attention, and ably discussed all probabilities for and against, thought otherwise. He considered the ruins at Kakaṛ Bukēra to be those of Dewal, and gives his reasons for thinking so. He says: "The Thata site is still more out of the question, it is surprising that its distance

[1] *Mihrān of Sind*, 328n.

[2] It was so called on account of a famous temple, or *dewal*, which Muḥammad Qāsim destroyed when he took the town.

from the sea, and the difficulty of navigation by keeled ships of such a river as the Indus have been overlooked by those who are 'certain' that it was once a famous port for sea-going vessels."[1] But he has himself overlooked the fact that Ṭhaṭhah was not at the distance from the sea in the time of Muḥammad Qāsim that it is today. It was, at most, only half that distance, if Raverty is right in his reasoning, and there seems every probability that he is.[2] Kakaṛ Bukēra, which he says is also known as Bēg Chugyo, would, at that time, have been upon the seashore. Elliot, also, has the same objection to Ṭhaṭhah as the site of Dewal, but thinks it was close to Karāchi.[3] This identification was the result of his accepting M. Reinaud's translation of Bilādurī, who makes him speak of the "Bay of Debal," whereas the correct translation is the "estuary" or "creek" of Debal. Raverty thinks Dewal was in the vicinity of Pīr Paṭho, but, perhaps, a little south-westward. This, again, puts it upon the seashore, according to his own showing, but Al Mas'ūdī tells us that the Mihrān fell into the sea about two days' journey from the town of Debal.[4] Cunningham considers Lāhorī Bandar to be the most probable position.[5] The *Tuhfatu-l-Kirām* distinctly says that what was once Bandar Debal is now Bandar Lāhorī. Yet it also says "Debal, now called Thatta, was in the land of Sākūra."[6]

But, before going any further into this much vexed question, I may as well state my own ideas, and it will then be seen how far they fall in with these many apparently conflicting accounts and, to some extent, explain them away. I believe that two different places have been confused, in the first instance, by native writers, most of whom wrote from hearsay and were never even near the locality; and those who were, wrote of things as they found them, not always as they were before their time. There was, then, Dewal proper, the city that the Arabs assaulted, and, later, as the state of the river necessitated, a port, nearer the mouth, to serve the city, where goods could be transferred to lighter craft for ascending the river. This port became known as Bandar Dewal (Port of Dewal) as the *Tuhfatu-l-Kirām* calls it. We have a modern parallel in Glasgow and Port Glasgow, the latter having been established for the same reason, the shallow state of the river Clyde, at one time, not allowing large sea-going vessels to reach the city. One writer says Lāhorī Bandar was so called after Lahor, being the port for that city. If so, this is another parallel. Bandar Dewal, first the port of Dewal, continued, for some time further, as the port of Dewal-Ṭhaṭhah. Later writers, losing sight of the connection of Dewal with Ṭhaṭhah, thus came to speak of Dewal Bandar as Dewal only. Raverty made a very serious initial mistake. He places Nīrūn, or Nīrūn Koṭ, some distance south of Haidarābād,[7] and upon this false premise he fixes the position of Dewal. If there is any one site in Sind, about which there is now no doubt whatever, that place is

[1] *Indus Delta Country*, 47.

[2] *Mihrān of Sind*, 236n, 317, 468n and 469n. Also see his maps of the coastline at different periods, reproduced as a composite map on the general map of Sind in this volume.

[3] *Indus Delta Country*, 42, and Elliot's *History of India*, I, 116.

[4] *Mihrān of Sind*, 322, and Elliot's *History of India*, I, 24.

[5] *Ancient Geography of India*, 279.

[6] Elliot's *Appendix to the Arabs in Sind*, 225, and *History of India*, 398.

[7] *Mihrān of Sind*, 228n.

Nīrūn, which, with universal consent, is placed at Haidarābād. The re-adjustment of position of Nīrūn would require that his site of Dewal should be shifted correspondingly further in a northerly or north-easterly direction to fall in with the distances given by the native historians, which he works upon. That move would bring the site close upon Kalyāṇ Koṭ or Ṭhaṭhah (see the map at the end).

Ibn Khurdādba tells us that the distance, from Dewal to the junction of the river Mihrān with the sea, is two *parasangs*.[1] Mas'ūdī says two days' journey.[2] Iṣtakhri says the distance from Manṣūra to Dewal is six days' journey. If one-third the distance between these last two places is measured off on the map and measured from Ṭhaṭhah southwards, it will strike the line of the coast as it probably existed in the tenth century when Istakhri wrote.[3] Ibn Hauqal thus describes Dewal: "The city of Debal is to the west of the Mihrān, towards the sea. It is a large mart, and the port not only of this but neighbouring regions. Debal is remarkable for the richness of its grain cultivation, but it is not over-abundant in large trees or the date tree. It is famous for the manufacture of swords. The inhabitants generally maintain themselves by their commerce."[4] Idrisi writes: "This [Dewal] is a populous place, but its soil is not fertile, and it produces hardly any trees except the date palm. The highlands are arid and the plains sterile. Houses are built of clay and wood, but the place is inhabited only because it is a station for the vessels of Sind and other countries. Trade is carried on in a great variety of articles, and is conducted with much intelligence. Ships laden with the productions of 'Umān, and the vessels of China and India come to Debal. They bring stuffs and other goods from China, and the perfumes and aromatics from India. The inhabitants of Debal, who are generally rich, buy these goods in bulk, and store them until the vessels are gone and they become scarce. They then begin to sell, and go trading into the country, putting their money out on interest, or employing it as may seem best. Going towards the west there are six miles between the mouth of the great Mihrān and Debal."[5] This account is, in its most essential points, in direct variance with the preceding, and can only be reconciled with it by supposing Idrisi was writing of the later Bandar Dewal or Port of Dewal, close to the sea coast, and in such a position as Lāhorī Bandar. The *Murāsidu-l-I'tilā* states that "Debal is a well known town on the shore of the sea of Hind, and a place of considerable trade, near which place likewise, the rivers of Lāhor and Multān empty themselves into the ocean."[6] As a specimen of gross inaccuracy in the accounts of native writers, the statement of the author of the *A'in-i-Akbari* may be given. He says: "Alore is now called Tatah and Debiel".[7]

The *Tuhfatu-l-Kirām* tells us that, immediately after the death of Muḥammad Qāsim, when a great deal of the country lapsed to native rule, only "the part of

---

[1] Elliot's *History of India*, I, 15.
[2] *Id.*, 24.
[3] *Id.*, 29.
[4] Elliot's *History of India*, 37.
[5] Elliot's *History of India*, I, 77, and Raverty's *Mihrān of Sind*, 224.
[6] Raverty's *Mihrān of Sind*, 230.
[7] Gladwin's translation, II, 115.

the country from Debālpur to the seashore remained in the possession of the governors of Islām." If Debal had been at Kakaṛ Bukera, and so practically on the seashore at that time, there could have been no land between the two for the Arabs to possess.

Cunningham thinks that Dewal was deserted about A.D. 1250, that is, between the visits of Jalālu-d-dīn of Khwarazm in A.D. 1221 and Ibn Batuta in A.D. 1333, when the latter visited Lāhorī Bandar, which had succeeded Dewal [? Bandar Dewal] as the great port of the Indus. Dewal was then in ruins. He fixes the site of Dewal on the western bank of the Baghar river, about five miles north of Lāhorī Bandar. He quotes Ibn Batuta as saying: "At a few miles from this city [Lāhorī Bandar] are the ruins of another, in which stones in the shape of men and beasts almost innumerable are to be found. The people of this place think that it is the opinion of their historians that there was a city formerly in this place, the greater part of the inhabitants of which were so base that God transformed them, their beasts, their herbs, even to the very seeds, into stones; and, indeed, stones in the shape of seeds are here almost innumerable."[1] The accompanying photographs (Figs. 18 and 19) taken recently

FIG. 18.—Ruins of Thambawāro *Masjid.*

by Mr. G. E. L. Carter, I.C.S., show some ruins a few miles north-east of Lāhorī Bandar, and not far from this site. They represent the remains of a *masjid* which had been constructed from the materials of a Hindū temple, and now called the Thambawāro Masjid. It will be seen how the Muḥammadans chiselled out the images from the niches on the pillars. The original temple probably belonged to about the twelfth century. Mr. Carter says the building is utterly ruined and lies in the centre of a salt waste (? the sterile plains of Idrisi) washed by the sea in the monsoon. He thinks it is probably the "Debul" or "Deul" of the map in Tavernier's travels. This place Raverty thinks must have been Damṛīlah, having already wrongly fixed Dewal elsewhere. Mr. Carter says there

[1] *Ancient Geography of India*, 295 and 299.

are no other ruins at the Thambawāro Masjid. It is hardly likely that it would have been a solitary building originally. Mosques are built to supply the wants of a settled population.

Cunningham says that, with "Abu-l-Fazl and the later Muḥammadan writers, Debal has been confounded with Ṭhaṭhah, but as Debal was no longer in existence when they wrote, I conclude that they were misled by the name of Debal Ṭhaṭhah, which is frequently applied to Ṭhaṭhah itself."[1] A parallel to this double name is Bamana-Manṣūra (see page 67). Haig says that the mention of Dewal in connection with Jalālu-d-dīn's visit in A.D. 1223 is one of the latest, if not quite the latest reference to the place as still existing and inhabited, and then continues: "It is possible that the Dewal of Jalālu-d-dīn's day was not the original Dewal [Here, I think, he gets near what I deem to be the truth—that there were two places of the same name, the city and its port], but some other town to which the famous name had been transferred. It is curious that El Biruni, writing in the first half of the eleventh century, does not name Dewal, but speaks of Lohārānī as apparently the Delta port of that time."[2] We are told that Jalālu-d-dīn founded a Jāmi' Masjid at Dewal on the ruins of an idol temple.[3] Possibly this is Mr. Carter's Thambawāro Masjid.

FIG. 19.—Pillars on the ruins of Thambawāro *Masjid.*

It remains now to give a few references to Ṭhaṭhah and Dewal by some European writers other than those already quoted, and perhaps one of the earliest of these is Captain Best, a Factor, in 1612. He says: "Concerning Sinda, no city is by general report of greater trade in the Indies than *Tatta*, the chief port, *Lowri bandar*, three days' journey from it; ....In two months from hence by water they go to *Lahor*, and return in one down."[4] Walter Paynton writes, in the same year: "*Tata*, a great city one day's journey from *Diul*, both cities standing in the Great Mogoll's Dominions."[5] Raverty

[1] *Ancient Geography of India*, 297.

[2] *Indus Delta Country*, 48.

[3] Raverty's *Mihrān of Sind*, 255n, and *Tabaḳāt-i-Nāṣirī*, 294n.

[4] Raverty's *Mihrān of Sind*, 319n.

[5] Raverty's *Mihrān of Sind*, 320n

says: "The ancient seaport of Sind, Debal, or Dewal, was well known to the English traders down to within the last two hundred years; and this part of the channel was navigable for small sailing ships up to within a short distance of Ṭhaṭhah."[1] M. de Thevenot, who commenced his travels in 1652, writes: "The chief Town of this Province is *Tatta*, and the most Southern Town, *Diul*. It is still called *Diul-Sind*, and was heretofore called *Dobil*. It lies in the four and twentieth or five and twentieth degree of Latitude. There are some Orientals, that call the Country of Sind, by the name of the Kingdom of *Diul*....... There is also a great trade at *Loure-bender* which is three days' journey from *Tatta*, upon the Sea, where there is a better Road for Ships, than in any other place of the Indies."[2] It appears from this that "Diul" and Lāhorī Bandar were separate places, and this is what we might expect if a slight change in the course of the river necessitated a change in the position of the port, the newer one, a few miles south, being called Lāhorī Bandar. "Diul," or Bandar Dewal, would still, for some time, continue to be an emporium of trade with its old established associations. Walter Paynton also mentions the two places. Captain Hamilton, who spent the years 1688-1723 in the East Indies, thus writes: "In travelling from Dungham towards Tatta, about four miles short of the city, on smooth rising Ground [the Maklī hill], there are forty-two fine large Tombs, which, from the Plain, appeared to be a small town. They are the Burying-places of some of the Kings of Sindy, when that Country was governed by its own Kings."[3] He then gives a description of these and goes on to say that, when he visited Ṭhaṭhah in 1699, the town was about three miles long and one and a half broad, and that, a short time previous to his visit, 80,000 persons had died of plague, and one half of the city was consequently uninhabited. Lieutenant H. Pottinger writes about these tombs in much the same strain, in 1816, in his *Travels in Beloochistan and Sind*, and tells us that when the Persian king Nādir Shāh entered Ṭhaṭhah in 1742, there were 40,000 weavers (Fig. 20), 20,000 other artisans, and 60,000 dealers in various departments.[4] The population

FIG. 20.—Ṭhaṭhah weavers.

[1] *Indus Delta Country*, 317.
[2] *Travels into the Levant*, p. 53.
[3] *A New Account of the East Indies*, etc., 1727, Vol. I, p. 12.
[4] Sind Gazetteer, 838.

in 1872, as determined by the census, was only 7,951. Captain Wood, in his *Journey to the Source of the Oxus*, also describes the place as he found it in 1837.

One of the most interesting writers on Sind was Captain Richard F. Burton[1] who gives some delightful accounts of the places he visited in his *Sind and the Races that inhabit the Valley of the Indus* (1851) and *Sind Revisited.* He spent much time in the country, and was well acquainted with its topography and history as told by the Muḥammadan historians. He says: "We are certain that the modern Tatta occupies the ground of the ancient Dewal, as the Arabs and Persians know it by no other name, 'Shal-i-Dibali' still being used to mean a shawl of Tatta manufacture."[2] With his description of the tombs upon the Makli hill I shall close this account of Ṭhaṭhah and Dewal. "Behind the Id-gah rises an infinite variety of mausolea and sepulchres, many ruined by the earthquake's shock, more crumbling to decay beneath the 'winnowing wings of Time,' a few, and but very few, preserved by the pious hands of descendants and disciples. Vaulted domes, arches, and towers; porticos, gateways, and colonnades, rise in long succession above shapeless heaps and mounds, whose remains no ivy, loved of Bacchus, invests with its green winding sheet. The piles of stone are naked, desolate, and unaltered as on the day when they sank to earth! here and there a tuft of parched-up grass and a thorny tree bowed by the winds and bare of leaves, adding desolation to the desolate spectacle. Many of the edifices, the tombs of the Amirs, Jams, and Sayyids, must have been the labour of years and years. In some the cupola, surrounded by a ring of smaller domes, rests upon a single or a double colonnade, enclosing a gallery and platform broken by pointed arches in each of the four fronts; others are girt by lofty stone walls, forming square courtyards, with gates leading to the different doorways. Some consist of heavy marble canopies, supported by light fantastic columns, and sheltering a parallel line of tombstones; and many are built of coloured and glazed Dutch tile and brick, which, by-the-by, might rival those of old Rome. No chiselled stone could have a sharper edge or a truer form: so carefully is the material mixed and burned, that it rings like metal, and breaks almost as clean as glass. When stained and glazed, they look as if enamelled; and nothing can be richer than the appearance of the inscriptions, in large white letters upon a dark purple ground. They were probably made by Persian bricklayers, who are celebrated throughout the East for their skill in this craft. The gaudy 'Chini Gumbaz' (porcelain domes), as they are called at Haydarabad in the Dekhan, have more the appearance of pleasure houses than mansions of the dead, as they stand out bright and singular from the general expression of monotonous melancholy; whilst upon all pours down the gay radiance of an Eastern sun, and the azure reflection of a cloudless sky, its hues of undying brightness contrasting tritely, yet how impressively, with the transitory memorials of earthly splendour."

[1] Afterwards Sir Richard Francis Burton, translator of the *Arabian Nights*, and explorer in Africa and Arabia.

[2] *Sind and the Races*, 380 n. McMurdo also says Ṭhaṭhah is known to the Arabs by no other name than Dibal. *Journ. R. A. S. I.*, 234.

"A closer inspection is by no means favourable to the view. There is a satiating minuteness in the details of decoration with which the tombs are carved; in the largest and most magnificent, every stone of the edifice itself, its walls and its gates, is elaborately carved in relief. Your eye rejects the profuseness of square and circle, spiral and curve, diamond and scroll-work, flowers, border-pattern, and quotations from the Koran in characters whose chief beauty is illegibility. In vain you look for a straight line; the architects were not sufficiently artful to succeed in the simplicities of art: they are like the goldsmiths of India, who can make anything but a plain flat surface. As a traveller justly observes, the effect of the tout ensemble is an 'appearance of tinsel tawdriness which results from injudicious over-ornament.'"[1]

[1] *Sind Revisited*, I, 142-154.

HAIDARĀBĀD.

HAIDARĀBĀD, the second city in Sind and the head-quarters of a district, is situated at a short distance from the east bank of the Indus, and about ninety miles north-east of Karāchi. It stands upon elevated rocky ground between that river and the old bed of the Fulēli, in which a canal now runs, and is some two miles long from north to south, at which end stands the old fort. It is supposed to occupy the site of the old fortified town of Nīrūn, which fell before the invading Arab army about the year A.D. 711, at which time the Indus flowed on the *east* side of the town; but its old bed is not to be confused with that of the Fulēli which was a modern stream having its head in the Indus, some twelve miles north of Haidarābād, and after the Indus took its new course to the west, about the middle of the eighteenth century.[1] Ibn Hauqal says: "The country of Nērūn is between Debal and Mansūra, but rather nearer to the latter."[2] Al Idrisi tells us "Nīrūn is a town of little importance, but it is fortified, and its inhabitants are rich. Trees are rare."[3]

The present town and fort of Haidarābād were founded by the Kalhōrah chief Miān Ghulām Shāh in A.H. 1182 (A.D. 1768), who made it his capital; and in 1789 Mīr Fatḥ 'Alī Khān, the then ruling Tālpūr chief, abandoning Khudābād near Hālā, also made it his capital, when he ran up buildings within the fort for his own accommodation and that of his relations. Some mosques were also built, among them those known as Mullā Rahmatullāh's Tālibshāh's near the fort gate, which had originally been built by Miān Ghulām Shāh, and Mā Khairī's,[4] all of which are said to have been built within nine months. It is

---

[1] Haig's *Indus Delta Country*, 54. Cunningham identifies Haidarābād with Patala (*Ancient Geography*, 285). Elliot places Nīrūn at Helāī, or Helāya, a little below Jarak, on the road from Ṭhaṭhah to Haidarābād. He says lakes abound in the neighbourhood, and are large enough, especially the Kinjar, to have admitted Muḥammad Qāsim's fleet (*Appendix to the Arabs in Sind*, 233), but he overlooked the fact that there was no connection between that lake and the Indus, there being high ground between; and, moreover, the river at that time must have been some distance further east than it is now. Elliot seems, here, to be mixing up the lake (Raverty and other writers say "river," not "lake") of Sakura or Sangrah, into which Muḥammad's boats put on leaving Debal, with the lake adjacent to Nīrūn called the Sonhari *Ḍhanḍh*, beside which he encamped on arrival at Nīrūn. Raverty puts Nīrūn at an old site close to Tāndo Muḥammad Khān, on the west, or at Shāh Kapur, or somewhere between the two (*Mihrān of Sind*, 228n). There is a Sonahrī *Ḍhanḍh* near Jarak, but it is only 25 miles from Ṭhaṭha, or 43 from Raverty's site of Dewal, whereas Muḥammad took 6 days to march from Debal to Nīrūn. The *Chach Nāmah* does not mention this lake by name. As Muḥammad arrived at this lake on his return from Sīwistān, it was, therefore, probably somewhere to the north of Nīrūn.

[2] Elliot's *History of India*, I, 37.

[3] *Ib*, I, 78.

French writers invariably transcribe the name as Birun or "Byroun," preferring to place the omitted dot beneath the initial letter rather than above it, so, بيرون instead of نيرون .

[4] Bibi Khairī was the mother of Mīr Fatḥ 'Alī Khān.

now an extensive and closely-packed modern town, the principal street running through its whole length from north to south and abutting upon the fort gate at its southern end. Upon the west of the town is the military cantonment, while, away to the north and north-west, stand the old tombs of the later Kalhōrah and Tālpūr rulers of Sind—the most conspicuous objects on the plateau. While the Kalhōrah mausolea are in rather a dilapidated condition, those of the Tālpūrs are in very good repair, being kept in order by descendants of that family. The former are large separate and isolated buildings, standing some distance apart, but the Tālpūr tombs are clustered in two groups.

The oldest building now standing is the tomb of Ghulām Shāh Kalhōrah, who died in A.H. 1186 (A.D. 1772), soon after he had built the fort. A few years ago its dome fell in, probably through some settlement of the foundations (Plates LXV—LXVIII and Figs. 21—23). It is a great massive square building, standing upon an extensive platform, with its one entrance upon the eastern side. The whole of the exterior of the walls was covered with glazed coloured tiles, in a great variety of geometric and floral patterns, but these were very badly damaged, and a great deal of what was left, a short time ago, was, unfortunately, plastered over by way of repairs. Plate LXVI shows the building as it was in 1896 before the repairs. The tiles were carried upon a six inch veneer of brick and plaster, which seems to have been added to the face of the walls as the latter rose from their foundations. As a result of the unequal settlement of the great massive walls, laden with the heavy dome, and this thin veneer, the latter has separated from the walls and has buckled outwards, thus springing the tiles which were attached to it, and causing them to fall away in great numbers. This may have taken place soon after the completion of the building. The great settlement that took place in the walls, which is seen in the dip of the flag-stones of the platform around the plinth of the building, probably cracked and rendered the dome unsafe, and was the incipient cause of its collapse. Its fall did very great damage to the white marble tombstone within, and its beautiful railing. The latter was broken to pieces, while some of the finely sculptured panel slabs of the platform of the grave were displaced and broken (Plate LXVIII).

FIG. 21.—Wagon-vaulted tomb.

The interior of the building has been very elaborately painted and gilded; and a deep band of coloured glazed tiles runs round the walls (Plate LXVII). A great deal of the decorated surface is made up of medallions, panels and bands of Persian texts in interwoven letters. Over one of the arches are inscribed certain verses "in what may properly be called Sindi-Persian, composed, it is presumed, by his eldest son Sarafrāz Khān, in 1771. The following is a translation of the verses, but the beauty of the original consists in not only giving the year of the demise of Ghulām Shāh in verse, but also in preserving the sense in connection with the context."[1]

1. Ah ! the unkindness of the ignoble heavens.
   Ah ! the freaks of the azure firmament.
2. The valiant cavalier of the race-course of fame ;
   The monarch of the capital of the empire.
3. The light of the Sun of the Zodiac of honour,
   Both the worlds paid allegiance to him.
4. By Divine grace his mandates
   Went forth in Heaven and on earth.
5. Kings entreated at his doors,
   Crowned heads prostrated themselves before him.
6. The emperor of the world, " Ghulam Shah, "
   The sky kissed the earth before him.
7. He passed away from the world into paradise.
   He received what he deserved at the door of God.
8. A dome over the tomb of that monarch
   Was erected like the vault of the starry skies.
9. The dome was as bright as the palace of paradise ;
   It was as delightful as the magnificent paradise.
10. For the date of his demise, the imagination of Sarafraz
    Was in great search with a great deal of pains.
11. Whilst in these thoughts an exclamation was made,
    By the Divine messenger : " For ever in Heaven."

A staircase in the thickness of the wall leads to the terrace roof which surrounded the dome. The low parapet wall, which runs round the edge of the platform, upon which the building stands, is constructed of thin slabs, or panels,

FIG. 22.—Portions of perforated rail.

of perforated stone supported by little pillars at intervals (Plate LXVIII and Fig. 22). The perforated patterns on these are very neat and pretty ; and, with

[1] *Gazetteer of Sind* (1876), p. 263.

some surface tracery upon a few corner stones let into the main building, remind one of similar work at Fatḥpur-Sīkrī. It has already been noticed at Ṭhaṭhah where it is lavished upon the tomb of 'Īsa Khān. The mausoleum and courtyard have been surrounded with high mud walls and bastions, which make the place look like a little mud fort.

Cut into the flagstones of the platform are a great number and variety of masons' marks, intended, no doubt, to indicate each man's work when it was being measured up for payment (Fig. 23). In place of symbols and signs such as these, initials and names are found used, for the same purpose, upon old Hindu temples.[1]

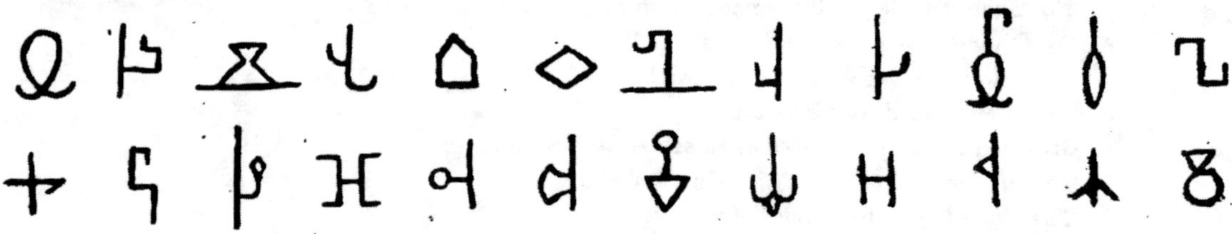

Fig. 23. Masons' marks.

At a short distance from Ghulām Shāh's tomb, to the south, is that of his brother Nabī Khān, who usurped the throne of Sind after Sarafrāz fled from the capital.[2] It is, like the last, a heavy massive building, which was in a very bad state of repair a few years ago. It differs from the last in that it is octagonal in plan, but the interior is square (Plate LXIX).

About half a mile further south, in a hollow below the hill, is the tomb of Sarafrāz Khān, which is still kept in repair, as he has become a *pīr* or saint. He, with other relatives, was murdered, in cold blood, by order of his uncle Miān Ghulām Nabī Khān. From an architectural point of view the building is very plain and of little note. Compared with the sepulchre of the *pīrs* or saints, the tombs of emperors or kings are of little account to the followers of Islām. Unless a ruler built his own mausoleum during his own lifetime, it was unlikely that any one would do it for him afterward; and, unless there were well-to-do descendants to look after it, it would, probably, not be kept even in decent repair.

There is a quiet dignity and stateliness about the first two buildings which is not found in those of the Tālpūrs, but much of this effect may possibly be due, indeed, to its very dilapidation—the hand of time, by the removal of much of their original gaudy coat of veneer, having left just enough colouring to make their *tout-ensemble* picturesque and pleasing. Like many a work of art, it is the better for the mellowing influence of time. They are fit sepulchres for those proud and sturdy old Kalhōrah chiefs.

The two groups of Tālpūr tombs, being of later construction, and being kept in repair, are in first rate condition (Plates LXX—LXXIII). Among the Mirs of Sind, who are buried here, and who succeeded the Kalhōrahs in

[1] These masons' marks are found in many old Muḥammadan buildings.

[2] The *Sind Gazetteer* says it is Sarafrāz Khān's, but this is a mistake.

the government of the country, are Karam 'Alī,[1] Murād 'Alī, Nūr Muḥammad, Naṣīr Khān, Shāhdād Khān, and Ghulām Shāh, beside many of their ladies and other relations. The buildings are covered with glazed tiles of the latest colours and patterns, which are very poor when compared with the older work at Ṭhaṭhah; and more colours are introduced than are found in the earlier work, such as showy greens, yellows and browns. This mixture rather tends, on the whole, to produce a tawdry effect, some of the patterns being very suitable for cheap linoleums; they would, in fact, provide an endless stock of new and uncommon combinations for makers of that material. The general construction appears to be better than in the Kalhōrah tombs, and the tiles have kept their places so far; but, as architectural efforts, these buildings are poor and cheap-looking, and shew a great decline in the art of building.

The tomb of Mīr Karam 'Alī, in the northern group, is a large square building, surmounted by a dome, with a turret over each corner: it is decorated

FIG. 24.—Mausoleum of Mīr Muḥammad Khān.

with marble fretwork, and is covered with coloured tiles. It was built about 1812. There are two graves in the mausoleum, the second being that of Mīr Hājī Muḥammad Khān. Behind this is a smaller building containing the graves of his two wives (Plate LXXI), the wife of Mīr Abdullāh Khān and an infant Mīr. To the north of Mīr Karam 'Alī's mausoleum is one containing five graves of Tālpūr chiefs, which, beginning from the eastern end, are those of Mīr Naṣīr Khan, Mīr Nūr Muḥammad Khān, Mīr Shāhdād Khān, Mīr Murād 'Alī Khān, and Mīr Muḥammad Ḥusain 'Alī Khān. The marble graves have the actual state

[1] Mīr Karam 'Alī Khān was the first Tālpūr to be buried at Haidarābād (A.D. 1828); before this all Talpūr chiefs were buried at Khudābād near Hālā.

turbans of these chiefs placed upon a projection at the end of each (Plate LXXIII). The building in front of this last, on the east, contains the remains of the wife and child of Nūr Muḥammad and the wife of Ḥusain 'Alī Khān. Other wives of two of these chiefs, and three young children, repose in the small tomb in the north-east corner. Still other Mīrs lie within the two small tombs at the south-west corner of Karam 'Alī's, and the remaining buildings contain the bodies of wives, daughters and children of some of these. In the southern group of tombs, the two principal mausolea, that nearest the entrance, on the east, and that immediately behind it, contain the graves of four Mīrs, while the rest are occupied by their wives and children.

The old fort, built by Miān Ghulām Shāh Kalhōrah, at the south end of the town, was, to all appearance, strongly and solidly built as a Sindhi stronghold. It is still in a tolerable state of preservation, though the buildings of sorts, that were once crowded within it, in the days of native rule, were nearly all cleared away by the British in 1857, who, for some time, used the place for the accommodation of troops, military stores, and as an arsenal. Of late there have been but two powder magazines, guarded by British soldiers, together with the old palace of the Mīrs, part of which had been converted into public offices. Burton, who saw the place in 1845, but a couple of years after the battle of Miāni, when the ruling Mīr was turned out of it, describes it thus: "The interior was a haute-ville with a promenade round the ramparts; a densely crowded town of wynds, cul de sacs, and narrow, crooked lanes; squarlets and guards; darbars and mosques, lines and barracks, palaces and dwelling-houses, harem and stables."[1] In the enclosure, around one of the magazines, are the tombs of two British officers who were killed at the battle of Haidarābād, and one of the enemy's gunners, who was given honourable burial by the British, upon whose grave lies the old disabled gun he so pluckily served to the last. A very high tower, which rises from the centre of the fort, may have carried a gun, or it may have served as a watch tower. Here, Burnes tells us, was deposited a great portion of the riches of Sind.[2] He visited the capital twelve years before it fell into the hands of the British. Along the crest of the walls of this fort, as well as the smaller one close by, are ornamental *kanguras*, or merlons, which, at a distance, owing to their attenuated necks, look like rows of heads stuck upon stakes. The smaller fort was built by Ghulām Shāh in A.D. 1772 to cover the main fort upon that side. There is here the grave of a local saint, Hājī Muḥammad Makai.

Within the old palace, which is a jumble of insignificant buildings, is a large room known as the "Painted Chamber," the best part of which is its ceiling. The walls are painted in the usual style, while, in the backs of four niches or recesses, are groups of figures, very indifferently executed, one of which is said to represent the meeting of Ranjit Singh, the ruler of the Panjāb, with Lord Lake in 1803. There was a considerable amount of gilding about the walls, but all of it has been scraped off, as was done at the Sāt Manzil

[1] *Sind Revisited*, Vol. I, 249.

[2] *Travels into Bokhara*, 2nd Ed., p. 43. Burton says this was not so.

at Bijāpūr, in the hope of reaping a golden harvest. There is still a very finely carved wooden door in the palace (Plate LXXIV).

Burton's further account of the interior of the fort may well be quoted here, since it gives a very good idea of the environment of the Mīrs in their own home. "The ground-plan of Haydarābād Palace was laid out as follows. You enter by a dwarf door, opening from a narrow impasse into a quadrangular courtyard: on your right was the private Musalla, or chapel, a low wall subtended by a stucco'd floor: opposite stood the stables; on the left rose the kitchen, the servants' huts, and the offices, while the body of the house monopolized the fourth side. The dwelling place consisted of a deep verandah, resting on wooden pillars and fronted by a chunam'd parapet: the men's, or public and state rooms, met you as you entered; those of the Zenanah, the Harem, as you call it, were under arrest behind them: low doors connected the several items and the interior was purposely made as dark as possible, to temper glare and secure privacy. Some apartments were lined with gypsum and elaborately decorated with coloured arabesques, somewhat in the style of our stencilling; the 'Painted Chamber' in Mīr Shahdād's house still shows the meeting of Ranjit Singh and Lord Lake; and Major Outram yet sits drinking with his wife. The tinting gave a pseudo-Moorish look to the interior, and in the richest houses the ceilings, with their large rafters, were lacquered, painted and heavily gilt. Some of the rooms were rivetted, like dairies, with painted tiles from Hālā and Multan. The inner walls held a number of Tak, or Niches, the cupboards and safes of the East, and when I first saw them in 1845, they were not a little dilapidated. The Amirs and their courtiers, taken by surprise at the results of Miyani and Dabba, hastily box'd and buried, more Asiatico, their gold ingots and jewels under the thresholds, in the house-walls, and in other places which a western would seldom visit with the hope of finding treasure. This secret, becoming generally known, caused abundant harmless excitement among the conquerors: Europeans as well as natives did little, for the first six months, but diligently rap with staves every foot of stucco, to judge by the sound whether the spot was hollow, and consequently worth the trouble of breaking into. There were, I believe, a few finds which did not reach the hands of the prize-agents." He tells us that, under the British, the "Painted Chamber" had become a state prison containing Sayyid Salim of Maskat, and, near it, another old apartment was serving a similar purpose.

Of the fort itself he says: "The defences appear as if a few rounds of grape would level them with the plain: an appearance the reverse of deceitful, the boasted stronghold of the boastful Tālpūr being one of the weakest of the strong looking fortresses in our corner of Asia."

Just outside the fort gate, in an enclosure attached to the houses of the town, is a long grave, 40 feet 6 inches long, which is said to contain the remains of Asābi Pīr, or the Nau Gāz Pīr (the nine-yards saint) who stood that height in his shoes. Such tombs are found all over northern India. Cunningham tells us he has seen upwards of a hundred, varying from 10 to 50 feet long.[1]

[1] Archæological Report, V, 104, 106, and I, 324. *Indian Antiquary*, XXVIII, 28.

SEHWĀN.

THE town of Sehwān is eighty miles north by west from Haidarābād, and is within a mile or so of the Indus, being also close to the Aral, a stream which, coming from the Manchar lake, falls into the Indus at this point. Sehwān and district have been referred to in most old accounts as Siwistān, though it has also gone by the names of Sharūsān, Sadūsān, Sadūstān and Sindūstān.[1] It is, without doubt, a very old place. Cunningham, agreeing with previous writers, identifies Sindomana of the Greek writers with Sehwān, and says: "Of its antiquity there can be no doubt, as the great mound, which was once the citadel, is formed chiefly of ruined buildings, the accumulation of ages, on scarped rock, at the end of the Lakkī range of hills."[2] There does not seem to be much in the way of scarped rock, the mound being chiefly composed of brick debris and earth. Al Idrisi thus describes the place: "Sharusan is remarkable for its size and for the number of its fountains and canals, for the abundance of its productions and for its rich commerce. It is much resorted to."[3] It was to Sehwān that Dalu Rāi's brother departed after the former's shameful overtures to his wife, and there lived in the odour of sanctity until his death. "His tomb is to be found in the city of Sīwān; many people flock to it on Fridays, and place full belief in its powers........When through the tyranny of Dalu Rāi, the river of the town of Alor became dry, the passage of the river of the Panjāb came to be made near Sīwān, and that town, which is still flourishing, became populated."[4] It was captured by Muḥammad Qāsim in A.D. 711, and by Maḥmud of Ghaznī in the beginning of the eleventh century. Ḥumāyun attempted to take it on his flight to Umarkoṭ, but it was subsequently taken by Akbar after a seven months' investment, and was dismantled.

On the north of the town are the remains of the great fort, or the Kāfir Qil'ah as it is generally called by the people, thereby indicating that its origin had no connection with the Muḥammadans. It is, indeed, said to date back to Alexander the Great, and to have been erected by him, but nothing of the

---

[1] McMurdo says it has been sometimes called Baghdād (*Journ. R.A.S.* I, 223).

[2] *Ancient Geography of India*, 264. See also the article on places in Sind by Captain De la Hoste in the *Journ. Bengal. As. Soc.* 1840, p. 913.

[3] Elliot's *History of India*, I, 79.

[4] The *Tārīkh-i-Tāharī*. Elliot's *History*, I, 280.

original walling, or of any subsequent fort, is now discernible upon the surface.[1] Nothing Greek has been found here except an occasional coin. But this only proves that the coin got there, not, necessarily, the Greeks. The nearest approach to such remains was when Burton faked a Greek vase, smashed and buried it in the line of excavation being made by an enthusiastic friend, and only confessed to his trickery in time to prevent a learned disquisition upon the find being published. The fort is now an immense mound of earth, measuring, roughly, 400×200 yards, and about 60 feet high, filled with potsherds, brickbats, broken china, bones, charcoal, ash and ghosts. The retaining walls which were, no doubt, of brick, having disappeared, the rains of countless seasons have washed down and furrowed the sides until it is, now, practically a shapeless and honeycombed mass. In the deeper portions of these fissures parts of brick and mud walls are seen in all positions, but they are too confused and ruinous to make anything of in a casual inspection. They are seen at different levels and probably show the rebuilding of the fort at different periods, one upon the other.

In the bottom of some of these gorges may be found a few of the very old style of Hindū bricks, of extra large size, which must date back to the early centuries of the Christian era. Towards the top are found quantities of large square tiles such as are still made in Sind for flooring and ceiling purposes. The sites of the old entrances to the fort are so obliterated that even traces are hardly to be found except at the south-east corner where the present road ascends. At some period the fort seems to have been raised to about twice its former height, possibly by the Muḥammadans. Upon the top and overlooking the town, is now perched a district bungalow.

At Sehwān are a few old tombs of no particular interest, but that of the saint Shāhbāz is considered of great account locally, as well as all over Sind, by both Muḥammadans as well as Hindūs. The building is profusely decorated with coloured tiles. Lāl Shāhbāz Kalandar *alias* Shaikh Usmān Marwandī was the most revered saint in Sind. He was one of the four saints who, when living, were called the "Four Friends." He arrived at Multān in A.H. 633 (A.D. 1235), and afterwards moved to Sehwān where he spent the rest of his life. He died in A.H. 673 (A.D. 1274). The present mausoleum is a comparatively late erection, having been built by a former governor, Malik Iktiyaru-d-din, about A.D. 1356.[2] It is recorded that Mīrzā Jānī Beg Tarkhān built a larger tomb, to which additions were added by his son, Mīrzā Ghāzī Beg, but it was not completed until A.D. 1639 when Nawāb Dindar Khān paved the courtyard with glazed tiles, and otherwise added to the place. The gate, as also the balustrade round the tomb, are said to have been of hammered silver, the gift, it is believed, of Mīr Karam 'Alī Khān Tālpūr, who also added silver spires to the top of the domes.[3] It is unnecessary to say that these last do not exist now. Sundry coloured cloths cover the tomb, which is further embellished with

[1] "Whenever a tourist of enquiring mind is shewn a ruin about which that venerable humbug, the 'oldest inhabitant,' knows nothing, or will not know anything, he considered himself justified in at once deciding it to be an 'Alexander's Camp.'" (Burton's *Sind Revisited*)

[2] The date is also given as 1340.

[3] *Sind Gazetteer*, 724.

suspended ostrich eggs, or imitations,—a favourite appendage to most Muḥammadan tombs—peacock feathers, beads, flowers, etc. The Indus is subject to the saint's commands, "and no vessel dares to pass his shrine without making a propitiatory offering at his tomb. Thousands of pilgrims flock to the consecrated spot, and the monarchs of Cabool and India have often visited the sanctuary. The drums which proclaim the majesty of the saint are a gift from the renowned persecutor Alla-o-deen, who reigned A.D. 1242; and the gate, which is of silver, attests the homage and devotion of a deceased Ameer of Sinde........The Hindu joins with the Mahommedan in his veneration of the saint, and artfully insinuates 'Lāl' to be a Hindu name, and that the Muhammadans have associated with the faith of their prophet, the god of an infidel creed." So wrote Lieutenant A. Burnes when he visited the shrine in 1831.[1]

"Burton, I think, says somewhere that Hindūs call the shrino at Sewan, known to the Muḥammadans as Lāl Shāhbāz, Rājā Bartārī, which, no doubt represents Bhartriharī, the name of the prince ascetic, and brother of king Vikramāditya, who lived in the last century before the Christian era. Colonel Tod says in his Rājāsthān (I, 776),[2] that Bhatriḥarī is reported to have lived for a time at Sēwan on the Indus, and no doubt the fame of so great a devotee would be wide-spread in Sindh as it was in all northern India."[3]

Burton gives a very interesting and facetious account of his visit to the tomb, which is worth reproducing as it is so full of the atmosphere that surrounds such places, and gives an insight into the every day human side of the saint and his mausoleum. He writes: "This quadrangle, with dome and lantern, is the honoured tomb of Usman-i-Merwandi, popularly called the Kalandar (honoris causa) Lāl Shāhbāz, or the Red Falcon of Merwand, his natal province. He owes his curious ecclesiastical titles solely to his own exertions. Having once sat for a whole year in an iron pot placed upon a broiling fire, to imitate Ibrahim,[4] his skin, when he issued from the place of trial, had, as might be expected, exchanged the pallor of sanctity for a deep rubicund hue. On another occasion he assumed a winged form to rescue a brother in Allah from the stake upon which an infidel king had exalted his venerable form. Hence he is called Lāl Shāhbāz, a name that at once embodies the heads of his exploits, and distinguishes him from his fellows, scarlet hawks being novelties in the animal creation. Heedless of this nonsense, you will probably judge him kindly when you hear that according to history he was a quiet, harmless old gentleman who, very like many a Fellow of Christ Church and Trinity College, preferred single blessedness; became highly moral as he advanced in years, and died, leaving behind him a high reputation as a grammarian, a logician, a philologist and a divine. There are points of difference in the comparison: the Kalandar I fear, was 'Low Church,' and probably never drank crusty old port. Among the Hindus he is Rajah Bhartari.

[1] *Travels into Bokhara*, 2nd Ed., p. 49.

[2] *Annals of Rājāsthān*. He says the "Castle at Sehwān" was Vikrama's.

[3] Haig's *Indus Delta Country*, 71n.

[4] Abraham, being unjustly accused of impiety by his father, Azar the idol-maker, was thrown by the wicked Nimrod into a fiery furnace, which forthwith became a bed of roses. So writes Moslem Holy Writ.

"The Masoleum, one of the Seven Wonders of the Sindian World, for magnitude as well as magnificence, would be a third-rate building in any semi-civilized part of India. In order to view the shrine, we must deposit our slippers at the threshold: then, perhaps, the jingling of a few rupees in our pockets may induce the surly, scowling crowd to open a ready way. Enpassant remark if you please the remains of splendour on the doors: anciently they were plates of massive silver, with gold locks, and hinges; now wood is more extensively used. The interior is dark, dingy, and insufferably close, filled in equal proportions with animal caloric, the fumes of rancid incense, and the heavy smoke of long-wick'd oil-lamps. Under the dome is the holy place, covered with a large satin pall, and hung over with a variety of silken, velvet, brocade and tinsel articles, shaped like your grandmother's pet pincushion or the little hearts which you may see in Southern Europe. The walls, dimly illumined by a ray of light from door or lamp, are garnished with votive offerings of every description: the darkness and the dirt with which antiquity has overspread them almost conceal them from our eyes profane.

"The tomb is surrounded by crowding devotees of all sexes and ages. Many people will travel from Haydarabad, a hundred miles or so, and even from more distant places, for the mundane and post-mundane benefits secured by the pilgrimage. Some are sitting here supplicating His Saintship to intercede for them with Allah, bribing him with promised dainties and rich clothes, which though he wants not, his successors do. That hopeless cripple wishes to take up his bed and walk; the blind beggar is determined to have his eyes opened; the pensive old 'party' with the long beard is praying for the ruin of a favourite enemy, and the wrinkled middle-aged matron for a son and heir. A few grateful hearts are only thanking the good corpse for past benefits, and many in whom the old Adam is, I fear, very strong, are savouring in anticipation the sweets of indulgenza plenaria, license to sin ad libitum. The men in the large turbans, with stolid faces, are the Mullas, or priests; the half-clad attendants are the Mujawirs, whose duty it is to sweep the floor and trim the lamps; the stout ruffian with the shaven head, beard, eyebrows, and moustachios is a promising young mendicant, who has just been affiliated to the order; and the two fellows sitting at the doors in the airy costume now familiar to your eye, and wrangling with every one, male or female, about the nature of his or her offering, are Murshids, or Masters in the mystic brotherhood of beggary. The latter, however, despite their dignity of free and accepted, do not always have their own way. Sometimes a swaggering Beloch, or a formidable-tongued Sindi dame will press in with no other present but a promise, and take place among the throng, seated, bowing and prostrating, groaning, mumbling ejaculating, blessing and cursing one another round the sepulchre. Should we stay here half an hour we are sure to see a kind of fight, if, at least, grabbing of garments and hauling of hair deserves that honoured name, between the collectors of church-money and the votaries of a cheap religion, and unpaid worship"[1]

[1] *Sind Revisited*, Vol. II, 185-193.

THE MIDSTREAM FORT OF BAKHAR.

PLANTED in midstream, between Sakhar and Rōhrī, is a chain of islands, the largest of which is Bakhar, once a fortified stronghold and the head-quarters of a petty government, and, later, of a district under Muḥammadan rule, but now covered with dismantled and forlorn ruins, across which the railway runs between the two sections of the Landsdowne bridge. It is a limestone rock, eight hundred yards from east to west, three hundred wide, and about twenty-five feet high. The walls of the fort, which were double, rose to a height of thirty or thirty-five feet, and were strengthened with numerous bastions. There were two gateways, one facing Rōhrī and the other Sakhar. It was at one time occupied by British troops, after which it was converted into a jail. Lieutenant Alexander Burnes, who visited it in 1831 wrote: "It has no strength in its works, and is formidable only from its position."[1] McMurdo states that it is recorded in the *Tuhfatu-l-Kirām* "that this town did not exist in the time of the Hindu Raj, and that it got its name Bakar ('the dawn') from Saiyid Muhammad Maki, of religious memory, some years after its foundation."[2] In the *Ā'īn-i-Akbarī* we are told "Behkur is a good fort. In ancient books it is called Munsoorah. All the six rivers, before mentioned, pass by it in a collective stream, and afterwards dividing into two, one goes to the south, and the other to the north of the fort. Here is very little rain. The fruits are delicious."[3]

It played an important part in the history of Sind, and was a centre from which many a foraging expedition set out. It was being constantly invested, taken and retaken, as the different factions fought out their quarrels in its vicinity, and it is often mentioned in connection with the important forts of Multān, Uchh, Sehwān and Thaṭhah. Surrounded by the river, it was naturally defended against its enemies, and, being in midstream, its garrison, whenever hardpressed or obliged to evacuate the place, were enabled to choose whichever side of the river suited their movements best. We learn that the fort fell to 'Abdu-r-Razāq, the Wazir of the Sulṭān of Ghaznī, when he invaded Sind in A.D. 1026. One of the most noted of local governors in Sind was Sulṭān Muḥammad Kōkaltāsh, governor of Bakhar, and son of Mīr Fāzil, who was appointed

[1] *Travels into Bokhara*, 2nd Ed., 256. A story of the origin of Bakhar fort is given in an article on "Khyrpoor and Fortress of Bakur" by Captain G. E. Westmacott in the *Journ. As. Soc. Bengal*, IX, Part 2, p. 1197.

[2] *Journ R.A.S.*, I, 225.

[3] Gladwin's translation, II, 112.

to that post by Shāhbeg, and subsequently confirmed in it by the emperor Akbar. He was the son of a Persian father and an Afghān mother, and continued governor of Bakhar for over fifty years. Shāhbeg, on one of his visits to the fort, divided up the ground, inside, into building sites for his chiefs and their families, and put the work in hand. At this time, "The bricks of the ancient fort of Alōr, the old capital of Sind, as well as the materials of the buildings belonging to the Turks and Sammahs, living round the town of Bakhar [on the north bank of the river], were brought and utilised in repairing the fort walls and building houses in it."[1] It was at first resolved to cut and remove the two hills to the south of Bakhar,[2] but, as the river flowed between, it was considered a sufficient protection for the town and so the plan of blasting the hills was abandoned as unnecessary. The repairs of the fort were then immediately taken in hand and finished in the course of one year. Further materials were, later on, carried away to Bakhar from the loot of Uchh when that fortress was razed to the ground by Mīrzā Shāh Ḥasan. It was at Shāhbeg's orders that Sultān Muḥammad, or Maḥmud as he is sometimes called, slew the Dhārejah chiefs one dark night, and pitched their bodies from one of the towers into the river, which was thenceforth called the Khūnīn Būrj or the "Bloody Tower."

Of the nature of the fighting that often took place beneath its walls the following story of an unsuccessful midnight escapade, which occurred in A.D. 1543, will give a lively idea. "Two months after this, Bakhshō Lāngāh collected people of the tribes of Lāngāh, Balōch and Nāhir in a fort near Multān, on the bank opposite Jūnpur, resolved to march against the fort of Bakhar, as he was informed that Shāh Ḥasan had gone to Tattā and all his governors and chiefs had assembled there under him. With that object in view he put his troops in 50 boats and sent them ahead to fall suddenly on the island at night, break open the gates and take it before his arrival. Accordingly these men landed at Bakhar about midnight, on the 15th of Jamādissānī, and set fire to the gate. The garrison, though small, tried their best to check the Lāngāhs. The assailants were at length repulsed and driven back to their boats. Some were burnt in the fire they had kindled and some were drowned in the river and the rest fled away. The next day, about noon, Bakhshō Lāngāh came on beating drums, hoping to see the fort already in the possession of his men. But as soon as he approached, guns and muskets were fired at him from the ramparts of the fort and he was obliged to go to Lōhrī [Rōhrī] where he spent three days and then went back to Multān, after plundering some of the villages in the country."[3]

A Mr. Joseph Salbanke, who journeyed from India through Persia in 1609, and about eight or ten years after the death of Mīr Ma'ṣūm, has written: "*Buckar* stands towards *Lahor*, where we received kind entertainment of the Governor. Sword blades are very good chaffer in this towne: my-self having

---

[1] *Tārīkh-i-Ma'ṣūmī*, translated by Mallet. Nādir Shah is said to have destroyed the works when he invaded Sind.

[2] So in the *Tārīkh-i-Ma'ṣūmī*, the *Tuhfatu-l-Kirām* says to the west of Bakhar.

[3] Fredunbeg's *History of Sind*, Vol. II, 87.

experience, who might have had ten pounds sterling for my sword, the blade being worth a noble in *England*. Close by this citie of *Buckar* runneth the Riuer of *Synde*, which falleth into the Ocean Sea, between the countries of *Gaudel* and *Guzerat*. On the Riuer passe Barkes of fortie and fiftie Tunnes, by means whereof, there is traffique into diuerse parts of *India*. *Sucker* is situated on an Iland [He appears to have mistaken Sakhar for Bakhar] in the Riuer, and consisteth most of Weauers and Diers, which serue the country round about. At *Sucker* we stayed four and twenty days for a safe conuoy to *Candahar*, and passed to *Candahar* in twenty days."[1]

Nicholas Whithington (1612) says: "Goods may be conveyed from *Agra* on camels to *Buckor* in twenty days, which is on *Sinda* Riuer, thence in fifteen days aboard the ships."[2] Sir Thomas Roe couples the names together so, "*Buckar Suckur*" which reminds one of such other names to be found in different parts of India as Ankāi-Tankāi and Rāvala-Jāvala—two pairs of twin forts—a pleasing jingle of similar sounds.

At the time of the arrival of the emperor Humāyun, Maḥmud Khān built an outer enveloping wall to the fort, increasing its circuit to 1875 yards, with four gates opposite those in the inner wall, and with 70 bastions. Enclosed within this were two gardens "Nuzurgah" and "Goozrgah." The fortifications were rebuilt and restored for the last time by the governor Nawāb Ghulām Sādik Khān about 1780-90, in the reign of Taimūr Shāh, to whom Bakhar then belonged. To obtain bricks he broke down the tombs of Pathāns which covered the heights of Sakhar, and reduced them to a complete ruin. Bakhar is one of the few pretty spots on the Indus in its course through Sind.

"The once flourishing city of Bukur contains now [Cir. 1840] only twenty-five houses, and exhibits a deplorable picture of desolation. The British have converted the governor's palace on the east wall into a powder magazine, and the entire area is covered with mounds fifteen or twenty feet high of bricks, the debris of buildings and ordure that have accumulated for ages."[3]

Under the Kalhōrahs the district of Bakhar is mentioned simply as a *tālūka* or petty subdivision. The fort then passed into the hands of the Āmīrs of Khairpūr, from whom it was taken over by the British government when it was required in connection with the building of a bridge of boats across the Indus at this point, resting upon the island midway.

Upon the lower side of the island of Bakhar, and separated from it by a short length of the river, is the pretty little island of Sāt Bēla, or Sādh Bēla, upon which, snugly ensconced in a thick grove of umbrageous trees, is a Hindū religious establishment, the various buildings connected with it being all more or less modern and gaily painted.

Upon the upper side of Bakhar, and joined to it when the river is low, is the compact little island upon which, under the cool shade of some large trees is the famous shrine of Zinda or Jinda Pīr, also known as Khwāju-ka-Thān

[1] Raverty's *Mihrān of Sind*, 494n.
[2] Raverty's *Mihrān of Sind*, 495n.
[3] *Journ. As. Soc. Bengal*, IX (1840), Part 2, 1187, Article by Captain Westmacot.

(Plates LXXV—LXXVII). The island has been raised and protected against the corrosion of the river by retaining walls of strong rubble masonry all around. The great gaṭeway to the enclosure, facing Rōhṛī, is a far more imposing structure than the mean little domed shrine itself, which occupies the centre of the island, and is a remarkably plain square building. The shrine has two doors one on the south, overlaid with silver plate, embossed with figures, and one on the east. In the west wall, opposite the latter, is a niche, in which. behind some miscellaneous draperies, is the *gadi* or seat of Khwājah Khizr, an ancient saint who, instead of departing from this world in the orthodox manner, merely changed his visible form for an invisible one, and continues to reside, in the place.[1] It is claimed on the authority of an inscription upon a slab set in the wall above the niche, that the shrine dates back to A.H. 341 (A.D. 952) (Fig. 25). General Haig translates the inscription thus in his *Indus Delta Country*:

FIG. 25. Inscription in Zinda Pirś shrine.

When this sublime temple (*dargah*) appeared,
Which is surrounded by the waters of Khiẓr,
Khiẓr wrote this in pleasing verse
Its date is found from the Court of God. 341.

The chronogram, he says, thus given in the words درگاه عالي (*Dargah 'Ālī*), gives the date 341.

Major Raverty, who is always very positive and dogmatic in his opinions and a stickler for accuracy, gives the following as a literal translation :[2]

[1] "Khwāja Khizar, *par excellence* the Muhammadanized spirit of the flood........ Khwājā Khizar is mixed up with Mehtar Iliās, the Muḥammadan and oriental form of the prophet Elias of the legends, to be traced in the same capacity in modern Russia. This god, and in some cases goddess, of the flood is traceable all over India even amongst the alien population of Madras." (*Indian Antiquary*, XXXIV, 144.)

"Khizr or Elias, sometimes confused with the prophet, Elias, and said to have been the Wazīr of Kai-Ḳubād, the ruler of Ī-rān Zamīn, is stated to have discovered and to have drank of the fountain of the water of life, and consequently, will not die until the sound of the last trump at the judgment day. Khwājah Khiẓr, for this reason, is also called the Zindah or Living Pir ; and it is out of this that the compiler of the' Gazetteer of Sind', when referring to this island, makes out the shrine to be worshipped by the Hindūs as a river god under the name of Jinda Pir. ....Khwājah Khiẓr is also accounted, in consequence, the patron saint of the waters or rivers, hence Muḥammadans of Hind are in the habit of offering him oblations of lamps and flowers, placed on little rafts, and launched upon the river, particularly on Thursday evenings (the Friday evening of the Musalmans, as the night precedes the day) in the fifth solar month, August. It is at this time that the festival of the *beṛā* or raft is held, when a raft is launched upon the waters in honour of Khwājah Khiẓr." (Raverty's *mihrān of Sind*, 492n.)

[2] But he makes a mistake in saying that the inscription is in a *masjid*, whereas the shrine, in which it is, is really a cenotaph, the *masjid*, alongside, has its own inscription. On the whole, the term "shrine" is best.

Know, that when this fabric was raised,
Khiẓr's waters encompassed it round about,
This pleasing hemistich Khiẓr wrote :—
In the 'Court of God' the date is found

"This, according to the *abjad* system, gives the date 341 H. (952-53 A.D.), which is just two hundred and forty-eight years after the conquest of Sind, and two years previous to the death (but some say it happened in that year) of Abd-ul-Malik, son of Nūḥ, seventh of the Sāmānī rulers, who was killed through falling from his horse while playing the game chaugān or Polo, when the sway of the Khilāfat over Sind was merely nominal, and part of it and Multān were in the possession of Karāmiṭah rulers, subsequently expelled by Sulṭān Maḥmūd of Ghaznih."[1]

In an article published in the *Journal of the Bom. Br. R. A. S.*[2] Mr. Eastwick expressed his opinion that this inscription commemorated a great change in the course of the river from the Alōr to the Rohrī side, and translated the first two lines thus :

When this Court was raised, be it known,
That the waters of Khiẓr surrounded it.

These gentlemen, no doubt, translated the inscription from the original. Mr Yazdani, the officer in charge of the Archæological Survey of H. E. Highness the Nizām's dominions, to whom a paper estampage was submitted, gives the following as its translation :

When this sublime shrine was built.
Which has the spring of Khiẓr in its precincts :
..........wrote in good style.

The chronogram (of the erection of the building) — "Sublime Court." And he appends the following note : "The inscription is in Persian verse, the metre being *Hazaj*. The name of the poet who composed the lines occurs at the beginning of line 2 ; the stone is damaged there and the letters are not distinct.[3] The chronogram *Dargāh 'Ālī* gives the year 341 A.H. (A.D. 952), which may be the date of the death of the saint. The inscription, however, seems to have been set up much later. because the *Nastā'līq* characters, and the style of composing chronograms in Persian verse were not in vogue in India in the fourth century of the Hijra." Mr. Yazdani was, at first, inclined to take the chronogram as *Az Dargah-i-'Āli* giving the year 349, but on further examination of the stampage he dropped the "*Az,*" which brings the date to 341, as shown in the figures on the stone. The upper loop of the figure ۴ does not show on the impression, but its fractured surface is clear upon the stone, as well as the other figures. But the eight years difference in the date is of little moment, what is of more importance is the correct rendering of the rest of the inscription, and the connection it has, if any, with the river. In commenting upon Mr. Eastwick's translation, Mr. Yazdani further remarks : "In his reading of the inscription Mr. Eastwick has upset the order of the hemistichs, and has made

[1] *Mihrān of Sind*, 492n. Mr. Eastwick gives another legend respecting the island of Khwājah Khiẓr or Khwājh kā Thān (*J. B. B. R. A. S.* I, 204).

[2] Vol. I, p. 203 (1843).

[3] It is rather the stampage which is defective owing to the way the stone is built in.

the first hemistich of line 2 as the second hemistich of line 1 and *vice versâ*. Besides, the ں of چوں in the first hemistich of line 1, and ش between تاریخش and از in the second hemistich in line 2 are superfluous and do not exist in the inscription. Mr. Eastwick's reading of the first word of line 2 as کفضر appears to be conjectural because the inscription in its present conditions is damaged there. The reading also makes the line lose its metre."[1]

Eastwick says, that just by the place where Clibborn's house stood, the river is exceedingly deep, and a whirlpool is formed by the opposition which the remains of an ancient building makes to the headlong waters. When the river is low this building can be distinctly seen, and is another proof, and one far more irrefutable than the inscription of K͟hwājah K͟hiẓr, that the stream migrated hither from Alor. Out of all this jumble of facts and fancies it is almost hopeless to arrive at any satisfactory conclusion. The Delphian obscurity of the inscription will remain a puzzle for all time, I fear.

It is doubtful whether the inscription slab is in its original position. It most certainly does not belong to the present building; or, rather, the present building was never erected so far back as the inscription would lead us to suppose. That it is intended to give that false idea is evident from the story that the *pīr* did not die but is still living though invisible. It could not, therefore, record the date of his death. The shrine is a mean little structure of comparatively recent date, and the slab has been inserted in a very clumsy fashion.

Flanking the niche are two common mirrors let into the wall. The domical ceiling, within, is painted, but it has been much blackened by the smoke of an oil lamp which is kept burning at night to keep the *pīr* company. The two leaves of the front or south door are overlaid with thin silver plate, worked over with some coarsely executed *repoussé* ornament in which a tiger, in relief, adorns the two central panels (Plate LXXVII).

At a little distance to the south-west of this shrine is an old ruined brick masjid, decorated with enamelled tiles, and containing an inscribed slab which, as it again refers to K͟hiẓr's spring, I give in full as translated by Mr. Yazdani :

> The great K͟hān, Sa'īd K͟hān, who in the world
> Is the ocean of munificence and the cloud of generosity ;
> One of the attendants of his court,
> Who is a loyal servant, of laudable qualities,
> Built this ambergris-scented mosque
> Which is auspicious like the Ka'ba.
> The purity of its water and air, waiving ceremony,
> Has made it a garden of the gardens of *Iram* (Paradise).
> The pen of Providence with the water of K͟hiẓr's spring (the fountain of immortality).
> Wrote—*Rauza*—as the chronogram of the erection of the building.

The chronogram, he says, gives the year A.H. 1011 (A.D. 1602). He says the inscription is in Persian verse, the metre being *Ramal*. The style of writing is *Nastā'līq*

[1] See Mr. Eastwick's article on Allore and Rohri in the *Journ. Bom. Br. R. A. S.* Vol. I, pp. 203-4.

of a very fine type. Another translation reads the name of the builder as Khān Sayyid 'Alī Khān, since it is written Khān 'Alī Sayyid Khān in the inscription, but Mr. Yazdani transcribes it "'Ālī", meaning "great" or "noble". This mosque, therefore, was built about the time Mīr Ma'ṣūm was building in Sakhar.

The other buildings on the island are poor modern structures of no interest; but the great gateway of brickwork, facing the south, decorated with tiles, is rather imposing. The tile work is, however, for the most part, poor late work, the best being that immediately around the doorway on the outside, which is of the same style as that on the old ruined *masjid* near the tomb of Mīr 'Abdu-l-Bāqī Pūrānī at Sakhar, and which is probably of about the same date as the tomb, namely A.H. 1019. The later-looking tile work is very similar to that on the Alamgir mosque at Alōr, of about a hundred years later. A thorough examination of the island, its retaining walls and buildings, failed to reveal any vestige of anything older. There used to be a great annual fair on the island, attended by both Musalmāns and Hindūs, but the two communities having quarrelled, it has fallen off considerably. The latter betook themselves to the Sakhar shore, where they established another "Jind Pir" of their own, though not, in this case, as a Muḥammadan saint but as a river god.

The old story of a maid and a powerful but unwelcome admirer is told in connection with this shrine. A merchant, "by name Shāh Ḥusain [Saifu-l-Mulūk, according to Raverty], was, with his daughter [handmaid, Bad'u-l-Jamāl: Raverty], travelling down the Indus by boat on his way to Makka. On his arrival at the city of Aror, Dalu Rāi [Dilū Rā'e: Raverty] the Hindū king of that country,[1] who had heard of the great beauty of Shāh Ḥusain's daughter demanded her in marriage, but was met with a refusal on the plea that it was impossible for a daughter of the Prophet to wed with a Hindū. Not content with this reply, the king determined to carry her off by force, but on the girl offering up prayers to Khwājā Khiẓr, she was answered by the saint, who directed the father to unloose the boat. As soon as this was done the course of the Indus changed, and the stream began to flow towards Rōhrī, whither also the boat was carried in safety. In gratitude for this miraculous deliverance, Shāh Ḥusain resolved to erect a shrine in honour of the saint who had thus befriended them; and, in answer to his prayer, he was directed to carry out his purpose on a small island a little to the north of Bakhar, and here the father built a mosque and tomb, which in after years was enlarged by wealthy votaries, who are said to have covered the door of the original tomb with sheets of silver."[2] This story probably induced Mr. Eastwick to think that the inscription in the shrine referred to the change in the river's course in A.H. 341.

What is evidently the same story is thus told in the *Tufatu-l-Kirām*: "It was also in the reign of one of these Sūmrah princes that Dalūrāi, a descendant of the Hindū king of the same name, who was the founder of Dalūr or Alōr, imitated the ruling Sūmrah princes of his own time in immoral behaviour by

---

[1] This occurred after the death of Muḥammad Qāsim, and before the rule of the Sūmrahs, when parts of Sind had thrown off the Arab yoke and were for a time once more under Hindū rule.

[2] Sind Gazetteer, p. 681. A full account of this is given in Raverty's *Mihran of Sind* 482, *et seq.*

attempting to seize Badīul Jamāl the beloved wife of Saifū'l Mulūk, a princely merchant travelling through his city and brought down the wrath of God that reduced the ancient towns of Alor and Bhanbra (or Brahmanābād) to ruins."[1] If these are two versions of the same story, Dalu Rāi, being a Sūmṛah prince, or even living in the time of a Sūmṛah prince, could hardly be placed in A.H. 341. If the story were true, and the diversion were caused by the merchant and his sympathisers placing some obstruction in the bed of the river, Raverty thinks it was not an impossible or difficult task to accomplish, owing to the loose soft soil of that part of the country north-west of Alōr. Burton says:[2] "The province is a sloping surface of silt and sand, through which the Indus cuts its varying way with a facility that passes description. The erection of even a few feet of brickwork built up in the bed of the Indus as it still flows, might divert the stream into another channel, cause the decline and downfall of a metropolis and twenty towns," etc. Whenever it was that this diversion took place, Raverty thinks that, in the first instance, it cut its way down into Sind some distance to the west of Sakhar, and, subsequently, veering more towards the east, forced its way between the positions afterwards occupied by Rōhrī and Bakhar fort. Finally it cut a loop around the north of Bakhar fort converting that place into an island.[3] So, if the inscription refers to the movements of the river at all, there are three different changes, at different periods, to connect it with. Some portion of the main river, after its diversion to the west, continued to flow, at the times of inundation, through the old bed of the Hakṛāh which was afterwards known as the Nārā.

Lieutenant Alexander Burnes, speaking of the "pulla" fish, for which the Indus is celebrated, says they never go higher than the fortress of Bakhar. "The natives superstitiously believe the fish to proceed there on account of Khaju Khiẓr, a saint of celebrity, who is interred at that town, from whence they are said to return without ever turning their tails on the sanctified spot,—an assertion which the muddy colour of the Indus will prevent being contradicted."[4]

---

[1] Fredunbeg's *History of Sind*, II, 37.
[2] *Sind and the Races*, etc. I, 202.
[3] *Mihrān of Sind*, 487-9.
[4] *Travels into Bokhara*, 2nd Ed., 1835. p. 34.

SAKHAR.

BETWEEN Sakhar and Rōhrī, in the north of Sind, the ever restless Indus seems to have found a fairly stable bed as it flows between the rocks which hem it in. As already pointed out, it was not always so; for, if we believe the traditions of the country and study the traces of the old waterways, it would appear that, not so long ago, as the Mihrān of Sind, it turned south before it reached Rōhrī, or, rather, the position Rōhrī afterwards occupied, and flowed past the old walls of Alōr, the old Hindū capital, into the alluvial plains beyond, where its vagaries may be followed by its old dried-up beds and the ruins of towns and villages in its course. Between the two towns, a fine cantilever railway bridge now spans its swiftly flowing waters. Along the river face on the Sakhar, or north side, runs an embankment and esplanade, nearly two miles in length, which always presents a very busy spectacle on account of the number of river craft loading and unloading along its bank. It is in strong contrast with the deserted looking bank opposite, which skirts the sleepy little town of Rōhrī.

Raverty tells us that such a place as Sakhar is not mentioned in history down to the time of the Sayyid, Mīr Maʿṣūm, styled Bakharī because he was a native of the Bakhar district.[1] It is not mentioned in the *Āʿin-i-Akbarī*, although Bakhar, Rōhrī and Arōr are. He thinks Sakhar was originally Bakhar before the latter town had been separated from the fort by the river. He has no idea of what the name Sakhar means, but Elliot ventures the meaning "embankment," and says it is better known to the inhabitants as Chipri-bandar. In my account of Bakhar I have suggested that the names Sakhar-Bakhar are simply a catching repetition of sound, which is often found in the names of two equally important places in close proximity to, or over against one another. The Hindū is very fond of this, and often carries it into his ordinary talk as well, such as *katcha batcha*, "young child."

The remains at Sakhar are neither many nor of much importance architecturally, but they have an interest of their own (Plates LXXVIII—LXXXII). The most conspicuous feature in the landscape is the tall *minār* of Mīr Maʿṣūm which, compared with the elegant one at Daulatābād, those at Ahmadābād, or the grander one at Delhi, is but a poor specimen of its kind. Its dropsical proportions, and uncertain undulating outline suggest putty or dough as the material of its construction rather than brick and mortar. Its lantern top,

---

[1] *Mihrān of Sind*, 492.

surrounded with an iron cage, makes it look more like an antiquated light-house perambulating through the country. Like the grille around the top of the Monument, this barred grating has been added by a solicitous municipality to induce people to go back by the way they came — the more convenient spiral staircase which winds down the centre of the *minār* — than to try short cuts from the top. It rises to a height of about a hundred feet, is eighty-four feet in circumference at the base, and is somewhat out of the perpendicular. It is said to have been commenced by Mīr Ma'ṣūm in A.H. 1003 (A.D. 1594), and finished by his son, Mīr Buzurg Manwar in A.H. 1027 (A.D. 1618). Over the door is an inscription which gives the date A.H. 1003 (A.D. 1594). The inscription reads :

> " This minaret was built in the time of the emperor
> Jalālu-d-Dīn Muḥammad Akbar Bādshāhi Ghāzī.
> Muḥammad Mā'ṣūm, who is the full moon of the high heaven,
> Who is (still) famous in the world for his good name,
> Erected this lofty minaret, on account whereof
> The blue heaven raised its head (or, It raised its head to the blue heaven)
> From the 'Arash,[1] the angels said about the date of its erection :
> ' That it is a famous Jahan Numa overlooking the whole world.'[2]
> Mīr Ma'ṣūm, who is highly dignified,
> Whose devotions are more holy than the law itself,
> Built this minaret in order that the people may say
> That it is in memory of the former ones [or, it is verily a monument for future generations: Yazdani].
> The old heaven said in response to its date, ' that it is a leg (or, support) of the great 'Arash.'[3]
> The composer of these verses is Sayyid Mīr Buzurg *bin*
> Mīr Muḥammad Mā'ṣūm.

Burton, describing the view from the top of this minaret says : " Particularly attractive is the view when seen at the morning hour. The sun slowly tops ' Fort Victoria on the Indus,' the new and all unknown name for Bakar, and washes with crimson the opposite part of the brown stream ; the airy depths sparkle with blue ; light mists cling to the wooded lowlands, giving a charm of indistinctness to the distant prospect, and the foreground is fawny as the Arabian desert. The first smile lights up the little archipelago of islets and holms, crowned with forts and ruins, and lends of glory not their own to the mausoleum of Adam Shah Kalhora ; to the various idgahs which crown the heights, and the adobe-built dead-walls of Rōhrī, based upon its plateau of shining-white nummulitic limestone. The general contrast between the features that stand out in the horizontal beams, and those about which the purple shades of dawn still linger, is as striking as any modern lover of landscape can desire."[4]

---

[1] The ninth heaven wherein is the throne of God.

[2] Or, according to Mr. Yazdani, " Nāmū's *minār* overlooks the Universe." These words indicate the date A.H. 1003 (A.D. 1594).

[3] These words also indicate the date A.H. 1003.

[4] *Sind Revisited.*

Under the shadow of the *mīnār* rest the remains of Mīr Muḥammad Ma'ṣūm Shāh, his father, and other members of his family, the Ma'ṣūmī Sayyids (Plate LXXIX). Over the graves are open canopies supported upon square, flat and octagonal stone pillars whose shafts are covered with Persian writing in relief and other ornamental tracery. Mīr Ma'ṣūm's grave is dated A.H. 1014 (A.D. 1605-6), and that of Mīr Ṣafā'ī, his father, which has several inscriptions, bears the date A.H. 991 (A.D. 1583). These buildings are in no way remarkable for their architectural features.

The inscription on the tomb of Mīr Ma'ṣūm runs as follows :—

Mīr Ma'ṣūm who is the moon of the noble constellation,
Is the sun of the Muḥammadan law and religion, and the glory of the universe.
He went to paradise on Friday, the sixth of Zi'l Ḥijj.
By order of God, who is the most glorious.
I consulted my mind regarding the year of his death,
It said that 'he was a famous master on the region of speech' [1] [poetry].
[Or, Nāmī was the lord of the kingdom of letters : Yazdani.]

This chronogram gives the date of his death, A.H. 1014 (A.D. 1605).

On the tomb of Sayyid Ṣafā'ī is the following inscription :

Sayyid Ṣafā'i is the moon of the Quraish tribe.
Heaven hoisted the flag of his light.
He suddenly left this world and went to the other.
Nāmī (name of a poet), in regard to the date of his death,
Said : 'May his tomb be filled with lights.'

Between Mīr Ma'ṣūm's grave and the base of the minaret is a domed octagonal building, apparently intended as a rest-house, which was built in A.H. 1004 (Plate LXXVIII). It has four arched entrances, those on the east and west having a cut-stone ornamental balconied window above each of them. It is built of brick and is decorated with coloured tiles. About fourteen feet from the floor, inside, is a gallery running round the walls, above which is an inscription consisting of extracts from the Qurān with a verse containing the date in a chronogram. There are also others over the small balconies. The verse reads :

This edifice is so magnificent and famous that
Its dignity has induced the heaven to become liberal.
As it has been the abode of liberality,
Its date is indicated by the expression 'Abode of liberality.'

Mīr Ma'ṣūm, who was born at Bakhar, and who assumed the poetical title of "Nāmī," the son of Ṣafāī Ḥusainī, was the writer of the history of Sind called after him the *Tārīkh Ma'ṣūmi*, which he compiled about A.H. 1009 (A.D. 1600). He wrote it for the instruction and improvement of his son, Mīr Buzurg, in order that "by reading it he might learn what good men of old did ; that he might discriminate between right and wrong ; between that which is useful and the reverse, and might learn to follow the paths of virtuous men."[2] His grandfather, Sayyid Mīr Kalān, took part in bringing about a reconciliation

[1] These words give the date A.H. 991 (A.D. 1583).

[2] Elliot's *History of India*, I, 213.

between the rival claimants for Sehwān when that fort was handed over to Mīrzā 'Īsa Khān, and Mīr Ma'ṣūm, himself, took part in a later attack upon the same fort in the time of Mīrzā Jānī Beg. On the occasion of a visit which he made to the emperor Akbar, in A.H. 999, the latter granted him the *parganahs* of Darbelah, Kākrī and Chāndikō in *jāgir*. He is credited with having possessed the philosopher's stone, which he threw into the river to avoid giving it to the emperor who had cast envious eyes upon it. "Mīr Ma'ṣūm founded many buildings, both here and at Rūṛhī, indeed, the founding of *masjids* and religious buildings may be said to have been his hobby; and, moreover, 'he ornamented them with his own designs in stone; for, in making chronograms and cutting inscriptions, he had no equal, and also in the elegance of his letters. When he accompanied the embassy to Persia, at every prominent stage, all the way from Hind to Tabrīz and Iṣfahān, he recorded the fact on the *masjids* and other buildings. The inscriptions over the gateway of the fort of Agrā are his work, and also those of the *Jāmi' Masjid* of Fatḥ-pūr, and other places.'"[1]

Approaching Sakhar by rail from the west, the hill, crowned with Adam Shāh's tomb, is passed on the right, but the buildings which surmount it look much better from a distance than at close quarters, being plain uninteresting structures having no architectural pretensions. The plain plastered exteriors are relieved by a few solitary bands of coloured tiles of very inferior make and colouring. Upon some of these is used a dirty brownish purple which is not found at Ṭhaṭhah, Haidarābād or Khudābād; it is muddy looking and uneven, and the general colouring of the tiles is coarse, the patterns being large and clumsily drawn.

Adam Shāh was an early Kalhōrah saint and freebooter who, about the middle of the sixteenth century, during one of his incursions into north-western Sind, was taken prisoner to Multān where he was put to death. His body was brought back by one of his followers, Aghā Shāh Muḥammad, Kotwāl of Multān, and was interred on the top of the hill at Sakhar. Another account says he went of his own account to Multān to pay a visit to Lāl Isāi, a celebrated saint, where a large number of disciples joined him, thus exciting the jealousy of the ruler of Multān who had him killed. He thus became a *shā'īd* or martyr, and became entitled to be remembered as a *pīr* or saint. He had been granted the *zamindarī* of Chāndūkah by the imperial government, through the instrumentality of Nawāb Khān Khānān who had come to Sakhar to pay his respects to the Miān and obtain his blessing. Two other graves on the hill are those of Jām Fīruz, the Tālpūr *faqīr*, who died in A.D. 1800, and Mast, son of Zinda, *faqīr* of the tribe of Joyah, who died in A.D. 1658.

Upon the plain, to the south-west of the Collector's house, is a small group of ruins, the principal building of which is the tomb of Mīr 'Abd-l-Bāqī Pūrānī; an inscription upon it runs as follows:

> Mīr 'Abdu-l-Bāqī Pūrānī, the Quṭb, who was the chief (*Lit.* model or pattern) of the descendants of the Prophet, the cream of the chosen people of God. Shaikh Qāzī Shāh

---

[1] Raverty's *Mihrān of Sind*, 493n. See also the *Ā'īn-i-Akbarī* (Blochmann), Vol. I, p. 514.

Muḥammad composed the chronogram of his death; 'Alas! Mīr 'Abdu-l-Bāqī Pūrāni gave his life.' 3rd of the month of Ramaẓān, night of Saturday, A.H. 1019 (A.D. 1610).

Close beside it on the west, the intervening space being crowded with graves, are the walls of two ruined buildings, probably both mosques, upon which still remain large areas of coloured tile work in designs and combinations of tints very different in their treatment to what is found in other parts of Sind (Plates LXXX and LXXXI). What makes this difference is the free use of plain unglazed brick or terra-cotta surfaces, alternating with the coloured tile work, and this produces a soft subdued tone to the whole which is distinctly pleasing. These ruined remains were in such a dilapidated condition when the drawings were made, which are reproduced in my volume on the Sind Tiles, that it is likely very little now remains at the time of writing this, many years later.

Near the river, and just below the reservoir on the hill above, is an enclosure in which are two small buildings, one an octagonal domed structure, and the other, before it, a mosque. These have been converted into residences by the insertion of glazed windows and doors, but they were originally built, as we are told by the inscriptions upon them, by Mīr Ma'ṣūm as a rest-house and place of prayer for the Muḥammadans. Lest the rest-house should be appropriated by any one as a convenient mausoleum, he invokes, in an inscription upon it, the curse of God's wrath upon him who should bury a body within it. Its general plan and design would have tempted many a Muḥammadan to have so used it had it not been for the curse. It is dated A.H. 1007 (A.D. 1598). The *masjid* has an inscription dated A.H. 1006, and refers to a pleasure house and the garden of Iram. Possibly these buildings were erected within a garden set apart for pleasure and recreation.

In old Sakhar, which is to the east of the new town, is the tomb of Shāh Khairu-d-dīn, whose bright blue enamelled dome, surmounted by a lantern, stands out conspicuously from the mass of buildings by which it is surrounded. Its gaily decorated façade and dome are the work of Sindhi tile-makers of some forty years ago, and its scheme of colour is after that on the Tālpūr tombs at Haidarābād. The setting of the tiles is, however, badly managed, when compared with that on the latter buildings, the joints being more obtrusive and the lines of the design are not always kept straight and true. Shāh Khairu-d-dīn is said to have been born at Baghdād in A.H. 898, and to have died at Sakhar in A.H. 1027 (A.D. 1492-1618), which is very improbable. He spent his youth in religious studies at Baghdād, visited Makka and Medina, and then journeyed through Arabia and India, settling down eventually at Sakhar as a religious teacher. His tomb was built between A.H. 1165 and 1174 (Plate LXXXII).

Sakhar appears to have had many other old buildings, the ruins of which have been cleared away for municipal and other improvements. Fragments of some still remain perched upon the rocks around, where they are fast crumbling away.

RŌHRĪ.

RŌHRĪ, or Lōhrī,[1] stands upon elevated ground on the opposite, or south side, of the river from Sakhar. Unlike busy Sakhar, it has a sleepy old world air about it, there being little or no external trade to speak of. The river craft glide past it with the current to unload at Sakhar on the other side. Its streets are narrow and tortuous, and its houses are closely packed upon its hilly site. It has no river face like that of its neighbour, except its ruined walls and bastions, and a few narrow passages leading down steep declivities or stairs, between the tall houses on either side, some of which overhang the river, to a few dirty *ghāts* where the washing of skins and clothes is the only visible sign of occupation. To the south and south-west are several rocky hills upon which are outlying parts of the town, old tombs, offices, and the railway station, but many of them are being slowly levelled by contractors in search of ballast, for the line. With the thick groves of palms along the river, below the town, these rugged hills, surmounted with old ruins, and backed by the river and bridge, present a very pleasing and picturesque aspect.

It is an old place, and signs of its antiquity are found in and around the town. The Sind Gazetteer states that it was founded in A.H. 698 (A.D. 1298) by Sayyid Ruknu-d-dīn, but who this person was is not very clear.[2] Captain Westmacott writes: "He [Sulṭān Maḥmud of Bakhar] died in 980[3] while Meer Eesa of the Turkhanee tribe from Thutta was besieging the fort. In the same year Sadood-deen, Son of Meran, of the lineage of Moohummud Mukaee Kuguree, was chief of the Suyuds of Bukur, amounting to seventeen hundred families. They had suffered great inconvenience and privations during the siege, and

---

[1] Burton says: "Rohri, which the people still call Lohri, is derived from the name of some fisherman; we find the word in other parts of Sind, notably in Ibn Batuta's 'Lahari' (A.D. 1333), and in Captain Hamilton's 'Larribundar' afterwards called 'Lowry Bundar.' According to the oldest authorities, its ancient name was Loharkot." (*Sind Revisited.*)

Raverty thinks Rohri, or as he spells it "Rūṛhi," to be derived from the Sanskrit रुढ, *rūḍh*, rough, stiff, rugged, hard, etc., but why he should think the Muḥammadans would resort to a Sanskrit root he does not say. He does not agree with Cunningham's derivation, and points out that it is not written Rori, as his derivation would require, but Rūḥri.

[2] There was a Shaikh Ruknu-d-dīn, son of Shaikh Sadru-d-dīn and grandson of the celebrated Multān saint Shaikh Bahau-d-dīn, who was in Multān in A.H. 696 (A.D. 1296), and who, in A.H. 728 (A.D. 1327), successfully interceded for the lives of the people of Multān. Then there was Malik Ruknu-d-dīn, who, during the reign of the emperor Firuz Shāh, in A.H. 752 (A.D. 1351), was, at Bakhar, appointed agent or lieutenant for Sind with the title of Ikhlās Khān.

[3] Fredunbeg says 982 (A.D. 1574).

determined with the consent of their superior to abandon the fort. They accordingly settled on the east bank of the river on the Lohuree hills, a little to the south of Bukur, and founded the city called, after the hills, Lohree, improperly Roree."[1]

Upon one of the hills, whose base is washed by the river, is a levelled platform or terrace upon which is a great number of graves, most of them having carved gravestones after the fashion of those on the Maklī hill at Ṭhaṭhah, with chain ornament around panels of ornamental extracts from the Qurān (Plates LXXXIII—LXXXV). The whole top, between the graves, has been paved, and a flight of steps leads up to it on the south side. Some of the tombstones have been placed upon high platforms or plinths, upon each of the four corners of some of which rises a little stumpy ill-shaped *minār*, which, from a distance, looks like a conical chimney-pot. Both they and the platforms are covered with enamelled tiles. Upon a high platform, at the extreme end, is a tombstone, in no way differing in style from many others dated from A.H. 1018, which Mr. Eastwick says is dated in its chronogram in A.H. 384[2] (A.D. 994). But he seems to have used only half the chronogram in his computation. The inscription, as translated by Mr. Yazdani, runs as follows :—

> The Mīr of noble descent, Ma'du-d-dīn,
> Who was expert and unequalled in every art,
> His heart became sick of this world,
> (And) he made Paradise his abode.
> When I asked my heart the date of his demise, it said
> "The pious Mīr entered Paradise."

The chronogram is thus contained in the words شد بفر دوس میر صاحب دل Eastwick calculated it from میر onwards. He transcribes the second word in this line as الفر whereas Mr. Yazdani makes it بفر, which would make the date 1070. Mr. Eastwick thus considers that this date helps to support the island inscription of 341 as the date of the diversion of the river, when "the population of Allore began to migrate to Rohri, and among them probably came the family of Seyuds, on the tomb of one of whom appears a date only fifty years subsequent to that of the Masjid of Khwāja Khizr." The earliest dated inscription on the terrace is dated in A.H. 1018 (A.D. 1609) and they run on to 1070 (A.D. 1659), when there is a gap until A.H. 1306 (A.D. 1888). The grave dated 1018 seems to be the most important one, as it, alone, is honoured with a lamp and lamp-post, which stands before it. It is the resting place of Mīr Abu-l-Qāsim. There is another Abu-l-Qāsim, buried on the hill, with the date A.H. 1045 (A.D. 1635).

In order to form the general flat surface on the top of the hill, which is steeply scarped all around, retaining walls have been built round the edge, and the intervening depressions have been filled up with masonry. In the masonry, upon the south side, is a suite of shallow rooms, connected together by a long passage, partly cut from the rock, which is occupied by the *mujāwars*,

---

[1] *Journal As. Soc. Bengal*, IX, Part 2, 1202.

[2] This should be 385, for he has, by mistake, calculated ح as 7 instead of 8.

or caretakers, and their families. The exterior of the walls has been decorated with enamelled tiles. These chambers are said to have been occupied, at one time, by seven virgin sisters—hence the name "Sātbhāin" which has been given to the place—who had shut themselves up here for life under a vow never to look upon the face of a man. Since their only light and air were obtained through partly stuffed-up little windows, beneath which man roamed at will, it is more than doubtful whether they were able to keep to their undertaking. The rooms, when I saw them—the women, for the time, being shut up in one of them, with a door not without a few useful chinks—are small dirty places with an ugly and untidy mud annexe. From certain points the hill is very picturesque, and forms a favourite subject for amateur sketchers. The place is, I believe, more correctly known as the *Thān* Qāsim Shāh, or place of interment of Mīr Qāsim Shāh Sabzwaris.

Scattered about in the town are several old *masjids*, more or less decorated with coloured tiles, but none of any special merit or interest. Among them are the tomb of Sayyid Sulṭān Faqīr, near the railway station, dated A.H. 1116; the Qāziān Masjid built by Muḥammad 'Umar in A.H. 1114; the Jāmi' Masjid, a heavy massive brick building with three domes and covered with coloured tiles, built by a military officer, Fatḥ Khān in A.H. 992, during the reign of Akbar; the Dīn Panāh Masjid, built in A.H. 1096, during Alamgir's reign, by Khwājah Muḥammad Ḥusain; another Qāziān Masjid, near the end of the Lansdowne bridge, built during Alamgir's time by Amīnu-d-dīn Ḥusain in A.H. 1062, as given in a chronogram; a *masjid* built by Shaikh Muḥammad in A.H. 1110, during Aurangzib's time; the *'īdgāh* on the hill to the south-west of the town, built by Mīr Ma'ṣūm, son of Sayyid Ṣafāī in A.H. 1002, and recently enlarged; Khwājah Sālih's mosque, built in A.H. 1122, and the Wār or Wāl Mubārak.

The Wār Mubārak was erected about A.H. 952 (A.D. 1545) by Mīr Muḥammad as a shrine for a hair of the Prophet, which is said to have been brought to Rōhrī by one Makdūm 'Abdū-l-Bāqī of Stāmbul. Once a year the relic is exposed to view to the Faithful.[1] "The hair, to which miraculous properties are ascribed by the faithful, is in amber, which again is enclosed in a gold case set with rubies and emeralds, the gift of Mīr Ali Murad of Khairpur. The precious relic is exposed to view in the month of March of each year,[2] when the hair is made by some mechanical process to rise and fall, a fact which the devotees are led to believe proceeds from supernatural agency."[3] The building, about twenty-five feet square, is in no way remarkable, except, perhaps, for its insignificant appearance.

Burton, in his *Sind Revisited*, thus describes a visit he paid to the shrine: "A rupee being well spent, we repair to the Shrine of the Holy Hair, which is

[1] Others declare that the relic, which was originally preserved by Umm Salma, was in the possession of a widow who, though intending it for Bokhāra, consented to deposit it at Rōhri. (Burton.)

[2] As the Muhammadan year is not of the same length as the Christian year, but is always advancing on the latter, this annual ceremony must be a moveable feast with regard to the latter, and cannot always occur in March. H. C.

[3] Sind Gazetteer, 680.

committed to the green robed Pir-Bakhsh Abdel-Sattar. Opposite the little room sit, in awe-struck reverence, a dozen Burka wearers, with latticed faces, and long dirty-white robes hiding their charms from head to heel. The same ceremony of peeling off some fourteen cloths, and at last we reach an etui, shaped somewhat like a short Persian inkstand; gold studded with rubies and emeralds, the gift of the Bahawalpur chief, as well as the silver-legged cot which supports it. Inside a leaf-shaped cover, also of gold, conceals the tube, formed like the segment of a small candle, and studded with fourteen rows of rubies: from its top projects the Holy Hair. The appearance of this "War Mubarak" is greeted with a murmur of profoundest reverence, especially by the women: to our Western eyes, it is mightily like a light-coloured bristle. When I first saw it, Sir, the colour was certainly darker and the length was greater; a sceptic suggested that the change is due to the insolvency and general ruin of the no longer 'Sublime Porte,' and of the anything but 'Grand Turk.' We know that the beard of the apostle of Allah was black, and we have, I have told you, a distinct tradition concerning its maximum length; we pay the fee and we go our ways."

Outside the town to the south-west, and just below the railway station, are the ruins of a very large mosque and enclosed courtyard, with a quantity of old tile work adhering to the building, but the ruin is too far advanced to make it worthy of any special care.

Mr. Joseph Salbanke, about 1609, wrote: "*Reuree* is a town consisting of husbandmen and painfull people, who deal also in merchandize, as cotton cloth, indicc, and other commodities, and are a peaceable people to deal withall."[1]

[1] Raverty's *Mihrān of Sind*, 494n.

LĀRKHĀNĀ.

LĀRKHĀNĀ, or Lārkhānāh, to the west of the Indus, is about forty-two miles in a straight line west by south of Sakhar, upon the North-Western Railway line. It is now the head-quarters of a district. In a garden, on the north bank of the Ghār canal, is the tomb of Shāh Bahāro, or Bahārah, who held a military command under Nūr Muḥammad Kalhōrah, and who died in A.H. 1148 (A.D. 1735-6). He is credited with having excavated several canals and built some forts. The tomb is not of much account except that it has a well-carved wooden door and an ornamental lantern which surmounts the dome. The lantern is a very unusual but pleasant feature, which improves the appearance of these rather heavy-looking segmental domes (Plate I, Frontispiece). It is only found, and that in a few cases only, in this part of Sind. Other instances of it are the three Thahīm tombs on the Drākan-Rotadero road and the tomb of Nūr Muḥammad Khān near Moro. Being octagonal in shape and overlaid with coloured enamelled tiles, it has much the appearance of a Japanese lantern. The great door is a very good specimen of wood carving. It is, as usual, in two leaves, each divided by ribs into ten panels, each panel being filled with raised floral patterns (Plates LXXXVI and LXXXVII). Carved borders run round the frames, while over the door, is a beautifully perforated arched light, which reminds one of similar work at Bijāpūr. Here we have in the spandrils, reproduced in carved wood, a design in foliated work similar in treatment to what is found elsewhere in Sind carried out in enamelled tiles. The woodwork is now rotting and falling to pieces.

Inside the building are some Persian inscriptions, in glazed tiles, which, translated, run :—

> The wonderful tower under heaven
> Is formed beauteously like the Pleiades.
> It seems like spring (when we) look at it.
> The world says that it is a pleasant paradise ;
> Its master's name was Shāh Bahār,
> Who planted in the world nothing but good deeds.
> When we enquired about its date they said :
> One thousand, one hundred and eighty-eight.
> The tower of Shāh Bahār. How benevolent and virtuous he was !
> The writer wrote on a slab all about his liberalities and good qualities.
> His servant, " Hut," enquired about the date when it was built.
> Then " Hatef " said that it is indeed " The esteemed paradise."
> This chronogram gives the date 1188.[1]

[1] Archæological Survey of Western India Memo. No. 8, p. 11.

This mausoleum is said to have been erected to his memory by Ghulām Shāh Kalhōrah in A.H. 1188 (A.D. 1774). There was a Bahār Shāh Faqīr who served under Nūr Muḥammad and Ghulām Shāh; and we are told that he was alive in A.H. 1158, when he led an expedition against the Hindūs of Kachh who had penetrated into Sind.[1] The *Faqīrs* were adherents of the Kalhōrah

FIG. 26.—Nūr Muḥammad's tomb near Moro.

chief, and, on several occasions, rendered him valuable military services.

Lārkhānāh has been called the "Eden of Sind." This, surely, could not have been applied to the town and its immediate surroundings, which is one of the dustiest places in the province. It is an Eden one would gladly quit in order to breathe pure fresh air again. But the epithet was probably meant to apply to the country around, which is exceptionally well wooded. In any case, an "Eden of Sind," to any one who knows the country, does not imply much. Captain Wood, who passed through it in 1837, calls it "a rambling-built town, situated in a date-grove, on the banks of a fine canal."

[1] Fredunbeg's *History of Sind*, Vol. II, p. 150.

K̲HUDĀBĀD.

THERE are two K̲hudābāds which are apt to be confused the one with the other, one of which is about two miles from New Hālā, which was the chief seat of the Tālpūr chiefs of Sind before they shifted to Haidarābād, and where several of them have been interred; and K̲hudābād upon the railway, between Sehwān and Dādū, about seven miles south of the latter place. It is the remains at the latter place that I am now describing. It was for some time the capital of the Kalhōrahs, whence they moved, first to Muḥammadābād and then to Allahābād—two newly established towns—and finally settled down at Haidarābād, It was the head-quarters of Miān Nūr Muḥammad, and it was a large town when the Miān's court was there; but it soon sank into insignificance, as all these mushroom towns did when the court abandoned them. It is now an extensive area covered with the ruins of its unsubstantial buildings. The *Tuḥfatu-l-Kirām* speaks of Miān Muḥammad Sarafrāz K̲hān, after the death of his father, G̲hulām S̲hāh, as returning to the newly-built town of K̲hudābād; and it was at K̲hudābād that, on the flight of Sarafrāz K̲hān, his brother, Maḥmud K̲hān, was placed upon the throne. Mīr Bijār also fixed his head-quarters for a time at K̲hudābād when he summoned Miān ʻAbdunabi from Haidarābād to the throne, the latter being lodged in the palace of Sarafrāz at that place, and here they made their head-quarters for the time being.

In the midst of the ruins of the old town, and within a quarter of a mile of the railway station, stands the great massive Jāmiʻ Masjid, a building now deserted and neglected (Plates LXXXVIII—XCI). It has been lavishly adorned with enamelled tiles, which have been shamefully damaged by people trying to pick them out. The corners of every tile, within reach, have been chipped away in the endeavour to lever the tiles out of their setting; but the cement refused to yield and so the walls have been left pitted all over by the vandals. On either side of the entrance to the mosque is a beautiful panel which is quite the best thing in tiles to be found in Sind (Plate XCI). Unlike the general run of designs which, however floral the pattern, are disposed, more or less, in geometrical forms, this design revels in its very realistic and unconventional treatment. It represents a tall and graceful plant of the lily order, whose lanceolate leaves, flowers, and buds sprout from the central stem and fall over right and left in easy natural curves. It has not the slightest stiffness, and is full of soft flowing lines, which produce a very pleasing effect. The whole plant is white upon a dark blue ground. Both panels, which are alike, have suffered at the hands of the despoiler, but not to the extent of the walls within. It looks as if the beauty of the panels had successfully appealed to the better feelings of some, and had held the hand of the barbarians whose mischievous fingers have disfigured the interior. Inside the three arched entrances to the mosque, is some very prettily designed vaulting.

The great tomb of Yār Muḥammad, the first Kalhōrah ruler of Sind, which is some little distance to the west of the Jāmi' Masjid, is a square massive building, the front of which is fully decorated with enamelled tiles (Plates XCII—XCIV). High up around the other three sides of the building, and lighting the gallery around the dome within, are rows of large arched windows fitted with perforated terra-cotta screens of delicate geometric tracery (Plate XCIV). Similar windows, upon the front, are fitted with perforated glazed tiles. Suspended around the tomb, within, is a great collection of clubs or stout sticks, placed there to show how easily Sind was taken from the Panwhārs by the Kalhōrahs, swords not having been necessary.

The great panel of coloured tiles above the entrance is a remarkable piece of work (Plate XCIII). Nearly ten feet square, it is made up of no less than 240 square tiles, no two, except in the outer border, being alike. The usual way in which these large single pattern panels are drawn out by the present makers, is by laying the plain tiles out upon the ground, closely packed to the same size as the panel, and then drawing and painting in the pattern as if the whole were one flat surface, and, with what success, may be judged from the photograph. The tiles are then again fired to fix the colours, and attached to the building in their respective positions to reproduce the design. In this case, the great size of the panel must have made this a difficult piece of work, considering the rough tools and appliances used. The result, however, is perfect. The large arched panels on either side of this, and below, are also worked out in the same way, though their designs, being that of a diaper, do not produce the same effect. The great central panel recalls, somewhat, the great rose windows in Gothic work.

It was Miān Yār Muḥammad who, after wandering about northern Sind and Baluchistān upon warlike expeditions, settled down at Khudābād on wresting it from the Panwhārs, and it was he who gave it that name. He died in A.H. 1131 (A.D. 1718).

The mausoleum of Miān Nūr Muḥammad, the son of Miān Yār Muḥammad, is situated seven miles to the north-east of Daulatpūr, and about eighteen miles to the east by south from Khudābād (Fig. 26). It, too, is a massive building of the same style as Yār Muḥammad's though not so fully decorated, whitewash entering more into the general scheme of decoration. It is surrounded by other smaller buildings. Like the tomb of Shāhbāz at Sehwān, the dome is surmounted by a lantern. There is nothing of any special interest about the building other than that it is the last resting place of the second of the Kalhōrah chiefs.

DRĀKHAN.

OF the same class of building as the tomb of Shāh Bahāro at Lārkhāna are the Thahīm tombs near the Drākhan and Ratodero road, about thirty miles west of Sakhar (Plate XCV). These are three large dilapidated structures with a smaller one beside them, all built of brick, with some enamelled tiles still adhering of those that formed a few ornamental bands upon them. Surmounting the domes are lanterns like that on Shāh Bahāro's tomb, but not quite so elegant: they are in great part destroyed. Towards the end of the reign of Abdu-l-Nabī Kalhōrah a battle took place, near Garhi Yasin, with the Pathāns, in which the Thahīms were killed. Two of the tombs were built by their wives, perhaps, about 1781, one in memory of Sāheb Khān Thahīm, and the other in memory of Dilāwar Khān Thahīm. Older than these is the tomb of Jalāl Khān; and the fourth is said to be that of Ja'fir Shāh. There is a legend which affirms that when the tomb of Jalāl Khān was being built, and its construction progressed badly, a voice was heard advising the construction of Jafir Shāh's tomb first, which was done, and all difficulties vanished.[1]

Three miles from Ratodero, on the same road, is the tomb of Bhando, whoever he may have been, built in 1740, in fair condition.

The tribe of Tamīn, from which the Thahīms were descended, were originally sent from Baghdād as lieutenants of the Khalīfahs. They were thus an old Arab family.

[1] Archæological Survey of Western India Memoranda, No. 8, p. 12.

BALŪCH TOMBS AND GRAVEYARDS.

THERE is a curious and extensive old Balūchi graveyard about four miles to the south-west of Jarak, on the Ṭhaṭhah road. Near the side of the road, the tableland, which it traverses, drops suddenly into low ground, surrounding the great westward loop of the Indus at this point. It is within this lower ground that the graveyard lies, and covers an area of, perhaps, half a square mile, which is thickly covered with graves (Plate XCVI). To the north-east side is a late-looking domed mausoleum, of the style of those of the Tālpūrs, at Haidarābād, decorated with Hālā tiles, which has a carved wooden door, the work upon which resembles, in the coarseness of its execution, the archaic-looking sculpture on some of the tombs. In a panel, above the door, is the Islāmic profession of faith in interlaced Persian characters. Near by, is a group of pillared pavilions, under which are graves, in picturesque ruin, with stone surface-carving like that on 'Isā Khān's tomb at Ṭhaṭhah.

There are, in this graveyard, a number of strangely fashioned tombstones. One class rises in stepped-out pyramidal piles, which are also found in many old graveyards between Karāchi and Haidarābād as well as in the districts of Balūchistān adjoining the Karāchi collectorate. They are usually known as *chaukandi* tombs.[1] The other class are tall, single, upright slabs, the front surfaces of which are coarsely carved in crochet-work patterns. Of the pyramidal class Sir John Marshall has written the following notes on some found in Balūchistān: "At Hinidan (in Balūchistān) on the Hab river, a series of structural tombs of a remarkable, and, so far as India is concerned, unique type was brought to the notice of the Archæological Department by Major M. A. Tighe, late Political Agent in Southern Balūchistān; they were subsequently visited by Dr. Vogel, and a number of drawings and photographs were obtained. The characteristic features which distinguish these monuments, are their pyramidal form of construction, the over-ground mode of burial, and the decorative slabs carved in relief with figures of men and horses. That they are of Muḥammadan origin there can be little doubt, and it is this fact that makes the presence of the ornamental slabs difficult to explain. Dr. Vogel suggests that the figures on these slabs are a Hindu survival, and he compares them with the figures on certain Sati stones in the Ḥimalayan district of the Panjāb, but one cannot help feeling that there is a suspicion of something un-Indian in these carvings,

[1] Mr. Carter, I.C.S., has listed over twenty such cemeteries containing similar tombs, some being within 18 miles of Karāchi.

especially in the more developed specimens; and the form of the tombs with their steps or tiers diminishing towards the summit, coupled with the name S͟hāmī (Syrian), given locally to the overground mode of burial, would certainly seem to connect them with the west rather than the east. Perhaps the immediate neighbourhood of Persia on the west might warrant the suggestion that these sarcophagi are the remote descendants of the early Persian structural tombs, like the famous one in the valley of the Murg͟h-āb, identified as the resting place of Cyrus, son of Cambyses; or it may be that they were actually introduced by immigrants from Asia Minor where many examples may be found of analogous structures."[1]

Mr. Carter, who has visited many of these, and is making a study of them, says he never heard the name S͟hāmī used in connection with them in Sind, but, if it has been, it would probably be on account of the fact that the Balūchis, whose tombs these are, originally came from Syria. He also thinks there was no over-ground burial in connection with them. In Dr. Vogel's photographs the tombs are more or less intact, boxed up all around with slabs, and this is so in those I photographed in the cemetery near Jarak; but, in some of the photographs taken by Mr. Carter, the lower sides and end slabs are all perforated with large arched openings through which the surface of the ground within is fully exposed. It is, therefore, manifest that bodies could not have been placed in these, and it is not likely that some bodies would be disposed of above ground while others were buried beneath by the same people at the same time. The carvings on some show a fully armed horseman, with his arms, such as the shield, sword, bow and arrow, and his signet ring, thus proclaiming that graves with these carvings are those of men. Moreover the men's tombs have a short stumpy pillarette projecting from the top, at one end, just as we find it in the tombs of the Tālpūrs, at Haidarābād (themselves Balūchis), where it is used to hold the turban of the deceased (see plate LXXIII). In these open air tombs the turbans would not last long. There is little doubt, I think, that the boss, or orb, as Mr. Carter calls it, surmounting many of these little pillars is, indeed, intended to represent a turban, and in some cases it is remarkably like those on the Tālpūr graves. Turkish tombs, in marble, are surmounted with a carved representation of the turban in the case of those of men, while a palm branch indicates those of women (*Encyclopædia Brit.* "Cemetery"). Similar little pillars are found at the heads of Musalmān graves elsewhere, without the turban, where they indicate that the deceased had died a *s͟hāhīd* or martyr. The women's tombs have not got this, but they are decorated with representations

FIG. 27.—Horseman on Balūchi tomb.

[1] Annual Report of the Archæol. Survey of India for 1902-3, 213.

of bracelets. As seen in my photograph, plate XCVI, which is that of a woman's tomb, two horizontal stones near the top project beyond the general outline, and they have a groove in the end of each. The meaning of this I do not know. The men's have similar projections with a rosette on the end of each. They look somewhat like the carrying poles of a bier. Some of these graves are placed under pillared canopies as we find them on the Maklī hill and at Mīr Ma'ṣūm's graveyard at Sakhar.

As for the style of carvings upon these, especially the horseman, it is not necessary to go so far afield as the Himalayan valleys for similar work, for it is found upon the *paliyas*, or memorial stones, which are found in thousands scattered through the adjoining districts of Kathiawād and Kachh.[1] The slab of perforated work at the top of the women's tomb, on plate XCVI, might have been a panel taken from the low stone rail around the tomb of Ghulām Shāh Kalhōrah at Haidarābād. It is of precisely the same design and workmanship. There can be but little doubt that these Balūch tombs and the mausoleum of Ghulām Shāh cannot be far apart in point of age, if not, indeed, contemporary. Compare the work on these tombs also with that on 'Isā Khān's tomb and adjacent ones at Ṭhaṭhah. The former are in most cases a bit cruder in execution, but that is more likely due to inferior and cheaper workmanship than as the stamp of older work. There are some good examples of these tombs at Landhi.[2]

---

[1] See Dr. Burgess' Volume on Kathiawād and Kachh for illustrations. The Kathiawād horsemen hold the spear above their heads, horizontally, and the horse walks with one foot off the ground.

[2] Report of the Archæol. Survey of India, Western Circle, for the year ending the 31st March, 1919, Plate VIII.

MISCELLANEOUS REMAINS.

NAṢRPŪR, in the Alahyar-jo-Tando *tālūka*, and 18 miles to the north-east of Haidarābād, is the remains of an old brick city, with three old Muḥammadan tombs. The place shows signs of antiquity, but there is not much remaining of those other days, when, for a time, it was a leading city in the province. The bed of the old river, long since dried up, is seen skirting it on the west, and the two dilapidated old brick *masjids* alone remain to tell of those bygone times. Elliot tells us that Naṣrpūr was founded, or rather rebuilt, on the river Sankra,[1] by Āmīr Naṣr, who was dispatched for that purpose, by Sulṭān Fīruz Shāh, with a thousand cavalry, in A.H. 751 (A.D. 1350). Naṣrpūr was subsequently the favourite residence of the Tarkhāns, and was greatly embellished by them during their brief rule.[2] McMurdo writes of it thus: "Nāsirpūr, now in ruins, was once the most beautiful and flourishing of cities in *Sindh*. Although I agree with some geographers in believing this to be the *Al Mānsura* of the Arabs[3] as is elsewhere explained, it is well established that the modern *Nāsirpūr* was founded by an officer named *Nasir*, who was left by *Sulṭān Firoz Shah*, of Dehli, to command in *Sindh* after that sovereign's attack on T'hatta in A.H. 751. Nāsirpūr was situated on the *Sangra* branch, at that time the main stream of the Indus, and its suburbs were highly ornamented by rich gardens, and pleasure-grounds filled with temporary or permanent villas for recreation. It was *Nāsirpūr* that the *Terkhan* dynasty, and that tribe in general, took so much trouble to embellish and improve. The precise date of the decay of *Nāsirpūr* is unknown; but it was coincident with the change of the stream to the westward of Haiderābād, which was prior to the entrance of the Delhi army in A.H. 1000." The Sind Gazetteer says Naṣrpūr is supposed to have been built by one Naṣr Muhāna in A.D. 989, and that the ol' tombs, which are adorned with glazed brick, were erected nearly two hundred years ago in honour of one Muḥammad Shāh.[4]

At Naṣrpūr there is a family of potters who still make the enamelled tiles, glazed and coloured vases, and other objects, and which is related to the potters of Hālā. Near Tāndo Ahalyar is a recently-built tomb which is elaborately decorated by them.

---

1 Raverty calls it the Āb-i-Sind, or Indus, *Mihrān of Sind*, 469.

2 Elliot's *History of India*, I, 372.

3 *Journ. R. A. S.*, I, 236.

In this identification he was quite wrong, for, as shewn elsewhere, Manṣūra was raised upon the site of Brahmanābād. This mistake was made by D'Anville, who probably followed the *Ajāib-al Makhlukot* which says so (*Journ. R. A. S.*, I, 20).

4 Page 592.

MOHEN-JO-DHAḌO lies seven miles south-east of Dokrī in the Lārkhānā district. The ruins here are thus described by Mr. Bhandarkar who recently examined them: "Here are spread the remains of an old place for about three-fourths of a mile (Fig. 28). Near the western edge is a tower on a mound nearly seventy

FIG. 28.—Mohen-jo-Dhaḍo mound.

feet high from the ground level, from which the mound gradually rises. Of the top portion only the inner core has remained, consisting of sun-dried brick-work. The bottom of it appears to have been reached most probably by treasure hunters who, I was told, frequently excavated the most promising spots here. Close by, towards the west and south, are six mounds, but of far less height, and there seems to have been a river once running between the tower mound and the other heaps. On the north side of the tower, again, are vestiges of an old brick road running up. The bricks, as a rule, are of modern type and are not of large dimensions like the old. There are, no doubt, some here which look old, but they are few and far between. Not a single carved moulded brick I was able to discover here........According to the local tradition, these are the ruins of a town only two hundred years old, and the *dhaḍo* or tower itself a part of the bastion guarding its west side."[1]

MAHORTA or Maihota. The great mound of Mahorta is on the bank of the Ghār river, 10 miles from Lārkhānā. It is mentioned by Cunningham and

[1] Prog. Report of the Arch. Sur. of India, Westn. Circle, for the year ending 31st March, 1912, p. 4. This short note may yet be expanded to a volume. My successor has lately carried out excavations here, and beneath the strata of the Buddhist period he has found evidence of a far more ancient civilization, the oldest yet discovered in India, making Taxila recent by comparison. Remains have been uncovered which are, unquestionably, as old as the Sumerian period of Babylonia, of about 3000 B.C., strikingly similar to objects found at Kish. See a preliminary article contributed to the *Illustrated London News* of the 20th September, 1924, by Sir John Marshall, and subsequent articles, in the two numbers following, by Prof. Sayce and Messrs. C. J. Gadd and Sidney Smith of the British Museum.

Masson.[1] The former identifies it with the Præsti, Porticanus or Oxykanus of Arrian, Curtius, Diodorus and Strabo. Masson describes it as the remains of an ancient fortress, on a huge mound, named Maihota. This mound has not yet been properly explored, but may possibly turn out to be another of the many *stūpas* which were built in Sind in the early years of the Christian era. Raverty has made a note of it in his *Mihrān of Sind*, in which he says: "Near Lar-khānah, on the Ghār channel, is the site of an ancient fortified town, on a great mound, and, in former times, must have been a place of some importance."[2]

FATḤPŪR. At Fatḥpūr, about six miles from Lārkhānā, is the tomb of Miān Shāhal Muḥammad Kalhōrah and his son, plainly built, upon an eminence, and decorated within with coloured tiles, but the outside decoration has gone. The building is about 22 feet square. The doorway to the outer enclosure is covered with coloured tiles. He was the grandson of Ādam Shāh and was killed in a fight near Fatḥpūr. It is said that his head chose his burial place by flying there in advance of his body, and that the latter was brought along by his followers. He is now numbered with the saints or *pīrs*, and the doorway of the courtyard and the mausoleum itself are adorned with votive offerings or thank offerings of those who have obtained answers to their prayers through his mediation, which consist principally of iron bells and strings of shells.[3]

HAKṚAH, about two and a half miles from Rōhrī, is the ruins of an ancient town. Captain Kirby, who visited the spot in 1855, thus describes it: "In excavating the great Nārā canal we occasionally came upon detached masses of brickwork, and at length, at a depth of about ten feet below the surface of the ground, the foundations of a very large number of houses were laid bare. These foundations consisted of stone, or of mingled stone and brickwork, and resembled those to be seen in the ruins of the city of Aror at the present day. Among the ruins were found a number of articles made of brick-clay, such as drinking cups, a khuja, some water-spouts, and a large number of children's toys. It appears that the town was built on the extremity of a rocky hill, and that it has been gradually covered by the mud held in suspension in the flood-waters of the Indus, which, even now, flow over the spot, indeed, its burial ground, which, according to the common custom in this part of Sind, was high up upon the rocky hill, is still uncovered.

"The name of the place, it appears, was Hakrah, a name still retained by a village in the neighbourhood, and it is, according to the natives of the country, mentioned by a prophet of the Mamoi caste of Fakirs, who says:—

> 'When broken shall be the bandh of Aror,
> And the waters shall flow over Hakrah,
> Where will be the fishing of the Samma?'

probably with the idea that when the *bandh* of Aror was broken, and the waters flowed over Hakrah, the river Indus would have taken that course and left its present bed dry. The *bandh* of Aror, however, is not yet broken, nor is there much chance of it being so, as it has been lately repaired, partly with the bricks

[1] Cunningham's *Ancient Geography*, p. 260, and Masson's *Travels*, I, 461.
[2] *Mihrān of Sind*, 314.
[3] *Sind Gazetteer*, 501.

removed out of its old neighbour, the town of Hakrah, when excavating the channel for the canal."[1] This site is deserving of further examination.

HELĀĪ, in the Ṭhaṭhah district and about 16 miles to the north-east of that town. Near this place is an ancient building in ruins, known as the *Māri*, or house of Jām Tamāchī, the fourth ruler of the Sammah dynasty in Sind. These ruins are situated on a hill at the northern end of the Sonahrī *ḍhanḍh*, or lake, and command a fine view. Captain John Wood of the Indian Navy, visited this place in 1837 and wrote: 'On the road [between Hilāī and the lake] we passed a small and venerable looking square enclosure of plain freestone, which our guide informed us was the tomb of Jam Tamatchi, the father of Indus fishermen."[2]

KHUDĀBĀD, near Hālā. This was the capital of the Tālpūrs before they moved to Haidarābād, and here rest the remains of the earlier chiefs of that family. The place is thus described by Captain Wood, as he found it at his visit many years ago: "The ruins of Khodābād are situated a little to the north-west of Hālā, and cover two square miles of ground. It was a favourite residence of the Talpurs, and here many of their chiefs have been interred. Under one dome, and side by side, lie the founder of the dynasty, Futi Ali Khān, and his brother Mīr Gholam Ali; while in an adjoining mausoleum are deposited the remains of Byram, Bejur, and Sobbdar, chiefs of the same house, who suffered severely from the tyranny and vindictive spirit of the latter Kalōrās. The mausoleum of Futi Ali is small yet neat, built entirely of red freestone, the only marble used being for the prayer slab that fronts his grave. The other tombs are of a still simpler construction (Plate XCVII). The three chiefs lie on the same platform, and their graves are protected from the elements by a light canopy supported upon pillars........The tombs just mentioned are the only buildings in Khodābād which are in even tolerable preservation; of the dwelling houses not one is entire. Little more than thirty years [now one hundred and twenty-five] have elapsed since this city rivalled Haidarābād in size and population. How perishable then must be the architecture of Sind! and, in a region such as this, how apt will the antiquary be to invest, in the ardour of his search, mounds of yesterday's formation with the sanctity of ages!"[3] Thornton states that in 1844, not one habitable dwelling remained. The mausoleum of Mīr Fatḥ 'Alī Khān is by no means a small building. It is nearly as large as that of Mīr Karam 'Alī at Haidarābād, and just as elaborately decorated with coloured tiles.

OLD FORTS. Sind is full of the ruins of old forts, dating from the hoary remains of that at Sehwān to the petty strongholds of the last of the Tālpūrs, some of which may cover the foundations of still earlier ones. Among the latest is Rāni-ka-Koṭ, about 7 or 8 miles from the town of Sann, a station on the older line of the railway. We learn from the Sind Gazetteer that "it is said to have been constructed by the Talpur Mīrs Karam 'Alī and his brother, Murad 'Alī, about A.D. 1812, at a cost of 12,00,000 of rupees, and has never been inhabited in consequence of there being a scarcity of water in and near it......

[1] *Sind Gazetteer*, 677.

[2] *A Journey to the Source of the River Oxus*, Ed. 1872, 9.

[3] *A Journey to the Source of the River Oxus*, Ed. 1872, 19.

The object of its construction seems to have been to afford a place of refuge to the Mīrs in case of their country being invaded. The hill on the north face is steepest, and, from the intelligence I received, must be at least 800 or 1,000 feet high; the opposite hill is of considerable height, and the east and west walls are built on level ground, and join those constructed on the hills; the whole is of stone and chunam, forming an irregular pentagon, and enclosing a space capable of containing 20,000 men."

Other similar forts are Charlo Fort, about 24 miles south-west of Sehwān; Chakar Koṭe, 17 miles west of Johī; Koṭ Drigh Mathi, thirteen miles west of the same place; Raniji Koṭ, 22 miles west of Sann; Koṭ Nūrpūr, 8 miles north of Manjhand; Koṭ Dharanjo, 5 miles north of Kotrī; and Dilandji Bhit. They are also found at Makan Dunichand, Kandi Tarāi, Yakor Khadi, Damach, Thunwari, Goth Arab Khān, Goth Sari, and Rattā Koṭ on the bank of the old Hakṛāh.

SHĀHAPŪR CHAKAR, in the Sākrand *tālukā.* Two and a half miles north from this are some tombs of the Mīrs of Khairpūr.

MĀO MUBĀRAK, ten miles north of Naushahro station, on the new loop line of railway. There is here an ancient mound, supposed to be the site of an early stronghold.[1]

OLD BADĪN, 62 miles south-east of Haidarābād, is now the head-quarters of a *Mūkhtyārkar;* near it is a ruined site which Raverty thinks may be that of Manjābāri.[2] The former site of the present town was on the right or western bank of the Ghāri Māndhar canal. The whole town was destroyed by Madat Khān, the famous Pathān, in his raid into Sind. The present town is supposed to have been built by Sawālo, a Hindū, about 182 years ago.[3]

VIKKAR. There are still a few indications of the shifting of the navigable waters of the delta and the Ran. Captain Wood found in the neighbourhood of Vikkar, near the Hajamrī mouth, the embedded hull of a Dutch brig-of-war, pierced for fourteen guns. He says: "She is built for shoal waters, as her sailing draft could never have exceeded six feet. Her construction, like the 'galliot,' is round-sided, flat-floored, with little depth of hold—all qualities adapted to shallow seas. Her length is seventy-one feet and her width of beam twenty-five. The post-sills are now about two feet and a half above the ground, and the nearest stream (the Sīyā'han) is distant 200 yards from the wreck. From 300 to 400 rounds of shot and shell, together with twenty musket barrels and some pieces of brass and iron ordnance, were disinterred from her after-hold. The shot was of every calibre from an ounce ball to a 12-pounder; and along with other rusty articles was forwarded to Haidarābād for the satisfaction of that court [the court of the Tālpūrs]. The Amīrs, we may well imagine, were better satisfied with this present than with a somewhat similar one since made them from Karāchī, when some 32-pound shot were lodged by H. M. ship "Wellesley" in the walls of its castle.[4]

---

[1] *Indian Antiquary*, XI, 7.

[2] *Mihrān of Sind*, 229n.

[3] *Sind Gazetteer*, 123.

[4] *Journey to the source of the River Oxus*, 3.

VIJEH-KOṬ, Wageh-Koṭ or Vigo-gad, an old site, five miles to the east of the Pūrān river, above the Allah-band, is said to have been a principal seaport when the Ran was a navigable sea. Its brick ruins were still visible in Burnes' time. About 1745 the wreck of a vessel, of a much larger size than any used in the gulf of Kachh fifty years later, was discovered at Wawania, sunk in the mud, about fifteen feet deep.[1]

SHĀH KĀPŪR[2] is a small village situated in the delta, about 30 miles east by south of Ṭhaṭhah, upon the left bank of the old Gungro channel. The extensive ruins about this village have been identified as those of the old Sūmṛah capital Muḥammad Tūr. The earliest mention we have of Muḥammad Tūr is in connection with the death of the Sūmṛah chief Sanghār (A.H. 485-500, A.D. 1092-1106), when, having no issue, "his widow Hīmū, who was ruling in the fort of Adak, managed to put her own brothers in possession of the towns of Muḥammad Tūr and Tharrī."[3] Later, owing to the misdeeds of the Sūmṛah chiefs, Sulṭān 'Alāu-d-dīn, upon being appealed to, invaded Sind and drove out the Sūmṛahs. "In short, the tribe of Sūmrahs was thus extirpated from Sind and their chief town of Muḥammad Tūr made desolate by the plunderous hands of the army of the Sultān of Dehlī. The Sammahs who succeeded the Sūmrahs built new towns near it, *viz.*:—Sāmuī and others, and considered the old site of Muḥammad Tūr, which was situated in the parganah of Darak, as a cursed and unlucky spot."[4] It is said that the Indus itself, at that time, flowed past the town.[5]

This site has been thus described by Mr. F. Phillips as he found it seventy years ago:—"The present village consists of not more than fifty houses, situated on a large watercourse, called the Old Goongra, to distinguish it from the stream of the same name flowing through another part of the country. Close round this watercourse and the present modern village commence the ruins of ancient Mehmetoor, which extend for upwards of three miles, in a south and south-easterly direction. They consist for the most part of burnt brick mounds of different dimensions, which stand in the plain perfectly isolated from each other, and are visible from a great distance. The largest mound is situated close to the existing village, and is about three hundred yards in circumference, and perhaps sixty feet in height. This has not been opened as yet. In places are seen large blocks of stone, which have, apparently, formed the foundations of buildings, and there is also a small burying ground containing a few tombs of carved sandstone, put together, as is common in Sind, without mortar. These, however, possess no inscription whereby to judge of their age, or the names of those whose memory they were intended to perpetuate.

* * * * * * *

---

[1] *Travels into Bokhara*, by Lieut. Alex. Burnes, 2nd Ed. 1835. 320-5.

[2] The correct spelling is Shāh Kāpūr, after a famous Kachh saint, who travelled through this part of Sind some 260 years ago.

[3] Mirza Kalichbeg Fredunbeg's *History of Sind*, Vol. II, 35. One of the succeeding chiefs was named Muḥammad Tūr, so it is possible the town was known by some other name up to his time when it was called after him.

[4] Mirza K. Fredunbeg's *History of Sind*, Vol. II, 41.

[5] Haig's *Indus Delta Country*, 5.

"Hitherto but few of the mounds have been opened, owing to the small success which has resulted from the operation. The excavations carried out have been made by sinking shafts and carrying the cut along all walls found in the ruins; the contents of the space so included have been dug up and sifted, but, as already stated, with small results; one silver coin only, lately sent to the Commissioner of Sind, has been found. The other relics consists of fragments of cornelian, agate, and other stones (apparently evincing that many lapidaries formerly resided in the place), and a large number of old copper coins, very small in size, and all so corroded that no inscription or legend, if any existed, is now to be traced; on some of the stones may still be seen faint traces of Arabic character, but not so distinctly as to convey a correct idea of their meaning."[1]

Major Raverty thinks these ruins may possibly be those of Nīrūn Koṭ or of Damṛīlah. He calls the place 'Shakr-pur.'[2] But Nīrūn has been definitely identified with Haidarābād.

The *Tārīkh-i-Tāhirī* says: "From the year of the Hijra 700 (A.D. 1300), until 843 (1439), that is to say, for a period of 143 years, the Hindū tribe of Sūmra were rulers of Sind; and that portion which is now flourishing was then a mere waste, owing to the scarcity of water in the Sind or Panjab river, which is known by the above name below Bhakkar. No water flowed towards those regions, and water is the very foundation of all prosperity. The capital of these people was Muḥammad Tūr, which is now depopulated and is included in the pargana of Dirak. Not I alone but many others have beheld these ruins with astonishment. Numbers of the natives of that city, after its destruction, settled in the *pargana* of Sakura, which was peopled in the time of the Jāms of Samma, and there they founded a village to which they also gave the name of Muḥammad Tūr."[3]

The *Tuhfatu-l-Kirām* speaks of the towns of Muḥammad Tūr and Tharrī about the beginning of the Sūmṛah régime. It was in the vicinity of the latter place that the tribe of Sūmṛahs first assembled. The Sammahs, in the beginning, seem to have made Tharrī their head-quarters.[4]

This place has been named by local historians Muḥatampūr, Muḥammad Tūr and Meḥmetūr. "Another capital of the Sūmras is said to have been 'Vijeh-Kot,' 'Wageh-Kot,' or 'Vigo-gad,' five miles to the east of ṭhe Pūrān river, above the Allah-band. The site of Tūr has been considered to be occupied by the modern Tharri, near Budina, on the Gūngrū river. There are, to be sure, the remains of an old town to the west of that place; nevertheless the position of Tūr is not to be looked for there, but at Shākapūr, a populous village about ten miles south of Mīrpūr [Mīrpūr-Batōra]. Near that village, the fort and palace of the last of the Sūmras are pointed out, whence bricks are still extracted of very large dimensions, measuring no less than twenty inches by

1 *Journal, Bom. Br. R. A. S.*, Vol. V, 541.

2 *Mihrān of Sind*, 229n. In his notice, "westwards" and "west" should be "eastwards" and "east."

3 Elliot's *History of India*, I, 256.

4 Mallet's *Mir Ma'sum*, 48. Mr. Carter tells me that the name Tharri or "Tharro" is really a generic one "strings of Tharros run across Sind just like Dāk Bungalows. Hilaya lies between two, one behind Jherruck and one just north of Tatta........Th› finest Tharro of all is the hill near Gujo."

eight [See Captain McMurdo, *J.R.A.S.*, I, 24, 226, 233]. Other fine ruins are scattered about the neighbourhood, and carved tombstones are very numerous. Fragments of pearls and other precious stones are occasionally picked up, which have all apparently been exposed to the action of fire. The people themselves call this ruined site by the name of Mehmetur."[1]

Lieutenant Pottinger writes: "At the village of Shāhkapūr, on the road from Kōtrī to Haidarābād [*Sic.*], and about sixty miles distant from the former place, there are the ruins of a large town, visible on the plain about a mile N-E of the village, to which the inhabitants give the name Hingūr, and which they describe as having been a very large and opulent place in the time of the *Sammās*; the remains, which are of kiln-burnt brick of a superior description, cover a very considerable extent of ground, and the circuit of the walls and positions of the bastions are plainly discernible.

"To the north-east of those ruins the forsaken channel of a very large river is also distinctly to be traced, and the people stated......that the river Indus, or a large branch of it, once flowed in this bed, and was navigable for large boats or vessels."[2]

In the neighbourhood of Shāhkāpūr, in the delta, are the ruins and sites of several old towns. There is a mound at a place called "Kakeja" or "Kakeyja," 30 miles south-west of Jarak. Another ruined site is at "Katbaman" of the maps, 24 miles east-south-east of Jarak; a third at "Shah Toorail," 9 miles north-north-east of Badīn, and rather less than two miles from the recent west bank of the Gūnī branch of the Indus; and a fourth collection of ruins at "Nindimanee," 5 miles east of Muḥabbat Dero.[3]

FIG. 29.—Hālā potter, in full dress.

HĀLĀ. There are two Hālās, the old and the new. Old Hālā, which is between New Hālā and the Indus, and about 30 miles to the north of Haidarābād, consists of the ruins of the original town, the new one having been built about 1800 by one Makh'dūm Mīr Muḥammad in consequence of Old Hālā, at that time, being threatened by the encroachments of the river Indus. There is in New Hālā the shrine or tomb of Makh'dūm Nūh, built by Pir Makh'dūm Muḥammad Zamān in A.D. 1790,[4] of brick and coloured tiles (Plate XCVIII). It is said that his remains

[1] Elliot's *History*, I. 403-404.

[2] *On the present state of the River Indus*, etc. J. R. A. S., I, 199.

[3] Raverty's *Mihrān of Sind*, 500n.

[4] Another date given is 1795.

were twice disinterred owing to encroachments of the river, his last resting place being New Hālā where he was laid about 1779. Tod names a later prince of the Sammah family as the founder of Old Hālā.[1] As already noted in the description of the tile work at Ṭhaṭhah, New Hālā is the principal home of the glazed and coloured tile industry of Sind (Plate C and Fig. 29). The fulsome hyperbole in which Muḥammadan scribes delighted to indulge when composing monumental inscriptions is exemplified in the inscription over the entrance of the tomb which says: "Blest be the Lord who gave power to build this heaven-resembling dome full of grace," etc.

MATIĀRI is situated 16 miles north of Haidarābād. There are here the tomb of Pīr Rukān Shah, built in A.H. 1179 (A.D. 1764); the *dargāh* of Pīr Hashim Shah, built in A.H. 1175, and the Jāmi' Masjid, built in A.H. 1218 (A.D. 1803), (Plates XCVIII and XCIX).

MĀTHELO, Nagar Māṭhela or Māṭhilah, the remains of an old fort, 6 or 7 miles south-east from Ghotkī railway station, is mentioned in the *Tuhfatu-l-Kirām* as being one of the six strongholds which Rāi Sahasi II ordered to be either built or repaired. It was captured by Abū-i-Ḥasan, the general of Sulṭān Maudūd in A.D. 1047-48, and it appears to have been the strongest and most important place in that immediate locality.[2] The old site is now very much obscured by the modern village, but in the bottom of cuttings, in the sides of the old mounds, may be seen the old Hindū bricks such as are found at Vijnōt about thirty miles to the east; but, above these, the town has been rebuilt more than once. This place had been used as a quarry for brick ballast for the railway. It is worth further examination and possibly excavation.

GHOTKĪ, a station on the main line of rail in the extreme north of Sind. In the town is a *masjid* of some note, known as Musan Shāh's Masjid which was erected in 1732. It has a dome covered with glazed tiles. This building is by far the largest of its kind in upper Sind. It is decorated with some carved and painted woodwork.

AMRĪ, eighteen miles below Sehwān, and on the same side of the river. Near the modern village is a mound of earth about 40 feet high, which the traditions of the country point out as the halting place of a king.[3]

NAGAR-PĀRKAR. This far away south-eastern corner of Sind, remote from any railway station or convenient means of communication, has not been properly explored, and its being so far off the beaten track has, perhaps, helped to preserve some few remains of ancient Hindū and Jaina architecture which has been so thoroughly cleared off the surface elsewhere in Sind. The peninsula has not been so easily reached by the long arm of Musulmān fanaticism. "This town is believed to be of some antiquity, and the existence of several ruined tanks in and about the place seem to show a more prosperous condition in times gone by than is the case at present. About a mile from this town is

---

[1] *Travels in Western India*, 474.

[2] Raverty's *Mihrān of Sind*, 428.

[3] Lt A. Burnes' *Travels into Bokhara*, 2nd Ed., 51.

Sardhāra, where there is a temple of Mahādeo and a spring of water sacred to the Hindus."[1]

BHODEŚAR, four miles north-west from Nagar Pārkar, close to the foot of the rocky hills which, for twenty miles in circumference, form the centre of the Pārkar peninsula, contains the remains of three old temples. Two of these were used as stalls for cattle, and the interior of a third is both beautiful and interesting, but had great rents in its walls and was blackened with the filth which its abandonment to bats and wasps had created. Mr. R. Giles, of the Sind Civil Service, had the occupants of these buildings ousted, and a wall built to protect them. A tank, 400 by 200 feet, is said to have been excavated in the reign of Bhoda Parmāra, son of prince Jeso Parmāra, who was induced by the Brahmans to sacrifice his own son to the goddess of the city in order that the tank might retain water. Very noticeable, on the banks of the Bhodeśar tank, and in other places in the neighbourhood, are the *satī* (self-immolation) stones, with their rude knights in armour carved on them, marking the spots where their faithful spouses followed them through the fire to the realms of paradise. On the roadside, near the tank, is a mosque with carved marble pillars which may have been brought from Pari-Nagar.

VIRĀVAH and Pari-Nagar. The ruins of the old city of Pari-Nagar are close to Virāvah, which is about fifteen miles north of Nagar Pārker. Pari-Nagar, or Pari-Nangar, as it is also spelt, stands on a slight elevation at the foot of the desert sand-hills with a perfectly flat plain immediately below it, in which, even now, it is easy to imagine that the water of the Ran stood, and boats laden with merchandize went to and fro. It was, perhaps a port, but whether it was destroyed by an earthquake, as the country people affirm, or by the troops of the Delhi emperor in A.D. 1226, as some say, it is impossible at present to decide. Virāvah, itself, appears to have been built over part of Pari-Nagar, and on its western side only one small stone temple still stands. It consists of an open group of pillars with carved capital and roof. In it, but clearly not of it, are some very ugly marble figures, and around are the foundations only of former buildings.[2] Among the foundations was found a beautifully carved block of marble, 6′ 9″ in length and 2′ 7″ in breadth. This stone was removed to the Karāchi Museum and is shown in Fig. 3. It is the door jamb of a Vaishṇava temple of about the eleventh or twelfth century, and is of similar workmanship to that of many of the old temples in the adjoining province of North Gujarāt. Pari-Nagar, with this exception, is a large brick heap. In a few places pieces of marble and bits of stone carving are met with, but all else has gone; and not so long ago either, for Captain Raikes, who had been there some time before Mr. Giles, found and described a good deal more of this class of remains, much of which will no doubt be found built into modern temples in the country around. Pari-Nagar is said to have been ruled by scions of the Parmāras of Abū.

---

[1] *Sind Gazetteer*, 384.

[2] These descriptions of places in the Nagar Parkar peninsula are from notes made many years ago by Mr. R. Giles, who was then acting Deputy Commissioner of Thar and Pārkar.

GORI, 14 miles north-west from Virāvah, possesses an old temple about 125 by 50 feet, built of marble. The oft repeated story of the dream, the buried image, and the breakdown of the cart containing it, at the spot where the temple stands, and the building of the latter for it, is told of this shrine. It is very similar, though superior to the one at Bhodeśar, but had been much defaced at various times by the fanaticism of the Sindhi troops. It is also said to have suffered from fire, and from gunpowder which was used by Colonel Tyrwhitt, at the time of the Nagar outbreak, in order to secure a Sodha chief who was supposed to be hiding himself in its passages. There is an inscription which was put up when the temple was repaired in A.D. 1715.

DHAMRAO, 6 miles from Badeh station on the Ruk-Kotri Railway, has extensive ruins of Buddhist buildings—*stūpas* and monasteries. Carved bricks are found in the largest mound, which is some 40 feet in height, similar to those at Mīrpur-Khas. Some of the bricks measure 18 to 20 inches in length by 3 inches thick. This site requires further investigation.

MITHO DERO, 6 miles north of Lārkhāna, has a great mound, probably the remains of a *stūpa*, which is over 50 feet high.

LANDHI, near Karachi. Remains of votive *stūpas* have been found here.

ANCIENT COINAGE IN SIND.

THE only coins, hitherto discovered, which can, with any degree of certainty, be looked upon as locally minted money in ancient Sind, are among those that have been found upon such sites as Brahmanābād, Vijnōṭ and Bhambōr, and which I have already referred to in previous pages. In rows 8 and 9, on plate CII, will be seen very thin copper pieces, more or less rectangular in shape, bearing sundry old *Devanagari* letters stamped upon them, but not sufficient to enable us to read any word or name. The last ones, at the right ends of the rows, are upside down: they are stamped with the same letters as the last but one in row 8. It is possible that these, which were found upon the site of Brahmanābād, belonged to the Hindū period immediately prior to the Arab conquest. The only mention in the *Chach Nāmah* of coins of this time is in connection with Dahir, who ordered that the name of his *wazir* should be struck on the reverse of his own coins for valuable services rendered.

The remaining coins, figured upon the plate, are Arab coins in silver and copper, the upper two rows being in silver. Some of these, the larger and thinner ones, in the rows 3, 4 and 5, were probably imported by the Arabs for use in the province, whilst the smaller, thicker, and stumpy ones were, without doubt, minted in the country, and, as I believe, by the primitive process described in my account of Brahmanābād.

There would appear to have been no gold coins, and there would hardly have been any necessity for such for ordinary currency, since we may gather from the very small copper pieces (row 7) that all commodities must have been very cheap indeed for such to have been in use. The only gold coin that we hear of, later, is what was called a *miskāl*, 100,000 of which were paid to Humāyūn as a solatium by Mīrzā S͟hāh Ḥasan in A.D. 1543, but whether these were local coins or not is not stated. Gold would be hoarded in the treasuries without much reference to its origin. Certainly, no gold coins of the early period of Arab rule have come to light.

We are told in the *Chach Nāmah* that Ḥāzam, one of Muḥammad Qāsim's lieutenants, gave the Sammahs, who danced before him, a present of 20 *dinars* of western gold. Being called 'western gold' would indicate that, if the present was in the shape of coins, they were probably from the K͟halīfah's mint. It was after this event, and after the fall of Multān, that Muḥammad Qāsim was instructed to strike local coins in the name of the K͟halīfah. Ibn Hauqal says, after describing Manṣūra: "The current coin of the country [of course, he means in his time, two and a half centuries after Muḥammad Qāsim's death] is stamped at Kandahar; one of the pieces is equivalent to five dirhams. The Tātarī coin also is current, each being in weight equal to a dirham and a third. They likewise use dīnārs."[1] Idrisi tells us that "the money is silver and copper. The weight of the drachma (dīnār) is five times that of the (ordinary) drachma. The Tātarīya coins also are current here."[2] The *Chach Nāmah* mentions "*dirams* of Silver"[3] in connection with the tribute that Muḥammad Qāsim levied from the people of Brahmanābād. And we are told that Ḥajāj informed Muḥammad that 60,000 *dirams* of silver had been sent him from the Khalīfah's treasury, from which we may gather that the *diram* was an Arab coin imported into Sind. His troops were paid in *dirams*. 'Tārtarīya *dirams*' are occasionally mentioned. Tamīn, son of Zaida-l-'Utbī, who, after Muḥammad's death, succeeded Junaid, is said to have squandered eighteen million of Tārtarīya *dirams*, which he found in the treasury of Sind[4].

Some of the early Arab coins have been examined. The earliest notice is, perhaps, that in Prinsep's *Antiquities*.[5] In reference to the Brahmanābād coins he says: "I am anxious to refer, though momentarily, and in a necessarily imperfect manner, both from the condition of the materials and the want of preparation on my own part, to an interesting series of Indian coins that have only lately been brought to light during the excavation of an inhumed city in the province of Sindh, which Mr. Bellasis, its enterprising explorer, designates, perhaps somewhat prematurely, by the title of the ancient Brahmanābād.

"However, be the site what it may, the laying open of this ruined town has made us acquainted with a class of essentially local money, of which the circle of our oriental numismatists had previously no cognizance. Unfortunately, for the due and full explication of their historical position, the pieces obtained from this locality are nearly, without exception, of copper; and in common with their more rare associates of silver, have suffered to an unusu extent during their prolonged entombment.

"The general character of the coins, numbering some thousands, and in mere bulk sufficient to fill a 28 lb. shot bag, is decidedly exclusive, involving Kufic legends with occasional provincial devices, and pertaining as I suppose, to the Arab potentates of Mansūrah, who ruled over the lands of the lower Indus after the decay of the central power of Mohammedanism at Baghdād. The money of Mansūr bin Jamhūr, the last governor on the part of the Umaiyid Khalīfs (about A.D. 750), heads the list. I do not advert to the earlier coinages of Central Asia, which have been transported, in the ordinary course, to the site of their late discovery; but commence the series with the coins which bear on their surfaces the earliest extant mention of the celebrated capital Mansūrah, the Arab reproduction of the still more famed Brahmanābād of classic renown.

[1] Elliot's *History of India*, 35.

[2] Elliot's *History of India*, I, 78.

[3] Fredunbeg's translation, 165 and 191.

[4] Elliot's *History*, I, 126. Mr. E. Thomas feels confident that the name 'Tārtariya is from Tāhiriya, the name of a dynasty dominant above all others in Eastern Asia at that period (*The Antiquities of Kathiawad and Kachh*, by Dr. Burgess, p. 71).

[5] Edited by Edward Thomas, Vol. II (1858), p. 120.

"I should be disposed to conjecture a considerable interval to have elapsed between the issue of this currency and that bearing devices somewhat in common, which displays the name of Abdulrahman (No. 3 *infra*), but I am not now in a condition to enter into any satisfactory speculations as to the precise identity of this monarch, or the dates of any of his successors, whose names can be but faintly traced on the worn and corroded surfaces of the coin, submerged with the town of which it necessarily constituted the bulk of the then existing currency. I await, in short, the further supplies of better specimens, promised me by the energetic antiquarians on the spot, and, individually, more leisure to look up the rather obscure history of the divisional government which these coins represent.

"I have one remark to add in reference to the peculiarly local character of these numismatic remains, and the restricted antiquity of the town, as tested by the produce of the habitations hitherto penetrated, in the fact of the very limited number of Hindū coins found among these multitudes of medieval pieces, and that even these seem to be casual contributions from other provinces, of no very marked uniformity or striking age."

MANSŪR.

No. 1.—Weight, 33 grains; size, 6.

Obverse :—

Area : لا اله الا الله وحده لا شريک له

Margin : illegible.

Reverse :—

Area : Central symbol nearly effaced, above which appears the name محمد, and below the words رسول الله.

Margin : (*sic*) بسم الله ضرب [هذا الفلـ] س بالمنصورة مما امربه منصر

No. 2.—

Obverse : Device altogether obliterated.

Reverse :

Area : Central symbol in the shape of an elongated eight-pointed star, above, محمد ; below, رسول الله

Margin : (*sic*). بسم [الله] ضرب ه بالمنصورة مما امربه منصر

ABDULRAHMAN.

No 3.—Copper : size, 5 ; weight, 44 grains.

Obverse :—Central device, a species of quartrefoil, or star with four points, on the sides of which are disposed, in the form of a square, the words محمد [رسول الله] عبدالرحمن the outer margin of the piece is ornamented with a line of dots enclosed within two plain circles, with four small dotted semicircles to fill in the spaces left vacant by the angular central legend.

Reverse :—A scalloped square, surrounded by dots, within which, arranged in three lines, are the words بالله عبدالرحمن لسلعار. The concluding word I am unable to satisfactorily decipher, it is possibly the name of Abdulrahman's tribe.

MUHAMMED.

No. 4.—A unique coin of apparently similar type—though with an obverse absolutely blank—replaces the name of Abdulrahman on the reverse by that of Muhammed. The concluding term is identical with the combination above noted.

ABDALLAH.

No. 5.—Copper.

Obverse :—Device as in No. 3 (Abdulrahman). Legend : محمد [رسول الله] عبدالله

Reverse :—Blank.

No. 6.—Copper : size, $3\frac{1}{2}$; weight, 18 grains.

Obverse :—Central device as in No. 3, around which, in a circular scroll may be partially read the formula لا اله الا الله وحده لا شريک له

Reverse :—Centre device composed of the name of عبدالله Abdallah ; the two portions عبد and الله being crossed at right-angles, in somewhat of accord with the scheme of the obverse device. The marginal legend is arranged in the form of a square and consists of the words محمد رسول الله [الا] مير

No. 7.—Silver : size, 2 ; weight, 8·4 grains. Devices are discontinued and replaced by simple Kufic legends, as follows :

Obverse :— لا اله الا الله وحده لا شريك له

Reverse :— محمد رسول الله الامير عبدالله

No. 8.—Copper, of similar legends. Other specimens vary in the division of the words, and omit the title of *Al Amīr*.

OMAR.

No. 9.—Silver : size, $1\frac{1}{2}$; weight, 9 grains. Five specimens.

Obverse :—No figured device. Legends arranged in five lines. بالله محمد رسول الله عمر Marginal lines, plain or dotted, complete the piece.

Reverse :—Kufic legends alone in three lines. بالله بنو عمرويه النصر

No. 10.—Copper : size, 4 ; weight, 35 grains. Common. Legends as in the silver coins, with the exception that the بنو is placed, for economy of space, in the opening between the ل's of بالله The die execution of these pieces is generally very inferior.

No. 11.—Copper : size, $3\frac{1}{2}$; weight, 21 grains. Unique.

Obverse :—Blank.

Reverse :—Centre : بنو — عمروية النصر

Margin : ?— س بالمنصورة سنة اربع —

OMAR (?).

No. 12.—Copper: size, 4½; weight, 36 grains. Mr. Frere, unique.

Obverse :—Central device, four lines crossing each other at a common centre, so as to form a species of star of eight points; four of these are, however, rounded off by dots. Legend, arranged as a square: محمد رسول الله with single dots at the corner angles, and two small circles filling in the vacant spaces outside of each word.

Margin :—Two plain lines, with an outer circle of dots.

Reverse :—Central legend in three lines within a triple circle composed of dots, circlets, and an inner plain line. I transcribe the legend, with due reservation, as: بنو بالله عمرويه النصر

The editor, in a footnote, says he is inclined to identify the above ruler with the Omar bin Abdallah, as the reigning sovereign of Mansūrah, at the period of the geographer, Masūdī's visit to the valley of the Indus.

It will be seen that the above descriptions relate to the class of coin shown in rows 3, 4 and 5 on plate CII. There is no notice of the smaller local silver and copper coins of rougher make as shown in the rest of the plate. They are, by far, the most plentiful, but at the same time, owing to their original rough surfaces and the fact of being cast and not stamped out of the more tough sheet metal, as the larger ones would seem to have been, it is only a very small percentage of the little lumps of verdigris that will yield such favourable impressions as those in the plate. But a subsequent note on some of these is given by Mr. Ed. Thomas in the *Indian Antiquary*,[1] where he describes two copper coins of Manśur bin Jamhūr (A.H. 107), one copper of 'Abd-ul-Raḥman, one of Muḥammad, three copper and one silver of 'Abdallah, one silver of Banū-Dāud, three copper and one silver ascribed to Banū-'Umar, one silver to Aḥmad, and one silver to 'Abdallah (Wali and Malik). Unfortunately the illustrations of these coins have been drawn by hand, but they present coins similar to those in the top two rows of plate CII, and some of the smaller ones in rows 6, 7 and 8.

In the Journal of the Bombay Branch of the Royal Asiatic Society[2] Mr. Rehatsek describes five similar coins in silver, which were found in the ruins of Vijnōṭ. He gives an illustration of one, again hand drawn, which is much like the smallest silver ones on my plate. Of these he says: "More information on this, and a few other ruins of interest in the Indus Valley, with the objects of antiquity discovered there, may be found in the 'Translation of Report No. 2879, of the 16th June 1873, from the Muktiarkār, Ubauro, to the address of the Collector of Shikarpur,' and in the 'Memo on the ruins of Vinjrote, Indus valley (State) Railway, Rohti Division.'" In the last Memo. Mr. Robertson

[1] Vol XI, p. 89. Some of these are noticed in a further account of these coins by Mr. E. Thomas in Dr. Burgess' volume on *The Antiquities of Kāthiawād and Kachh*, page 71 to which the reader is referred. Sufficient has been said here to give a general idea of their leading characteristics.

[2] Vol. X. p. 165.

after saying that he has forwarded the above five coins, states that some of the same kind, but rather more legible, were sent to the Chief Engineer, who sent them to General Cunningham. Mr. Rehatsek considers the coins to be silver *dirams* with Kufic legends. He says he cannot be positive about the legend but thinks it reads "Conquest of Sind in the year 88," but that the date is indistinct and dubious, and he gives the whole as a conjecture. His reading is very unsatisfactory.

A few coins of earlier dates than the Arab invasion have been found in Sind. There is little doubt that those which were found *inside* the Mīrpūr-Khās *stūpa*, with the relics, are of a much earlier period; and, though all signs of impressions were absent from their surfaces, their shape and size suggested the punch-marked type.

In a perfectly satisfactory state of preservation were the six Sassanian gold coins discovered in the Larkhanah district, about 1908, and shown in Fig. 3. The Honorary Secretary of the Bombay Branch of the Royal Asiatic Society, to whom they were submitted for examination, thought that they probably belonged to about the 5th century A.D. Dr. Codrington, writing on these, from the photographs of casts made from them, says:

"I have looked through all the books and notes I know of but found nothing like these gold coins of Sassanian pattern.

"All six are of the same pattern on the obverse, but struck from 2 or 3 different dies. The same may be said of the reverse of five of them, but the sixth—right end of bottom line—is different, being a fire altar without the attendants at the sides, a pattern found in some of the Sassanian coins.

"Unlike all Sassanian coins, as far as I know, in gold and silver, these have no Pehlvi inscriptions on them, except, perhaps, that some of the marks above the altars on the reverse may be parts of letters. Above the forehead of the king, on obverse, a crescent and star, and in front of the king's face is a symbol or figure which I cannot identify, ʒ. This may be meant for the Arabic كعف ; it reminds me somewhat of the Arabic names in front of the king's head on the Sassanian Tabaristan coins حزير هاني شعيد عمر and others who were governors in that region, but I do not know of a governor with a name like K'af. The crescent in front of the king's headdress first appears on the coins of Yezdegird I (A.D 397-417), and is again on coins of Firoz (A.D. 459-486) on which also is a crescent and star above the altar on reverse, and are doubtfully seen on these coins.

"On the whole I think the king's head more resembles that of Yezdegird I than any other. The attitude of the attendants at the altar, with swords advanced, is also the same as on his coins."

Other very early coins found in Sind were those discovered by Mr. Bhandarkar when opening up the old *stūpa* known as Sudheran-jo-dado about six miles north-west of Tāndo Muhammad Khān. Among them were one Indo-Parthian, two Kushana, and one Kshatrapa, all, to some extent supporting the opinion that the *stūpa*, with others of the same class in Sind, dates back to the first century of the Christian era. The Kshatrapa coin is unique, inasmuch that it is the only copper coin of Mahākshatrapa Rudrasena II that has yet been found.[1]

The coins of the later rulers were generally those of the powers under which they were more or less tributary—at one time under Kabul and at another under Delhi.

[1] Described in his article in the Annual Report of the Archæological Survey for 1914-1915.

PLATE II.

Right View

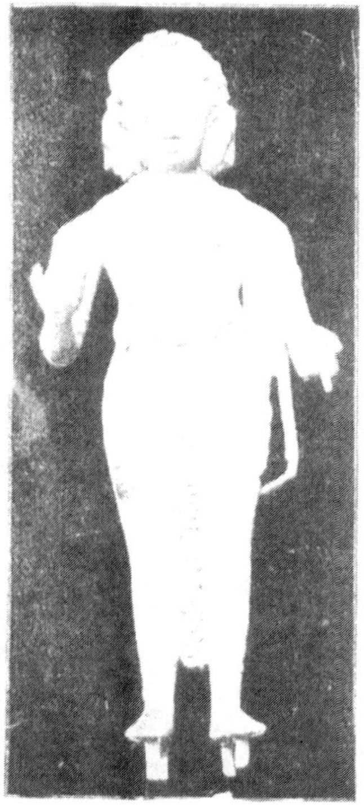

Front View

Back View

Left View

BRAHMA : BRONZE : KARACHI MUSEUM, SIND.

PLATE III

ALTAR. MOL VALLEY.

CARVINGS AND INSCRIPTIONS. ALTAR IN MOL VALLEY.

PLATE IV

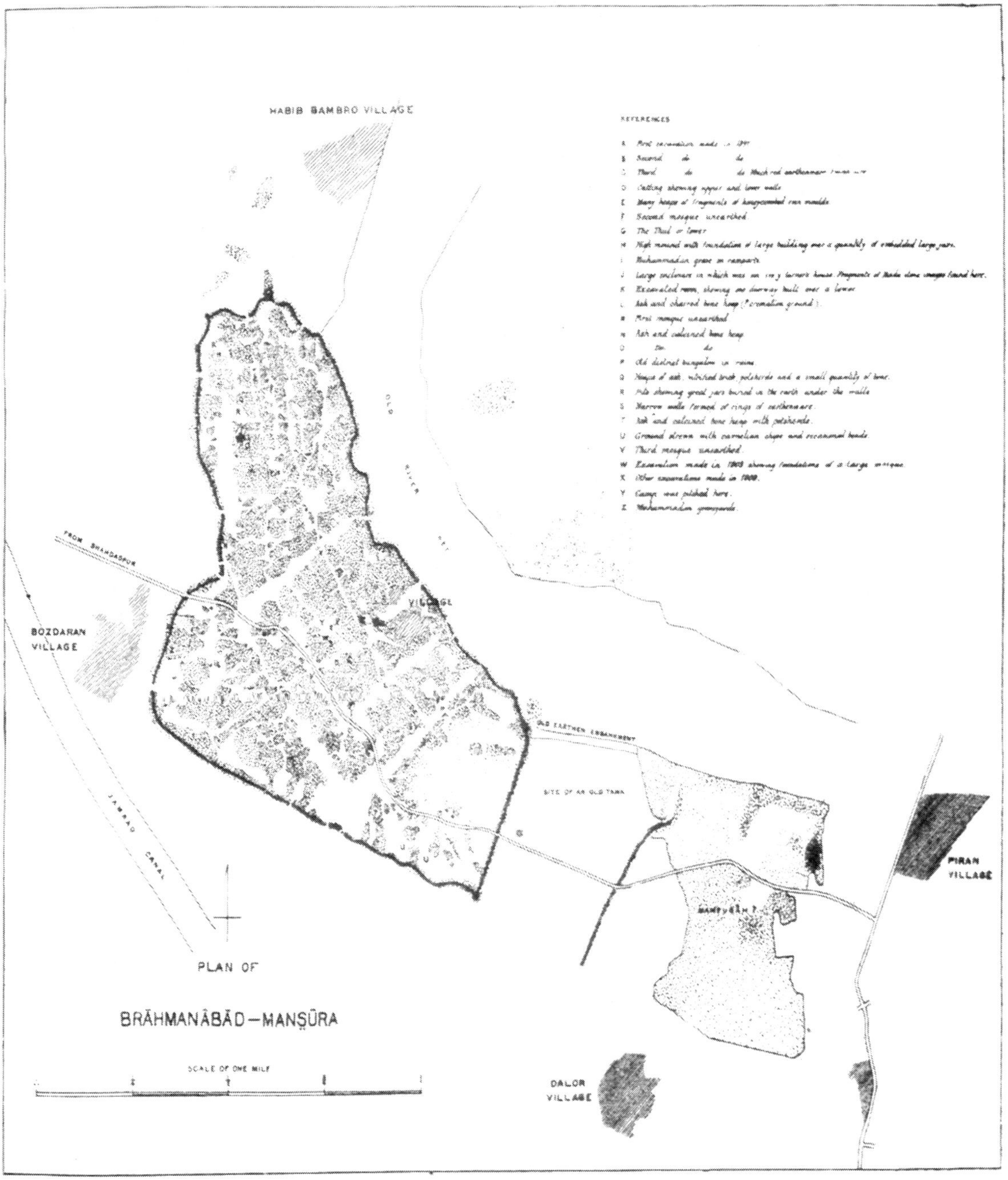
HABIB BAMBRO VILLAGE
REFERENCES
OLD RIVER BED
FROM SHAHDADPUR
VILLAGE
BOZDARAN VILLAGE
OLD EARTHEN EMBANKMENT
SITE OF AN OLD TOWN
JAMRAO CANAL
PIRAN VILLAGE
MANSURAH ?
DALOR VILLAGE
PLAN OF
BRĀHMANĀBĀD—MANṢŪRA
SCALE OF ONE MILE

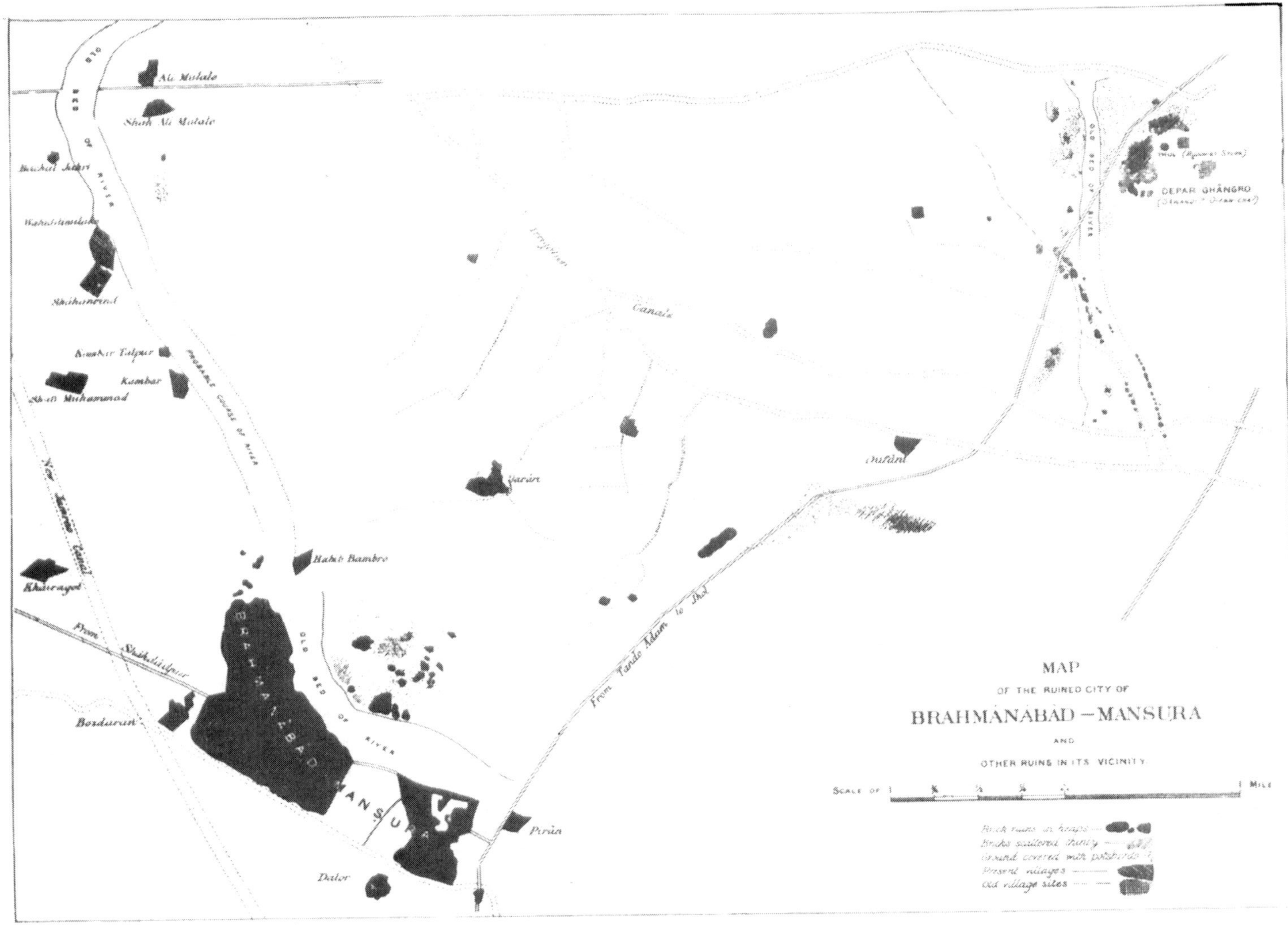

MAP OF THE COUNTRY AROUND BRAHMANABAD

GENERAL VIEW OF THE HEAPS OF BRICKBATS, AT BRAHMANABAD

RUINS, SHOWING EARTHEN BOWLS, AT BRAHMANABAD.

PLATE VIII

OUNDATION OF MOSQUE, SHOWING MIHRAB BUTTRESS, AT BRAHMANABAD

LARGE BRICK FOUNDATIONS OF A MOSQUE (?), AT BRAHMANABAD

BRICK DRAIN UNDER GREAT BRICK FOUNDATIONS, AT BRAHMANABAD

LIBATION SLAB, AT BRAHMANABAD

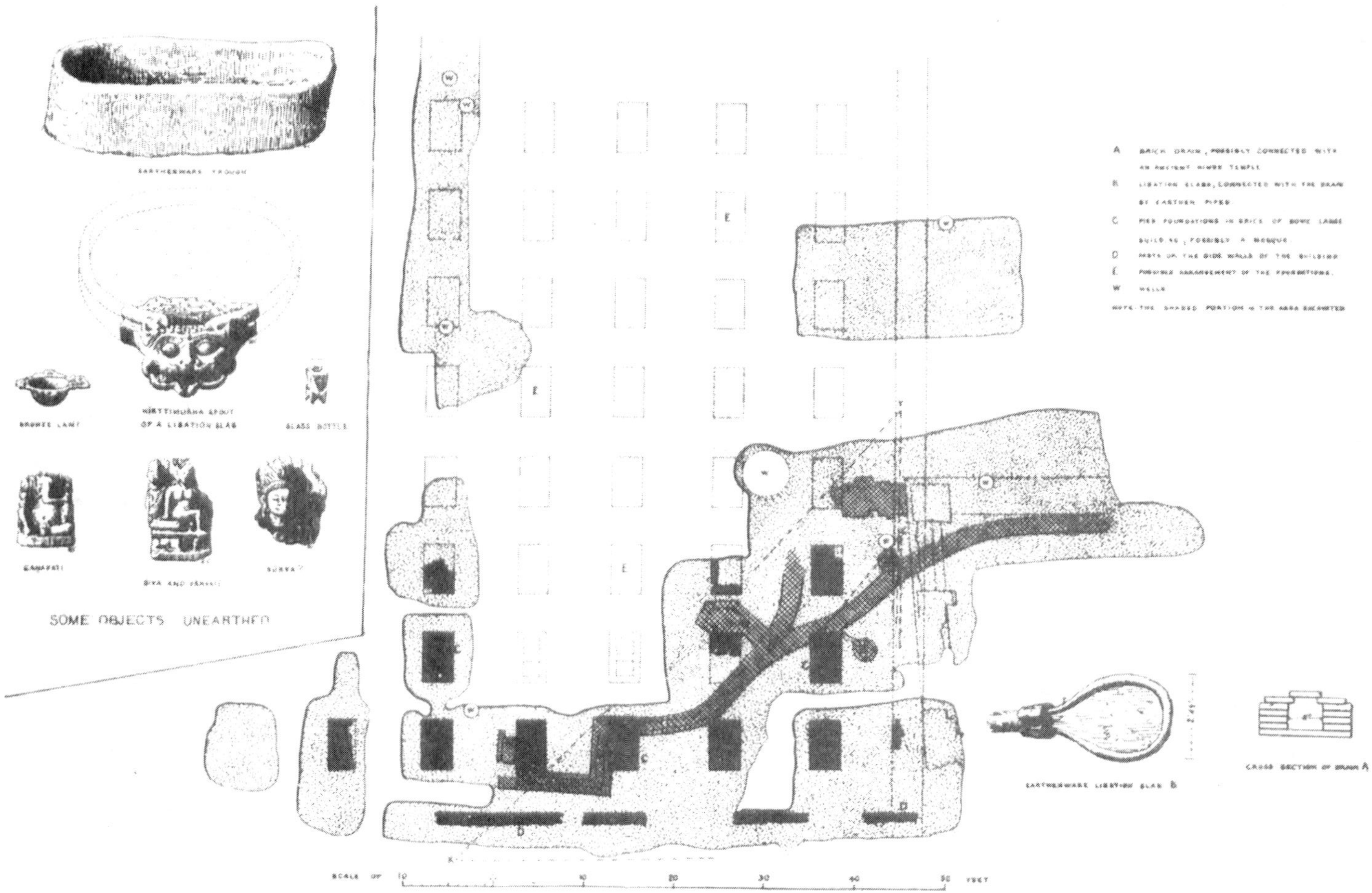

PLAN OF EXCAVATIONS AT BRAHMANABAD.

PLATE X

POTTERY EXCAVATED ON THE SITE OF BRAHMANABAD.

BALLS, FRAGMENTS OF IMAGES ETC., FROM BRAHMANABAD.

CARVED BRICKS FROM RUINED STUPA, AT DEPAR GHANGRO

PLATE XII.

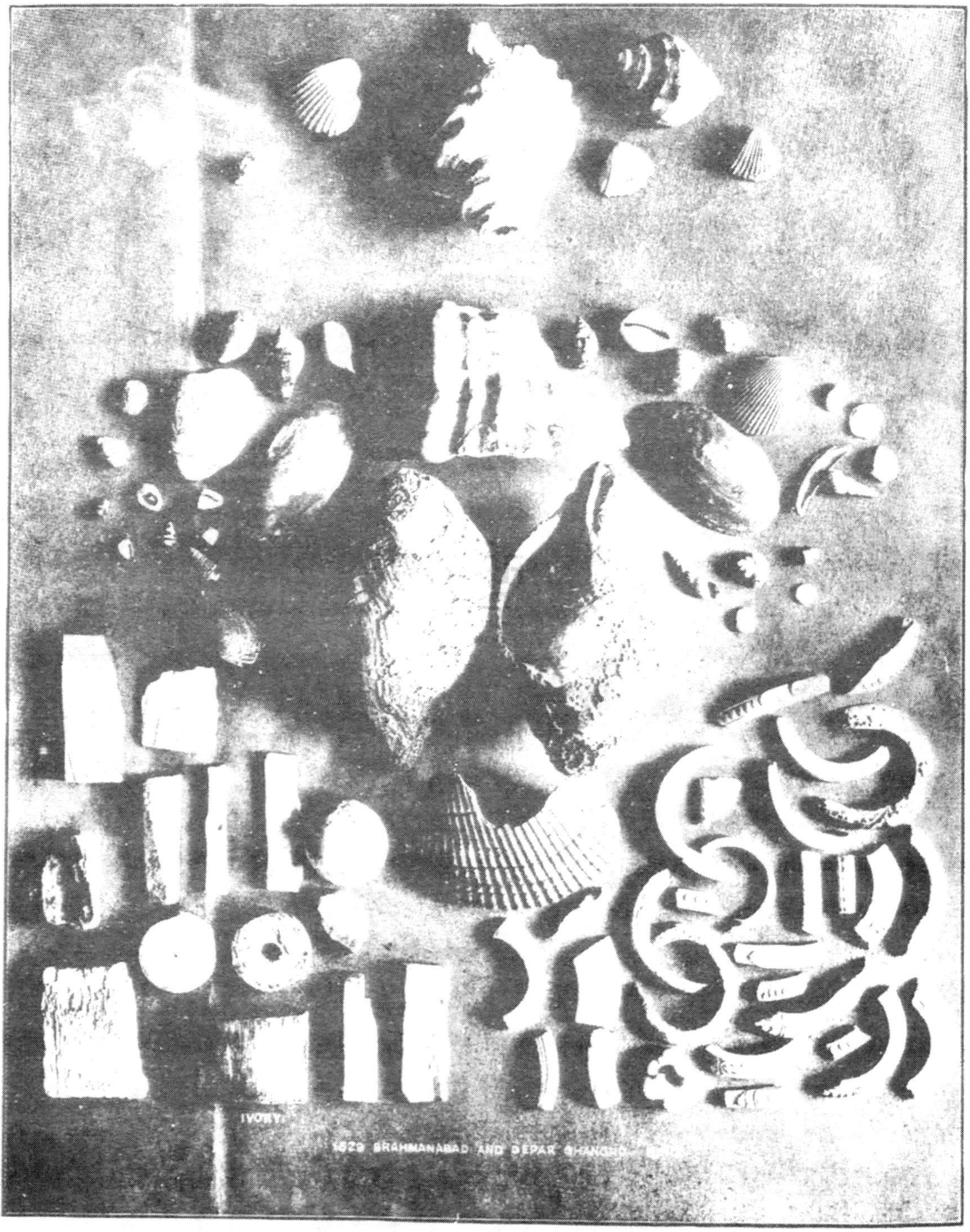

SHELLS FOUND UPON THE SITE OF BRAHMANABAD.

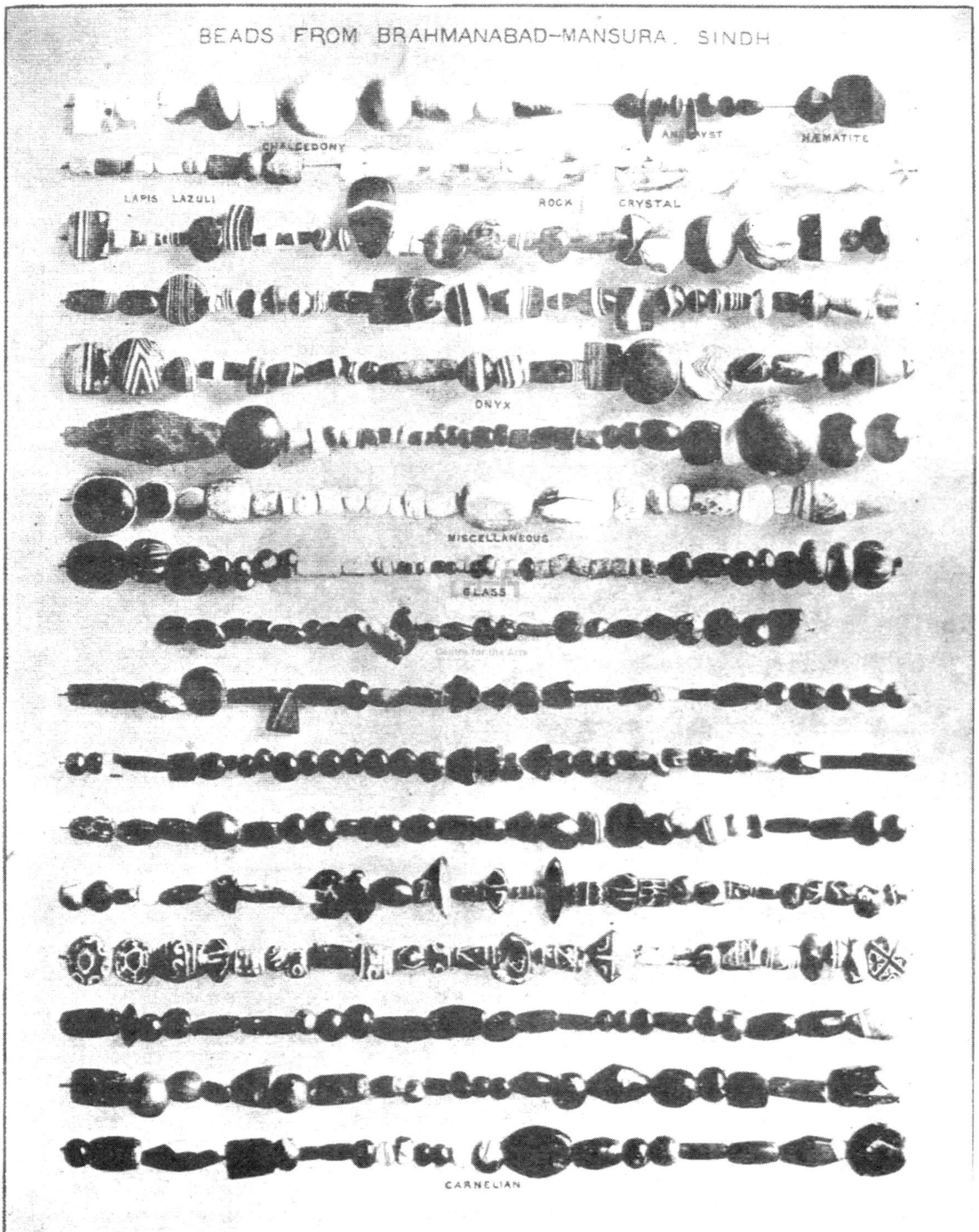

BEADS OF SORTS FOUND UPON THE SITE OF BRAHMANABAD.

FRAME OF AN IMAGE, FROM BRAHMANABAD.

THE THUL AT BRAHMANABAD.

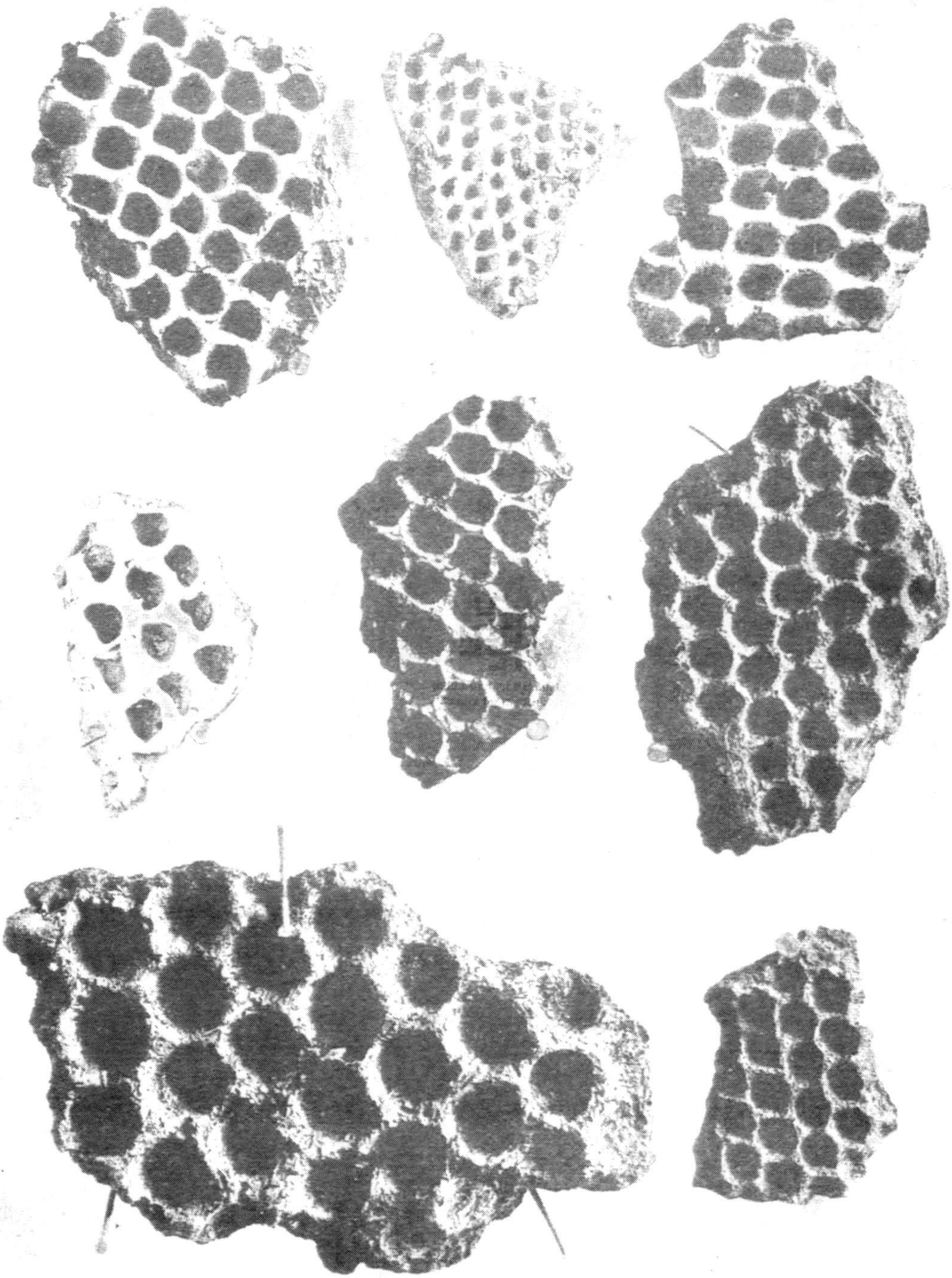

1536. BRAHMANABAD & BHAMBOR—SIND. COIN MOULDS.

PLATE XVI

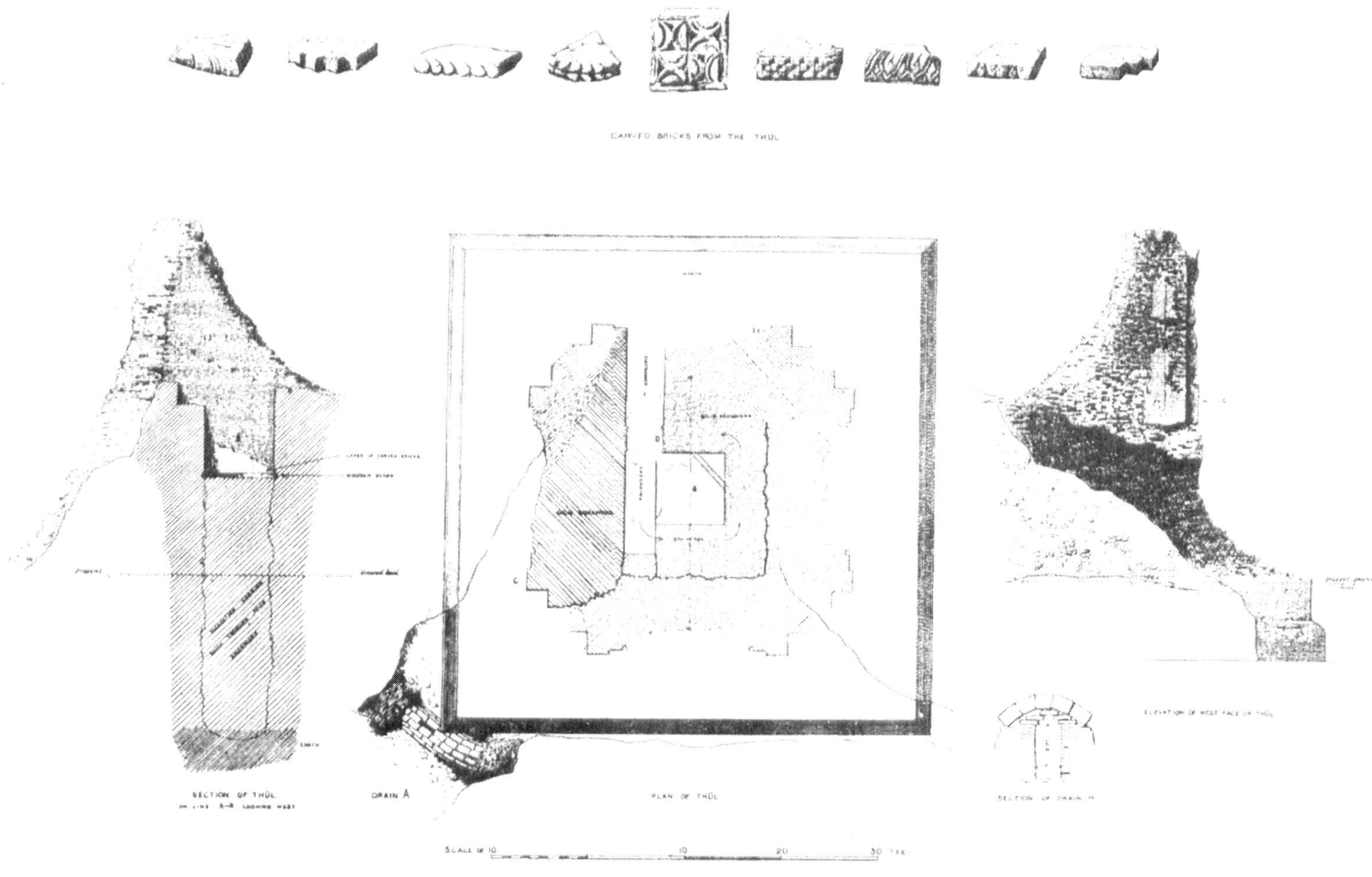

PLAN OF THE THUL AT BRAHMANABAD.

THE THUL AT DEPAR GHANGRO.

THE STUPA AT MIRPUR-KHAS FROM THE S.W.

PLATE XVIII

a. IVORY BALUSTERS OF FURNITURE RAIL (SO CALLED CHESSMAN) ETC., FOUND BY MR. BELLASIS IN 1854. AT BRAHMANABAD

b. OBJECTS FOUND BY MR. BELLASIS IN 1854. AT BRAHMANABAD.

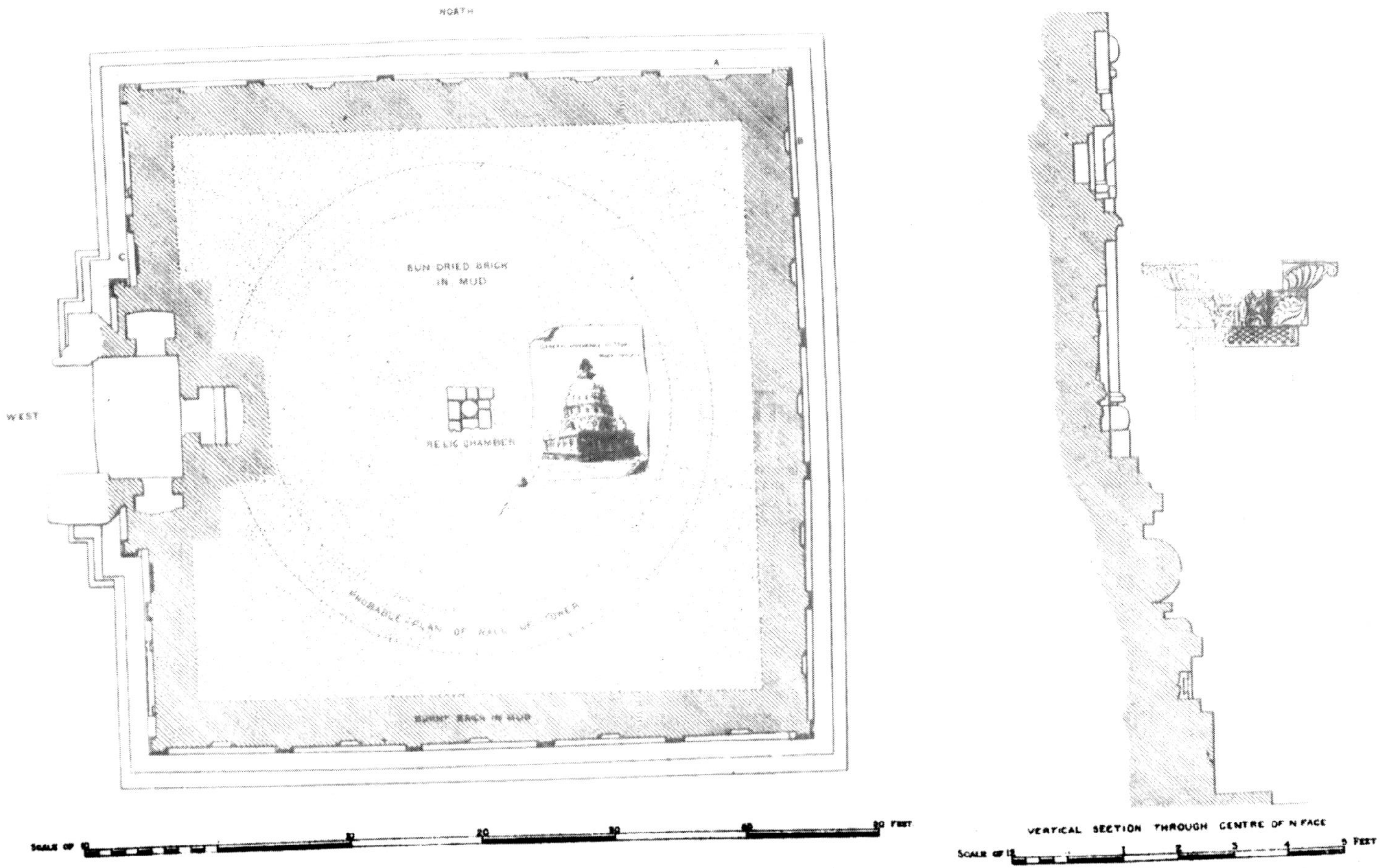

PLAN OF THE STUPA AT MIRPUR-KHAS.

PLATE XX.

ELEVATION OF THE STUPA, AT MIRPUR-KHAS.

PLATE XXI.

GENERAL VIEW OF THE STUPA AT MIRPUR-KHAS AFTER EXCAVATION

THE STUPA AT MIRPUR-KHAS, BEFORE EXCAVATION.

THE STUPA AT MIRPUR-KHAS, AFTER EXCAVATION.

THE STUPA AT MIRPUR-KHAS, FROM THE NORTH-WEST.

THE SOUTH SIDE OF THE STUPA, AT MIRPUR-KHAS.

MIDDLE AND NORTH SHRINE IN WEST SIDE OF THE STUPA, AT MIRPUR-KHAS

MIDDLE AND SOUTH SHRINE IN WEST SIDE OF THE STUPA, AT MIRPUR-KHAS.

THE RELIC CHAMBER AND COFFER IN THE STUPA, AT MIRPUR-KHAS.

RELICS (ASHES), MAGNIFIED. FROM STUPA AT MIRPUR-KHAS.

PLATE XXIV

CARVED BRICKS FROM THE STUPA, AT MIRPUR-KHAS

MOULDING OF BASEMENT OF STUPA, AT MIRPUR-KHAS

CARVED BRICKS IN THE BASEMENT OF THE STUPA, AT MIRPUR-KHAS

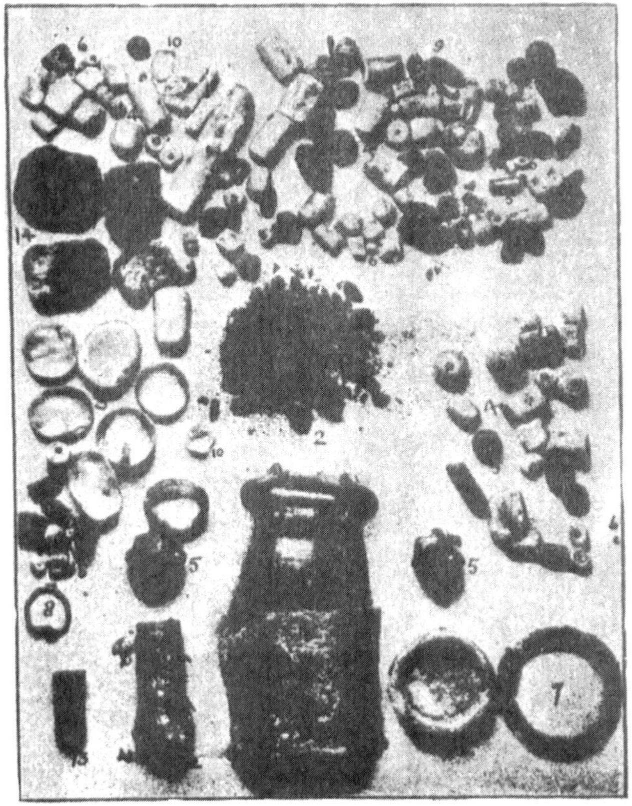

RELIQUARY AND OFFERINGS FROM THE STUPA. AT MIRPUR-KHAS.

1 Reliquary (Crystal).
2 Relics (Charred bone ash).
3 Crystal beads.
4 Coral beads.
5 Gold beads.
6 Minute Seed pearls.
7 Copper ring.
8 Gold ring.
9 Wheat grains.
10 Diamond-shaped cut Crystals.
11 Cap of reliquary.
12 Silver box.
13 Gold box.

TERRA-COTTAS FROM THE STUPA, AT MIRPUR-KHAS

PLATE XXV A

CARVED BRICKS IN THE BASEMENT OF THE STUPA, AT MIRPUR-KHAS.

PORTION OF TRUE ARCHING ON THE STUPA AT MIRPUR-KHAS.

IMAGES FROM THE STUPA, AT MIRPUR-KHAS.

PLATE XXVII

IMAGES AND VOTIVE TABLETS FROM THE STUPA, AT MIRPUR-KHAS.

THUL MIR RUKAN.

PLATE XXX

SUDHERAN'S STUPA, BEFORE EXCAVATION.

SUDHERAN'S STUPA, AFTER EXCAVATION.

PILASTER AND DETAILS OF MOULDING FROM THE THUL MIR RUKAN.

PLATE XXXI.

CARVED BRICKS FROM STUPA TWO MILES NORTH OF SUDHERAN'S STUPA.

SUDHERAN'S STUPA-NORTH SIDE

REMAINS OF A STUPA TWO MILES TO THE NORTH OF SUDHERAN'S STUPA

CARVED BRICKS BUILT INTO BASEMENT OF SUDHERAN'S STUPA

PLATE XXXIII.

EXTERIOR OF JAM NIZAMU-D-DIN'S TOMB AT THATHAH.

SAMPLES OF GLAZED TILES.

Half Scale

JAM NIZAMU-D-DIN'S TOMB: INTERIOR, SHOWING MIHRAB, AT THATHAH.

PLATE XXXV

CHATTRIS NEAR SAYYID ALI SHAH'S TOMB, AT THATHAH.

NAWAB AMIR KHALIL KHAN'S TOMB, AT THATHAH.

ISA KHAN'S ZANANAH TOMBS, FROM S. W., AT THATHAH.

TOMB OF DIWAN SHURFA KHAN AT THATHAH.

PLATE XXXVIII

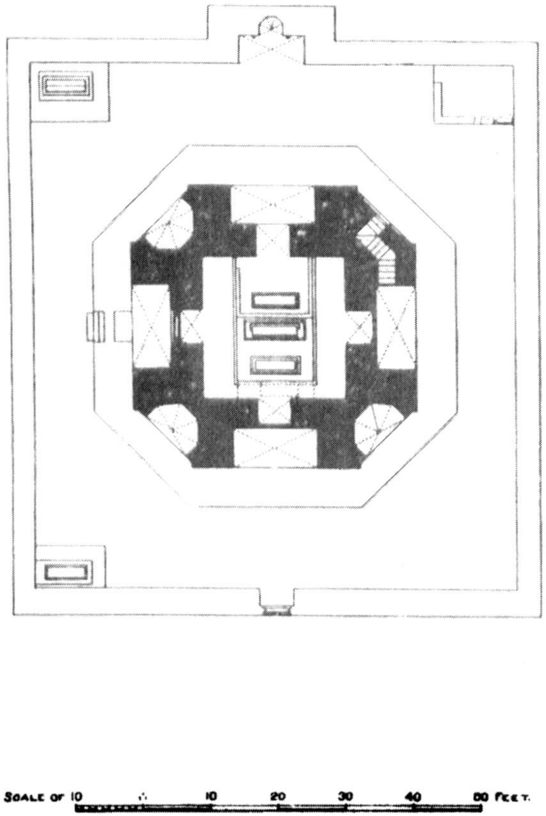

PLAN OF MIRZA JANI BEG'S TOMB, AT THATHAH.

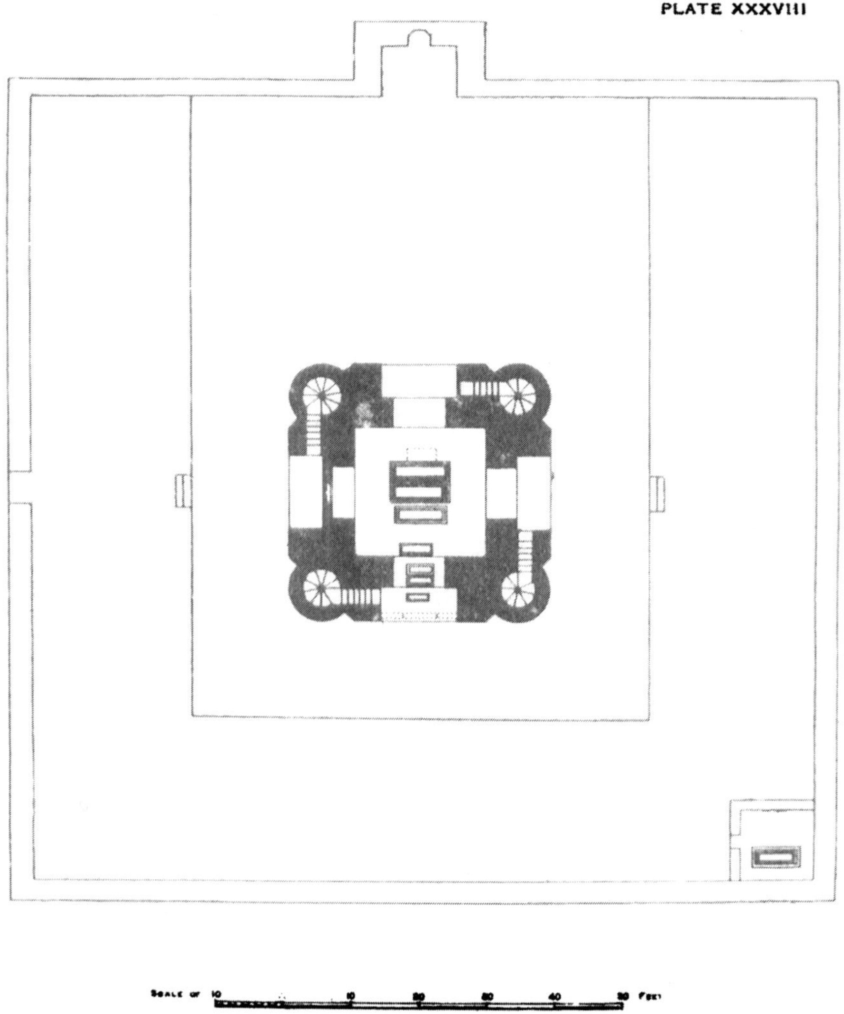

TOMB OF DIWAN SHURFA KHAN PLAN, AT. THATHAH.

PLATE XXXIX

GRAVE STONE IN DIWAN SHURFA KHAN'S TOMB, AT THATHAH.

PLATE XL

FRONT, BACK AND SIDE ELEVATIONS OF GRAVESTONE IN DIWAN SHURFA KHAN'S TOMB, AT THATHAH

MIRZA ISA KHAN'S TOMB AT THATHAH.

PLATE XLII

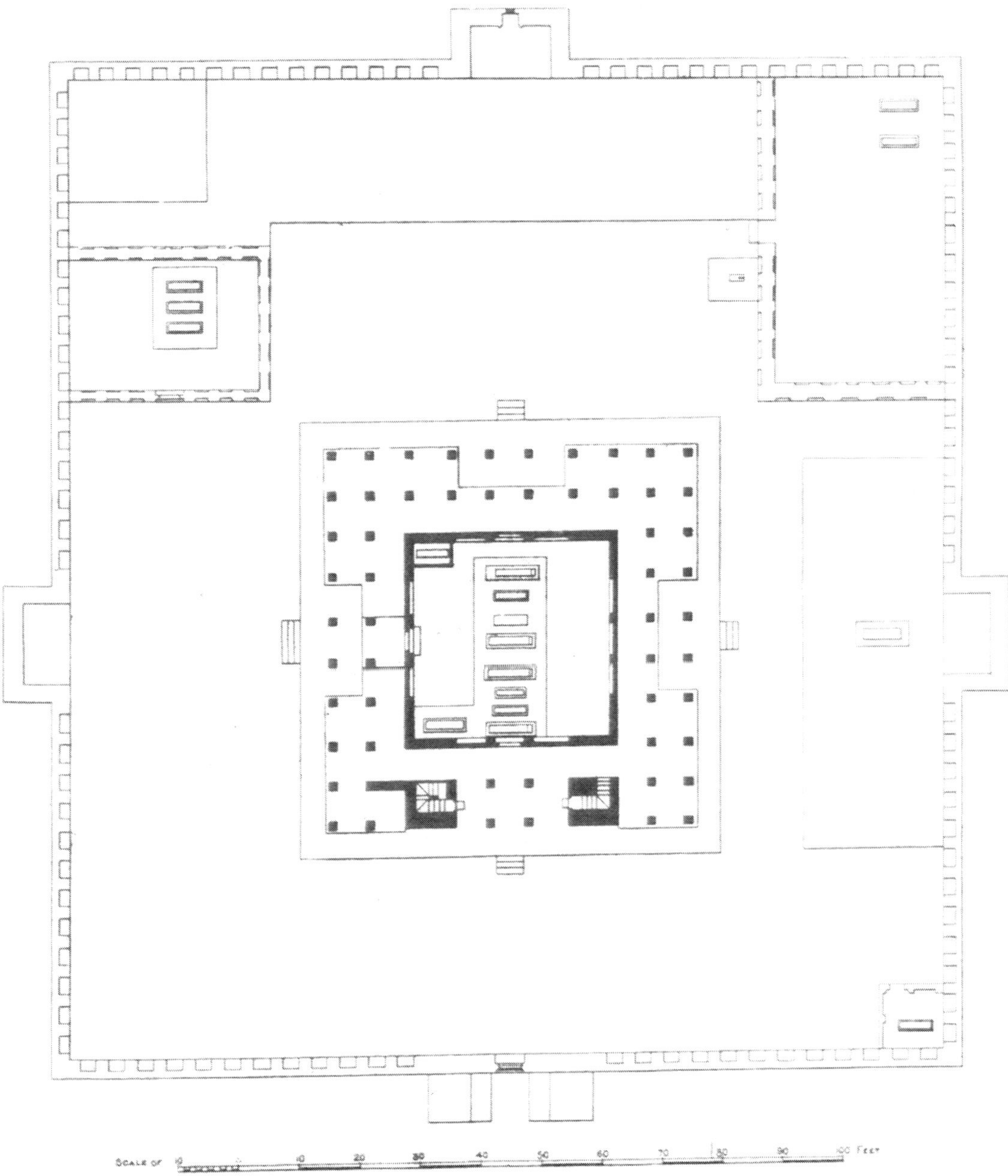

PLAN OF MIRZA ISA KHAN'S TOMB, AT THATHAH

PLATE XLII

COLONNADE IN TOMB OF MIRZA ISA KHAN, AT THATHAH

WALLS OF ENCLOSURE ROUND MIRZA ISA KHAN'S TOMB, AT THATHAH.

PLATE XLV.

NORTH WING OF THE ENCLOSURE OF MIRZA ISA KHAN'S TOMB AT THATHAH.

PILLARS FROM MIRZA ISA KHAN'S TOMB. AT THATHAH.

ENTRANCE TO MIRZA ISA KHAN'S ZANANAH TOMBS, AT THATHAH.

MIHRAB IN MIRZA ISA KHAN'S ZANANAH TOMBS, AT THATHAH.

PLATE XLIX.

BACK OF THE MIHRAB AT MIRZA ISA KHAN'S ZANANAH TOMBS AT THATHAH.

PLATE L

DETAIL FROM ISA KHAN'S ZANANA AND JANI BEG'S TOMBS, AT THATHAH.

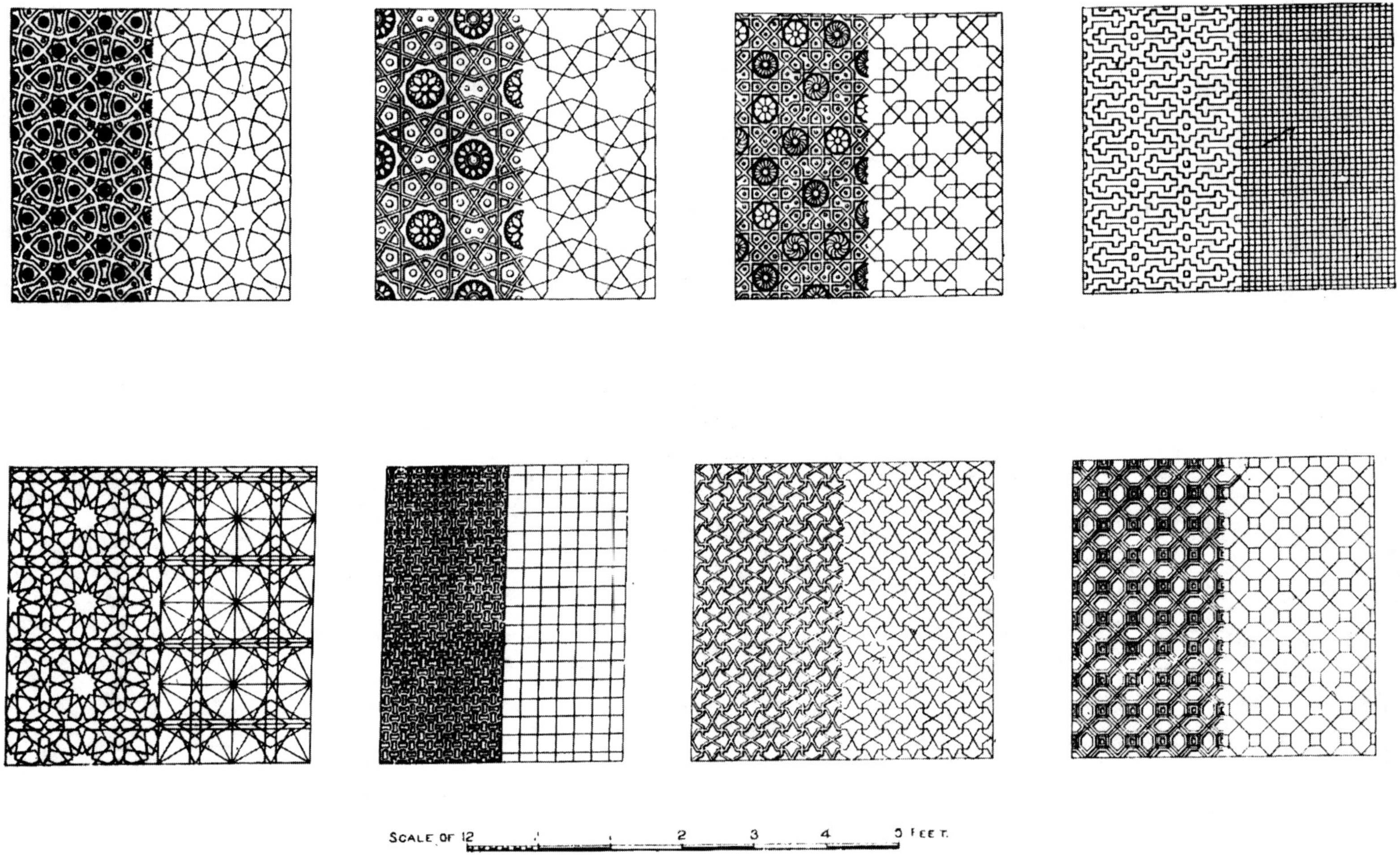

STONE TRACERY FROM ISA KHAN'S TOMB, AT THATHAH

JANI BEG'S TOMB AT THATHAH.

PLATE LIII

ENTRANCE DOORWAY TO MIRZA JANI BEG'S TOMB, AT THATHAH.

MIHRAB OF MIRZA JANI BEG'S TOMB AT THATHAH

OUTER ENTRANCE TO MIRZA JANI BEG'S TOMB AT THATHAH

MIRZA TUGRAL'S TOMB, AT THATHAH.

INSIDE OF PAVILION NEAR MIRZA TUGRAL S TOMB, AT THATHAH.

PLATE LVII.

THE JAMI MASJID AT THATHAH

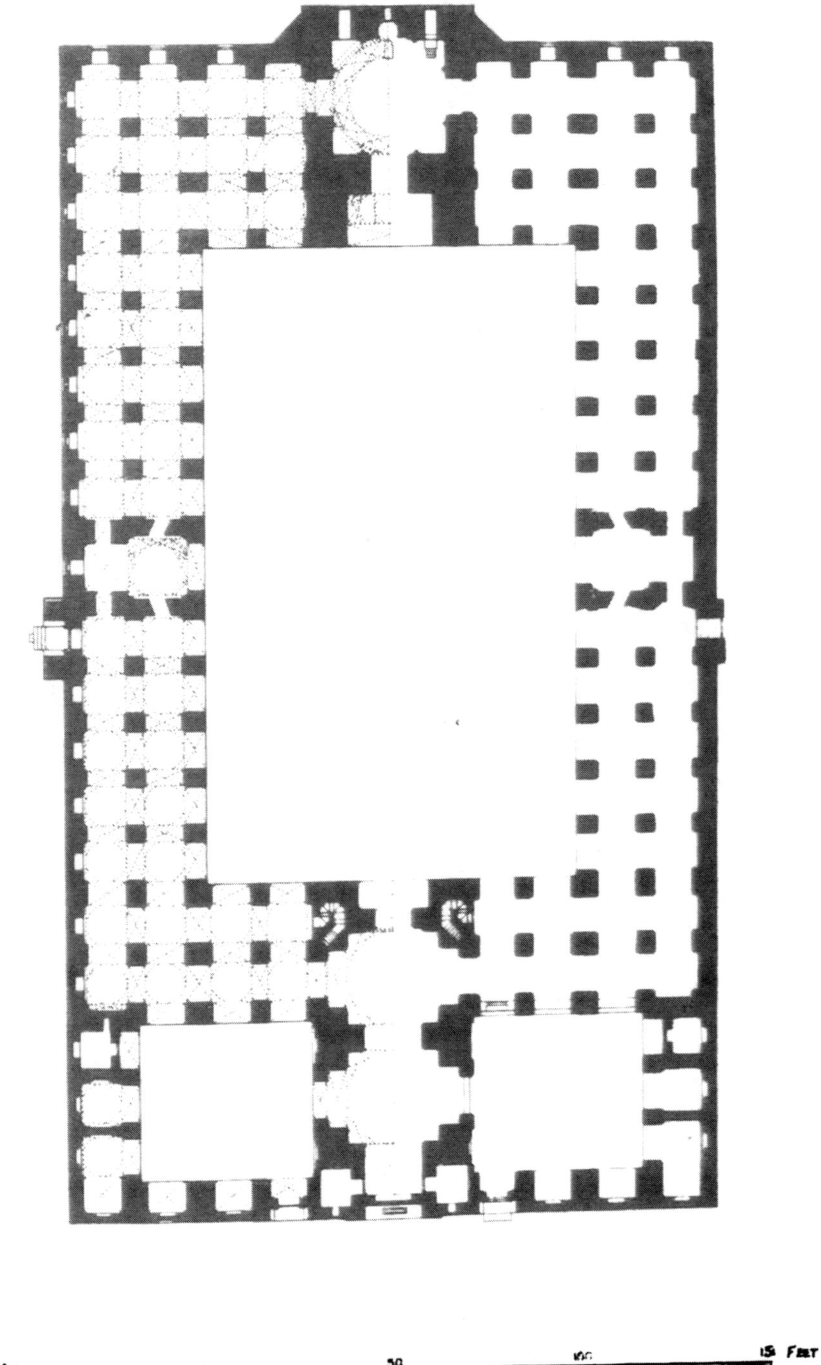

PLAN OF THE JAMI MASJID AT THATHAH

CROSS SECTION OF THE JAMI MASJID PLAN. AT THATHAH.

THE MIHRAB OF THE JAMI MASJID, AT THATHAH.

INTERIOR OF JAMI MASJID, LOOKING DOWN THE SOUTH AISLE, AT THATHAH.

DECORATIVE TILEWORK AT ENTRANCE TO THE JAMI MASJID AT THATHAH

CENTRAL DOMED CEILING OF THE JAMI MASJID. AT THATHAH.

THE DABGIR MUSJID, AT THATHAH.

THE DABGIR MASJID AT THATHAH. THE INTERIOR.

BACK OF THE DABGIR MASJID AT THATHAH

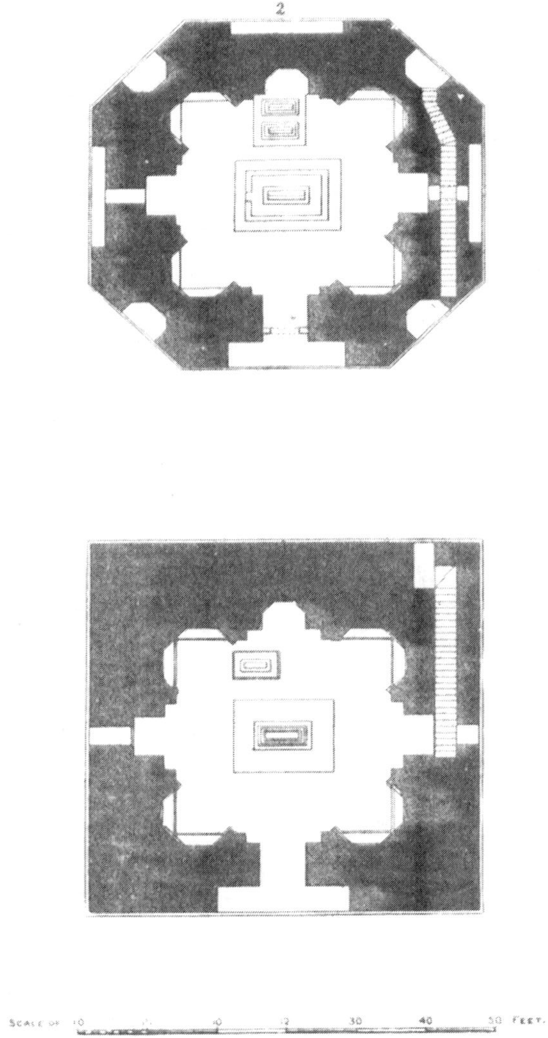

PLANS OF NABI KHAN'S AND GHULAM SHAH'S TOMBS. AT HAIDARABAD

PLAN OF THE DABGIR MASJID. AT THATHAH.

GHULAM SHAH'S TOMB AT HAIDARABAD.

INTERIOR OF GHULAM SHAH'S TOMB AT HAIDARABAD.

MARBLE PANELS AND RAILING IN GHULAM SHAH'S TOMB. AT HAIDARABAD.

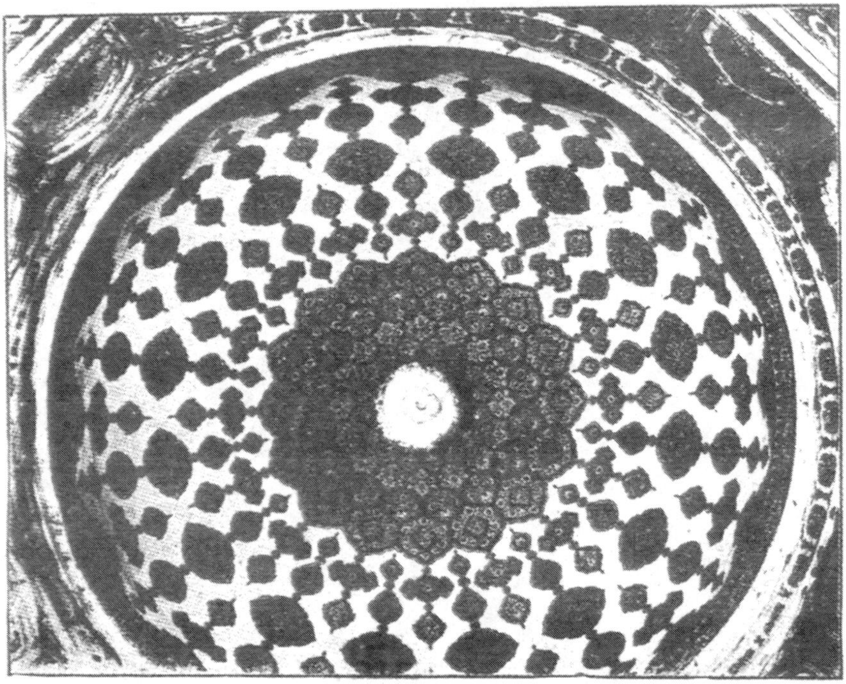

PAINTED CEILING IN TOMB OF MIR HAJI MUHAMMAD KHAN'S WIFE, AT HAIDARABAD.

TOMB OF M. KARAM ALI KHAN AND M. HAJI MUHAMMAD KHAN, AT HAIDARABAD.

PLATE LXXII

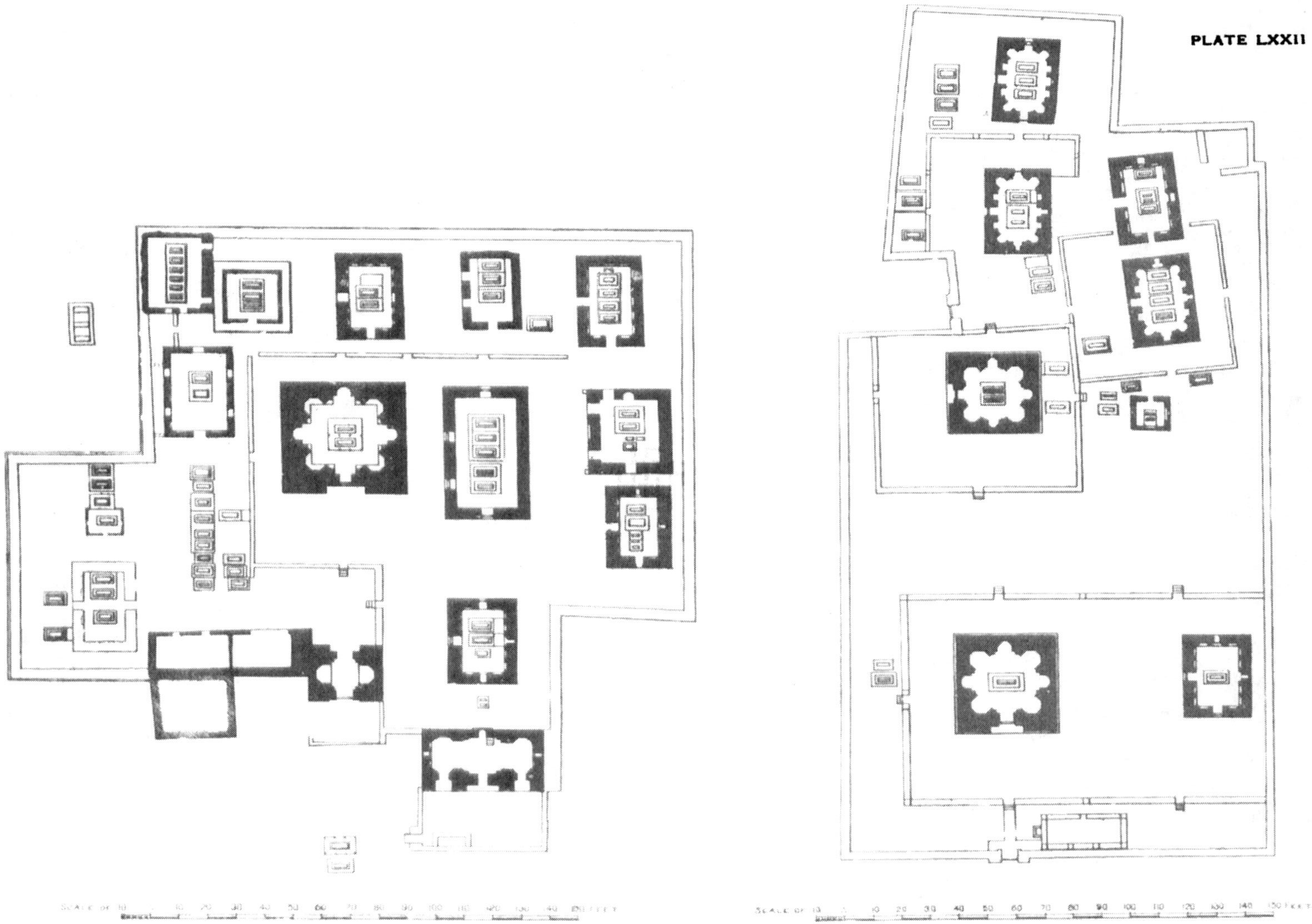

PLANS OF THE TWO GROUPS OF THE TALPUR TOMBS, AT HAIDARABAD.

PLATE LXIX.

NABI KHAN'S TOMB AT HAIDARABAD.

THE TALPUR TOMBS AT HAIDARABAD.

PLATE LXXIII

INTERIOR OF ONE OF THE TALPUR TOMBS, AT HAIDARABAD.

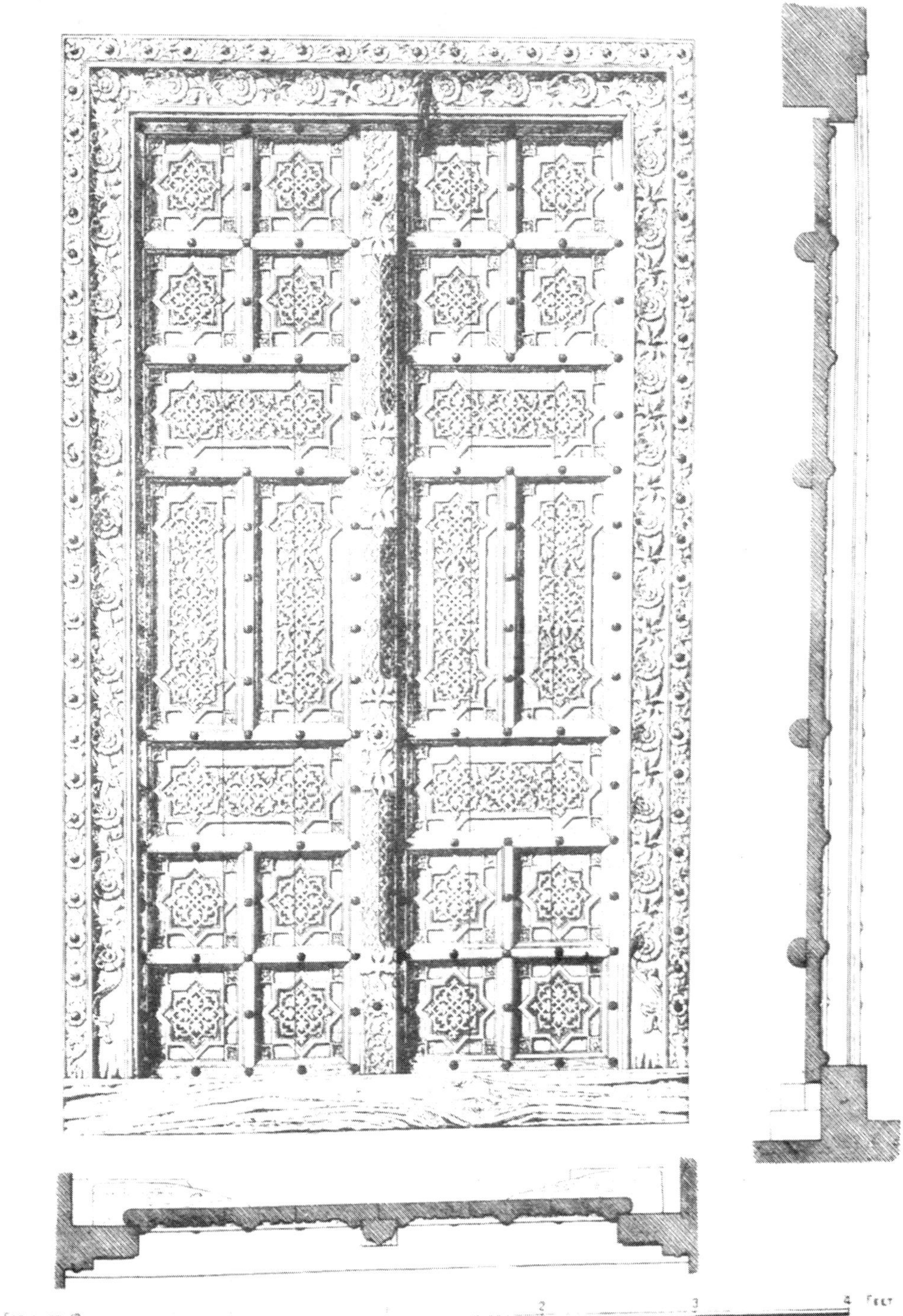

DOOR FROM THE FORT, AT HAIDARABAD.

THE ISLAND OF ZINDA PIR, NEAR BAKHAR.

THE SHRINE OF ZINDA PIR, NEAR BAKHAR.

PLATE LXXVII.

MINAR AND TOMB OF MIR MASUM, AT SAKHAR.

PLATE LXXIX

THE TOMB OF MIR MASUM AT SAKHAR.

MOSQUE NEAR MIR ABDUL BAQI'S TOMB.

CENTRAL BAY OF MOSQUE NEAR MIR ABDUL BAQI'S TOMB, AT SAKHAR.

SHAH KHAIRU-D-DIN'S TOMB AT SAKHAR.

THE SATHBAIN TOMBS AT ROHRI.

THE SATBHAIN TOMBS AT ROHRI VIEW ON THE TOP

PLATE LXXXV

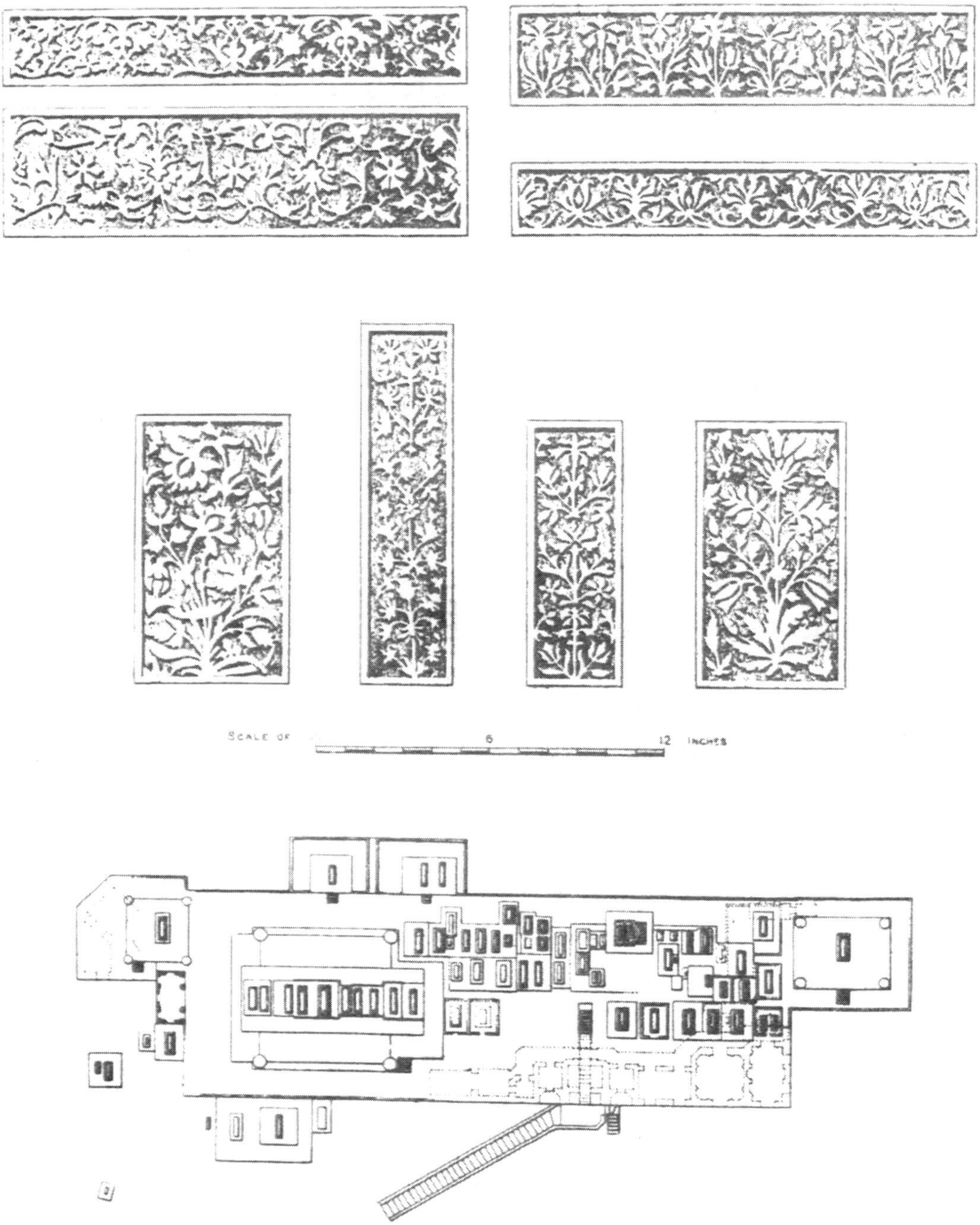

PLAN, AND DETAILS OF TRACERY ON THE SATHBAIN TOMBS, AT ROHRI.

DOOR OF THE TOMB OF SHAH BAHARO, AT LARKHANA.

DOORWAY OF THE TOMB OF SHAH BAHRAO. AT LARKHANA.

THE JAMI MASJID AT KHUDABAD

THE JAMI MASJID AT KHUDABAD, FROM THE SOUTH-EAST.

PLATE XC.

THE JAMI MASJID AT KHUDABAD, FROM THE NORTH-EAST.

PANEL IN GLAZED TILES IN THE JAMI MASJID, KHUDABAD.

THE PANEL, WITHOUT BORDER, MEASURES ABOUT 4 BY 11 FEET.

YAR MUHAMMAD'S TOMB AT KHUDABAD

PLATE XCII

YAR MUHAMMAD'S TOMB AT KHUDABAD. CENTRAL PART OF THE FACADE.

PLATE XCIV

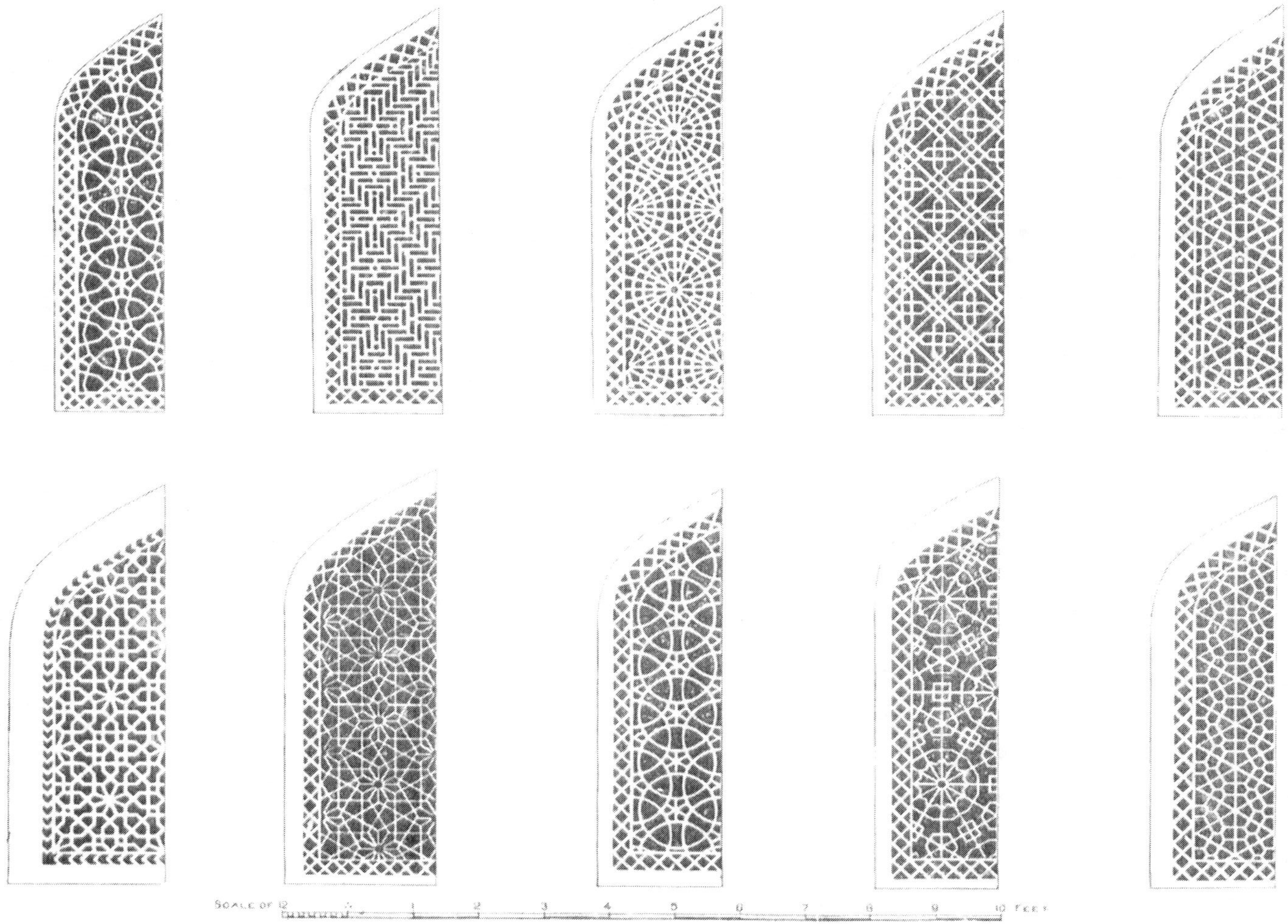

PERFORATED WINDOWS FROM YAR MUHAMMAD'S TOMB, AT KHUDABAD.

PLATE XCV

THE THAHIM TOMBS AT DRAKHAN.

TOMBSTONE IN GRAVEYARD NEAR JARAK.

TOMB FRO... KHARKHARO, SHOWING WOMAN'S BRACELETS.

TOMB FROM SONDA GRAVEYARD

TOMBSTONE IN GRAVEYARD NEAR JARAK.

DOOR OF TOMB IN GRAVEYARD NEAR JARAK.

GRAVEYARD NEAR JARAK.

FATH ALI KHAN'S TOMB, AT KHUDABAD, NEAR HALA.

TOMB UNDER PAVILION, AT KHUDABAD, NEAR HALA.

TOMB OF MAKHDUM SAHEB AT HALA.

PIR HASHIM SHAH'S TOMB AT MATIARI.

THE JAMI MASJID AT MATIARI.

PIR RUKAN SHAH'S TOMB AT MATIARI.

HATA POTTERY. THREE VASES AND A TABLE TOP. THE LARGE CENTRAL VASE IS 38 INCHES HIGH.

HALA POTTER.

Indira Gandhi National Centre for the Arts

HALA POTTERS' FURNACES.

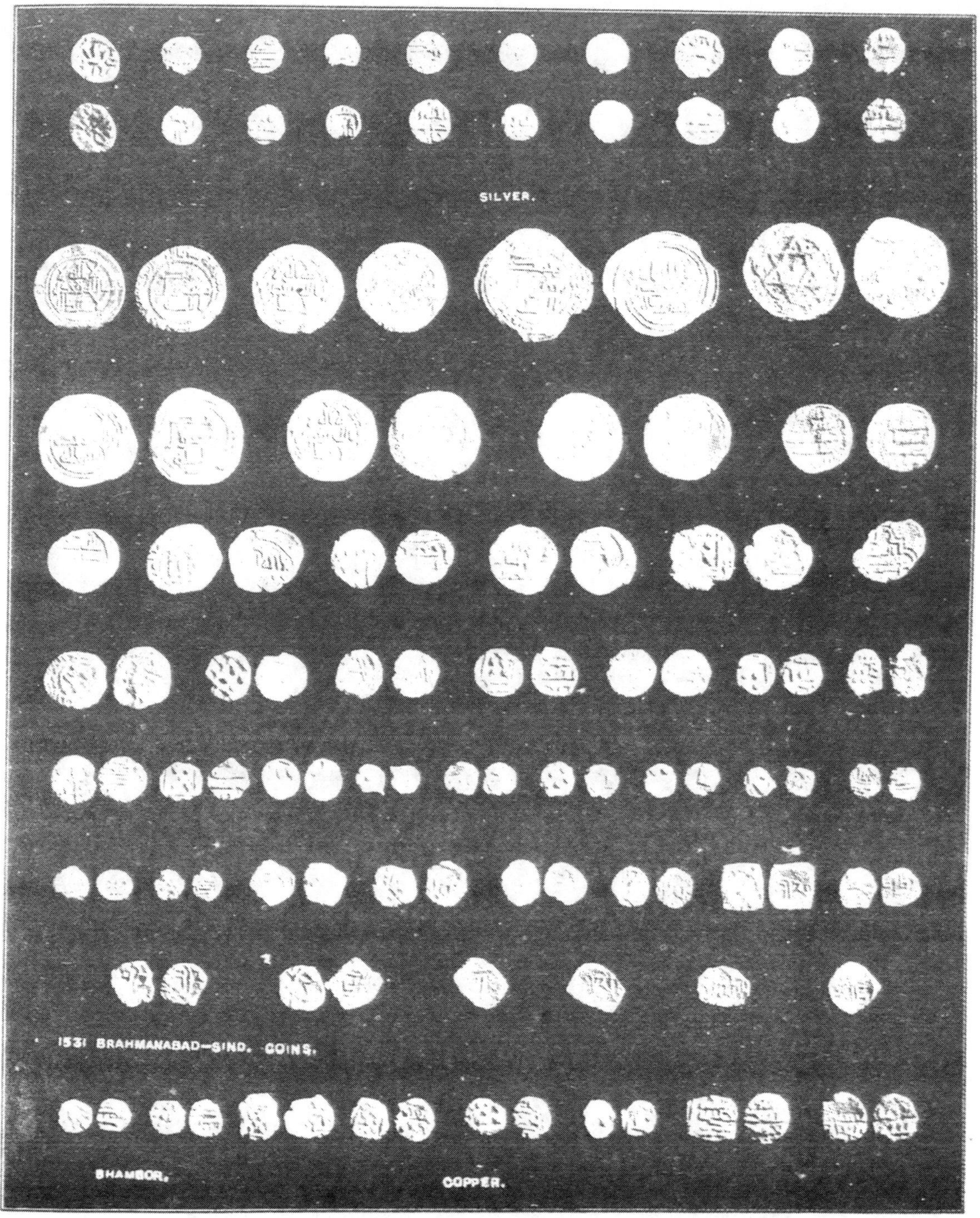

SIND COINS

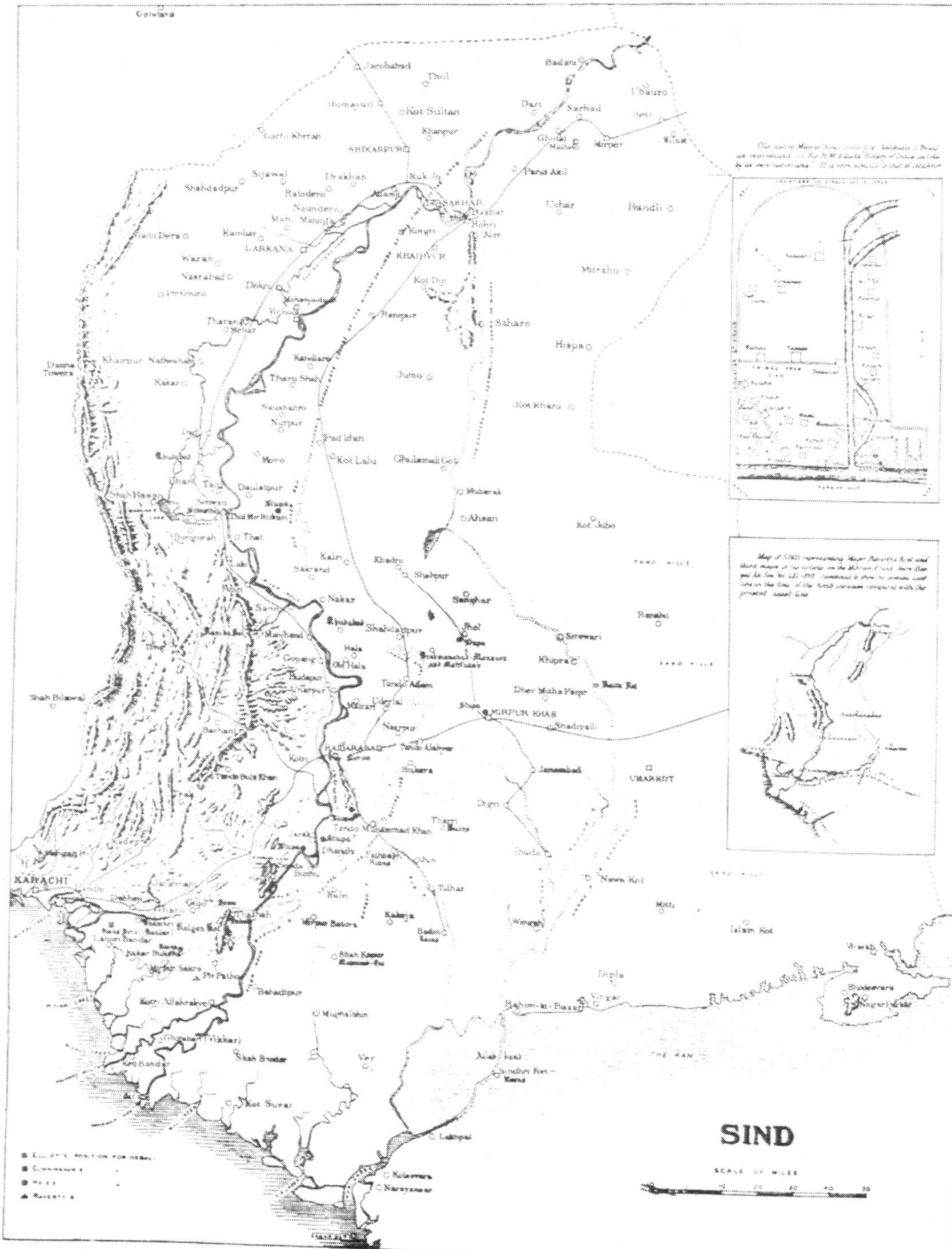
SIND
SCALE OF MILES
KARACHI
HYDERABAD
MIRPUR KHAS
UMARKOT
LARKANA
SHIKARPUR
SUKKUR
THE RAN